HOOVER'S VISION

ORIGINAL

THINKING

FOR

BUSINESS

SUCCESS

HOOVER'S VISION

GARY HOOVER

TEXERE

NEW YORK · LONDON

Published by
TEXERE

55 East 52nd Street
New York, NY 10055
Tel: +1 (212) 317 5106
Fax: +1 (212) 317 5178
www.etexere.com

In the UK

TEXERE Publishing Limited
71–77 Leadenhall Street
London EC3A 3DE
Tel: +44 (0)20 7204 3644
Fax: +44 (0)20 7208 6701

This publication is designed to provide accurate and authoritative information in regard to the subject matter covered. It is sold with the understanding that the publisher is not engaged in rendering legal, accounting, or other professional services. If legal advice or other expert assistance is required, the services or a competent professional person should be sought.

Library of Congress Cataloging in Publication Data is available.

ISBN 1-58799-059-8

Printed in the United States of America

This book is printed on acid-free paper.

10 9 8 7 6 5 4 3 2 1

Acknowledgments

This book is dedicated to all the great teachers I have had—my parents, the Anderson (Indiana) public school system, the Anderson Church of the Brethren, all my colleagues at enterprises from T. W. Bus to TravelFest, and the community of scholars constituting the University of Chicago from 1969 to the present. I also acknowledge the outstanding efforts of my editor, Karl Weber, and the entire Texere Publishing team, led by Myles Thompson, in shaping the idea of this book into reality.

Contents

PART TWO

Essence: The Power of Vision

PART THREE

Execution: Enterprises at Work

Introduction

The Art of Enterprise:
Thinking Differently

I consider any great and lasting enterprise a work of art. Perhaps this is surprising. When we speak of art, we usually think of it as the work of a solitary creator—a painter, a poet, a sculptor. But there are also collaborative works of art, including some of the greatest. The art of architecture, for example, depends on the combined efforts of many people. The Empire State Building would not exist without the contributions of dreamer-developers John Raskob and Alfred Smith, the architectural firm of Shreve Lamb and Harmon, and the construction partnership of Starrett Brothers and Eken. On just one day in 1930, the hands of 3,439 people contributed to its building, from 281 bricklayers and 269 carpenters to 20 water boys and 1 ornamental iron inspector.

Any motion picture is the result of a complex collaboration among producers, directors, composers, screenwriters, cinematographers, actors, and editors. No one would be watching *Lawrence of Arabia* today were it not for an extraordinary combination of human resources: the courage of producer Sam Spiegel, the directorial brilliance of David Lean, the haunting music of Maurice Jarre, and the acting talent of then-newcomer Peter O'Toole. When we hear a symphony, we hear the work of many—even including the work of the instrument makers and symphony hall architects (or sound recordists).

In the same way, any successful enterprise depends on the efforts of many people with diverse backgrounds and a multitude of skills. Through the enterprise of men and women working together we have landed men on the moon, defeated plagues, created the Internet, and enabled billions of people around the world to live richer, more productive, more interesting lives. The creation, leadership, and growth of a great enterprise are astonishing human achievements. That's why I consider people who launch and sustain great enterprises to be artists just as truly as great composers, playwrights, or painters are.

During much of the twentieth century, dialogue about the nature of enterprise has often remained stuck in old debates: capital versus labor, big business versus small business, private sector versus public sector, for-profit versus nonprofit. It is time to move on. At its heart, successful enterprise is all about people joining together to serve other people. That's why I define enterprise simply as a group of people working together to accomplish a shared goal or a common dream.

Perhaps anthropologist Margaret Mead said it best: "Never doubt that a small group of thoughtful, committed citizens can change the world. Indeed, it is the only thing that ever has."

With this definition in mind, we can see that enterprises—collections of people joined together to accomplish shared goals—are at work around us everywhere. Some have transformed the way we live. In different ways, this is true of Microsoft and Amazon, Disney and Sony, Ford and Federal Express, Wal-Mart and The Gap. Others have a more modest impact: they "merely" bring us shops that sell more delicious coffee, tennis shoes that are more durable, or even the proverbial better mousetrap. Many enterprises, like the ones we've already mentioned, are run on a for-profit basis. Many others, from private foundations to universities, hospitals, schools, and churches, are not, although they, too, exist to pursue the shared goals of a group of people. Every year, thousands of new enterprises are founded. Many achieve their goals, but many fail to do so. For the past thirty-eight years, I have been on a mission to discover the sources of success for enterprises of all kinds—what separates the winners from the losers. *Hoover's Vision* presents the findings of my search.

This book is meant for you if you . . .

- Own your own business

- Dream of creating a new business

- Are an executive of or lead a department or division of a large enterprise

- Are charged with thinking about enterprise strategy

- Are looking for enterprises in which to invest your money or time

- Serve on the board of directors or trustees of a for-profit or not-for-profit enterprise

- Have a leadership role in the nonprofit world or in government

- Are passionately devoted to pursuing any goal that can be achieved only though the combined efforts of a group of people

If any of these descriptions applies to you, you need to understand the *real* keys to the success of any enterprise. *Hoover's Vision* was written with you in mind.

To begin our quest for these keys, let's step back in time for a moment. . . .

In 1970 Sears ruled the retail world. The people who ran Sears had a clear vision of the future—a future in which Sears continued to be the world's number one retailer. This vision was shared by most of Sears' suppliers, employees, and stockholders. It was even shared by many of the company's competitors, who watched Sears' every move—and copied Sears as often as possible.

One fellow had a different view. His name was Sam Walton, and he ran a company that competed with Sears. From his own uncommon perspective, Walton thought that he could win that competition, even though the company he led was only a tiny fraction of Sears' size.

In the early 1980s, giants American, Delta, and United dominated the world of airline travel. They were led by smart, experienced executives who had confidence in their understanding of how airlines should be run and what it would take to prosper in the future. Few industry observers doubted that the big three would continue to rule the airways for decades to come.

A man named Herb Kelleher, who ran a small Texas-based airline called Southwest Airlines, had a different idea. He thought that Southwest could steal customers, market share, and profits from the airline juggernauts.

At the same time, the computer industry was ruled by IBM, one of the world's largest, most respected, best-managed, and most profitable companies. IBM sold far more computers than any other company and was also the world's largest software company. The company's future as the industry's leader appeared clear to everyone. Everyone, that is, except a few nerds, punks, and upstarts at companies like Microsoft, Intel, and Dell. They had their own unique outlook on the world of information technology and how it might evolve.

Everyone knows what happened. In each case, the conventional wisdom was wrong. The upstart with the oddball concept or the offbeat strategy overtook the industry leader. Furthermore, these stories have parallels on every street corner: the pizza place that died when a new restaurant moved in around the comer, the insurance agency that prospered while the larger one across the street shut its doors.

There's no shortage of experts who are ready to draw lessons from these tales of competitive warfare. They tell us to study Wal-Mart's logistics management, Southwest's sense of humor, Dell's direct-sales model. "The key to success," they proclaim, "is to copy the best."

My long-term study of enterprises large and small suggests a different conclusion. I've found that copying the current leader is not the formula for success. Success is based not on thinking like today's winner, but on thinking differently, thinking in original and creative ways.

Don't get me wrong—I believe in studying the best in every business. There's a lot to learn from Wal-Mart, Southwest, Dell, and many other well-run enterprises. But trying to build the next great enterprise by imitating them would be like Sam Walton studying Sears in 1970 and trying to ape their business model, or Michael Dell trying to mimic the methods of IBM.

What separates the Waltons, Dells, and other successful enterprise builders is precisely that *they did not follow a formula.* Neither Sam Walton nor Michael Dell had a Harvard M.B.A. Neither followed a roadmap drawn up by a team of industry experts or consultants. Heck, Michael Dell didn't even listen to his own parents when they warned him not to drop out of college to pursue his "little computer sales idea." Rather than listening to the advice of experts, they became their own experts. They listened to potential customers. They listened to themselves. And they obviously heard a different tune from the songs sung in the boardrooms of Sears and IBM.

Great businesses succeed because of their leaders' ability to see things that others do not see. To ask questions that others do not ask. And then to chart their own course, combining insights and strategies into the blueprint for a uniquely focused enterprise.

You know the old saying, "Give a man a fish and you feed him for a day; teach a man to fish and you feed him for life." This book is about how to fish. My goal is to give you tools for developing your own unique view of the world, one that relates to your dreams and aspirations and those of your enterprise. In the process, we'll look at dozens of businesses in various industries around the globe, past and present. Their stories illustrate how others have found their own paths to success. More important, these stories can serve as triggers for your own fresh thinking about opportunities in your industry, in your hometown, in your lifetime. All are drawn from my own lifelong quest for the keys to business success.

Hooked at Age Twelve

I grew up in the 1950s and '60s in a General Motors factory town, Anderson, Indiana. GM was then the world's largest industrial enterprise, at the height of its power. All my friends' parents either worked for GM, provided services to GM employees, or were suppliers to GM itself. In my junior high school homeroom, the girl sitting on my left was the daughter of a top GM executive, and the boy on my right was the son of a United Auto Workers leader. (During strike negotiations, they were not allowed to talk to each other.) General Motors *was* Anderson, Indiana.

Meanwhile, in social studies class, our teacher was talking about San Juan Hill and Gettysburg, Teapot Dome and the WPA. One day, I held up my hand and said, "What about General Motors? Tell us about them."

The teacher said, "Well, they make cars. They make Chevrolets, Pontiacs, Buicks, Oldsmobiles, Cadillacs, and GMC trucks. Now can we get back to our history text?" I wasn't satisfied. I wanted to know the history of GM, where it came from and why it existed. Were the people who ran it smart or stupid? Why did they do the things they did? What was important to these people? What motivated them? How would they react to the new Japanese car, the Toyopet, made by an obscure company called Toyota? And in the back of my head was the ultimate question: If I wanted someday to start or run a business as successful as GM, what would I need to do? What would I need to know? How did the system really work? What were the sources of success?

After class, I tried to explain all of this to my teacher. I'm sure I didn't convey it very well. She told me that if I wanted to find out more about General Motors, I should look in the reference books in the public library. But there was no entry for General Motors in the dictionary, or even in the *World Book* encyclopedia. While all the kids in town and their parents were always talking about GM—about the latest car models, problems at the plant, the chance of new hiring in the next few months—no one at school seemed to want to talk about it. And certainly no one seemed to be asking the fundamental questions to which I wanted answers. I felt frustrated.

Then, one day, my family stopped at a newsstand. My sister quickly gravitated to the horse and dog magazines, my brother to the magazines about cars and planes. But as I scanned the racks of periodicals, I caught a glimpse of an oversized magazine called *Fortune*. Staring me smack in the face was the cover story: "The Fortune 500: America's Largest Industrial Corporations." I grabbed it and began scanning the pages. I was stunned to discover a list, topped by General Motors itself and including 499 other creatures of the same species. At last, I'd stumbled across the first source that might help answer my questions.

Soon I convinced Mom and Dad to get me a subscription to *Fortune*. A few months later, the cover story was an excerpt from a new book: *My Years with General Motors,* by Alfred P. Sloan, the man responsible for GM's rise to glory. That did it. I was hooked on the study of human enterprise, the hows and whys of building great and lasting organizations.

I went on to study economics at the University of Chicago. Three of my teachers later won Nobel Prizes. (I'm not sure how they did it without me, the one who was always cutting classes to start little businesses with my dorm-mates.) I then worked for three of those giant Fortune 500 companies, starting as an analyst on Wall Street and later helping to guide strategy and acquisitions for one of the world's largest retail companies. Eventually I started three companies from scratch, two of which went on to change the nature of their industries, while the third tried but failed.

The first industry in which my friends and I pioneered was book retailing. We created the BOOKSTOP and BOOKSTAR chains. At a time when some thought that the dominant book retailers, B. Dalton's and Waldenbooks, were invincible, and others thought that the book business was a mature, dead-end industry, I studied demographic and retail trends and came to very different conclusions. Superstores, I realized, were the wave of the future, and the aging baby boom would want more and more entertainment and information—often in the form of books. We started building very large (for the time) off-price bookstores with broad selections of books in cities from Miami to San Diego.

We built some of the first distribution centers in book retailing and pioneered bookstore customer loyalty (that is, membership) programs. When our company was seven years old, Barnes & Noble bought it for more than $40 million and went on to build the largest book superstore chain.

Our other pioneering effort was in creating Hoover's, Inc., to provide company profiles. Most observers viewed business information as the exclusive turf of Standard & Poor's, Moody's, and Dun & Bradstreet. It was considered a dull, dry business—not a sexy opportunity. But I studied the trends and foresaw a coming rise in the need for readable, affordable, accurate information about the world's enterprises. I anticipated an explosion in interest in business and investments and the consequent growth of business journalism. We began by providing this information in book form, but my friend Patrick Spain foresaw the rise of online information and took the company onto the Internet in the mid-'90s. Today Hoover's is a public company that tracks more than 17,000 enterprises worldwide. Web users generate 400 million page views per year at www.hoovers.com.

My third pioneering venture—the one that failed—was an effort to change the way people shop for travel. In the innovative TravelFest Superstores in Austin and Houston, we combined the best of travel books, luggage and other travel gear, travel videos, travel classes, and travel planning and ticketing. Customers loved us, but the airlines didn't—they dramatically reduced the commission on airline tickets just as we were struggling toward profitability. It was a fantastic—and painful—learning experience.

Throughout this education, I have remained fascinated—no, obsessed—with the study of enterprise. What makes a successful enterprise? What makes a loser? How do people work together to get things done? Why do some enterprises that seem so potent disappear, while others that "don't have a chance" go on to greatness? And, over and over again, I have seen the same answers emerge to these questions.

The Secrets of Success

It'll take all the remaining chapters of this book to answer those questions fully. But here, in a nutshell, are the three keys to business success as I've observed them in action:

1. Observing and understanding other people and how their needs, desires, interests, values, and tastes change over time

2. Serving other people by making their lives better

3. Developing a business style that expresses your own dreams and passions even as it serves the needs of others

Stated as generalities, these ideas may sound obvious. But in the pages to follow, we will not be talking about generalities. We will be talking about real companies, about real success, and real failure. I'll share my own experiences and the lessons I learned from them. Companies like Sears and other leaders of the past lost their positions of power by thinking the answers were in the boardroom or on Wall Street. In truth, the answers are on Main Street—and in your heart. This book is all about how to see them and act on them to turn your dreams into reality.

Throughout this book, I stress the importance of learning new ways of thinking. Successful leaders see things that others do not see. They seize opportunities where others see only chaos. In writing this book, I've tried to provoke fresh thinking and at times to stir up a little controversy. If you disagree with one of my ideas, write out your thoughts. (If you like, you can send them to me at www.hooversvision.com, where you will also find additional materials, discussion, and links.) It is through the give and take of debate and the confronting of paradox and contradiction that we grow mentally. If *Hoover's Vision* isn't first and foremost a challenge to your comfortable ways of thinking, then I've failed as an author.

Sequential thinking is a little outdated. Twenty years ago, we had the cassette tape. It was sequential: you couldn't get to track three without going through track one. Today we have CDs, which permit you to instantly access any track and to program tracks in an infinite variety of sequences. In the same way, I have found that the secrets of success are not so much 1-2-3 steps as they are mindsets at work at all times, over-lapping, interplaying, and intersecting. But for purposes of this book, the ideas are divided into three parts, which we'll consider in this order: Exploration, Essence, and Execution.

Exploration: Where Do Great Ideas Come From?

The leader of a successful enterprise is, above all, curious. He or she lives for knowledge, for an understanding of the world around us and how it works. That world includes everything from the lines at the supermarket to the aging of the baby boom, from the power of the Internet to the rise of China, from the latest fad in teenage clothing to the newest technol-ogy for creating signs.

Information about the world and its peoples is all around us, flood-ing our senses each day from a thousand directions. The key is to have some idea of how to make sense of all those inputs. Piecing together the puzzle and integrating what you know is the first subject covered in this book. Seeing things that others do not see, wrapping your mind around the big picture, developing fresh perspectives and fresh defini-tions, looking at things from many angles, and effectively observing people are topics covered in chapters 1 through 8.

As I will show, the people who build and lead great enterprises are generally students of the past as well as the future. They understand what is going on around them in time (history) and in space (geogra-phy). Chapters 9 through 13 examine some of the most important trends of our times, as well as techniques you can use to better under-stand how things are changing over time in your own industry.

In researching this book, I traveled to every continent except Antarc-tica. As I'll explain, history and geography combine to give rise to many developments that the would-be enterprise builder must understand. The rise of China, the spread of technology, the explosion of cities, and the trend toward economic and cultural globalization—all of these world-altering movements occur at the intersection of history and geography. An understanding of these and similar other geographical concepts is critical to the success of virtually every enterprise. They are examined in chapters 14 through 21.

Essence: The Power of Vision

Observing and learning about the world around us isn't by itself a sufficient basis for building an enterprise. It's also critical to develop an idea and turn it into an articulate and well-defined vision. That vision must stand on four pillars—*clarity, consistency, uniqueness, and service.* The result is what I call the essence of the enterprise. Essence must come from within—it must be true to the personality of the enterprise. The essence of an enterprise does not change with time. Technologies, marketing methods, pay scales, and thousands of other details adapt continuously and often quickly. But the essence of the successful enterprise remains the same despite all these changes.

Success or failure of an enterprise can usually be attributed to the strength or weakness of these four pillars. The ambiguity and dullness of corporate-speak, the inconsistency of management-by-fad, the me-tooism of timid leaders, and the myopia of focusing internally rather than on your customers are enormous forces that often trip up big companies. Past success tends to breed complacency and arrogance. The only remedy is to remain focused on the four pillars and constantly strive to improve, enhance, and strengthen them.

Chapters 22 through 25 describe the first three pillars—the clear vision, the consistent vision, and the unique vision.

The most difficult of the four pillars may be service. A genuine desire to serve others, to somehow make the world a better place, is at the heart of all great enterprises. But many enterprises, including some of the largest ones, seem to think that other things are more important—getting approval from the FTC for the latest merger, planning the product launch party, or spinning last quarter's results to Wall Street. Therein lies great opportunity for the competition, big or small.

Execution: Making the Enterprise Work Every Day

With the precepts of curiosity, clarity, consistency, uniqueness, and service in mind, the final chapters of the book focus on what happens in the real world. There is much to be learned by studying key industries and today's most interesting and innovative companies—as well as those that are floundering. Chapters 29 through 31 explain how to look at industries and companies.

The book closes with a review of the key mind-sets and attitudes that must pervade the enterprise if it is to truly excel, starting with the leader who thinks like an entrepreneur. The keyword for this closing chapter is *passion*. Without it, nothing worthwhile takes place.

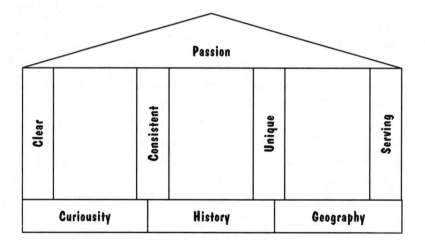

Are You Eligible for Success?

Have you ever taken one of those little quizzes with titles like, "Do you have an entrepreneurial personality?" I have. Some I passed, many I failed. There have been many scholarly studies of the nature of entrepreneurship. Some researchers focus on where entrepreneurs went to school, their parents' social status and income, or how happy their home life was. As far as I'm concerned, these studies are often off the mark. The truth is that successful leaders and entrepreneurs are as diverse as the population at large.

Some are tall, some are skinny. Some talk fast, some talk slow. Some have Harvard M.B.A.'s, some are high school dropouts. A few are born rich, but many are born poor. Some have great connections in the world of business, but many more "didn't know a soul" when they started out.

What entrepreneurial leaders *do* have in common is a burning desire to build something worthwhile. They have an intense energy that seeks new answers, a drive and dedication that propels them toward their goals. They are not put off by obstacles, competitors, or the doubts of naysayers. In their heart, they *know* they can achieve their dreams.

But such passionate self-confidence is for naught if the purpose of the enterprise is not worthwhile. When I first began studying entrepreneurship in the 1960s, the catch phrase was, "Find a need and fill it." Those words are still the best description of how to dream up enterprises that are likely to succeed. Successful enterprises consistently and continuously serve people and adapt to the changing needs and desires of their customers or clients.

Given a powerful desire to serve others, anyone—absolutely anyone—can learn and use the ideas contained in this book. If this describes you—great! Let's get started.

PART ONE

Exploration:
The Foundation for Finding Your
Own Path to Success

EXPLORATION I
Curiosity: The Fountain of Creativity

What is the first step toward building successful enterprises? What distinguishes the great entrepreneurs? Where do they begin? It all starts with curiosity.

Roy Spence, the president of GSD&M, Texas's largest advertising agency, once said that three of his most impressive clients—Norman Brinker of Steak and Ale and Chili's, Herb Kelleher of Southwest Airlines, and Sam Walton of Wal-Mart—were also among the most curious people he had ever worked with. They asked questions about anything and everything; you simply could not stop the flow.

In today's world, we praise the ability to think "outside the box." We put creative people on a pedestal. We value the power of innovation. But all of this power proceeds from curiosity—from asking, looking, and seeing.

The following eight chapters explore curiosity and its application. If you already have more ideas than you can ever put to work, you may find some new techniques to add to your arsenal. If you don't know where to start, or feel you need to be more creative, or are even looking for an idea for a new product or business, these chapters are written for you. Chapter 1 deals with preparing the mind, making sure it is a ready sponge for information. Once readied, we can begin to gather information, mainly by asking the types of questions illustrated in chapter 2. As we acquire information, it is easy to get information overload—chapter 3 gives a few of the many possible techniques for knitting this information together into a comprehensive whole. Chapter 4 deals with the first step in building innovative understanding—redefining and reclassifying our world.

With these techniques in mind, we can begin to look around the world for new ideas and get rid of old ones. This starts with getting out of our natural patterns, out of our ruts—illustrated with real business examples in chapter 5. There are many places to look for ideas and opportunities. Chapter 6 looks at how to see what others miss. Chapter 7 deals with applying different lenses to what we see—seeing the world from multiple perspectives. The last chapter in this section, chapter 8, points out how much can be learned by looking right under our nose, at the most mundane details that are all around us. These chapters contain numerous tips (labeled "Try This") and sources of ideas ("Gateways") for your further investigation and provocation.

1

The Open, Absorbent, Ready Mind

Mind Before Matter

As a sculptor Michelangelo was a great craftsman, skilled with his hands. But before he could begin to create his magnificent works, he had to see them in his mind. His art had to exist in his head before he could use his hands to bring it to life. It's the same with all of us. Before we can act, before we can begin to build toward the future and turn our dreams into reality, we must first look at the world around us and think about it.

In the daily heat of business, we often say, "Plan the work and work the plan." The overall enterprise—in fact, life itself—is no different. In every building process, in every construction of a great thing, we must study before we begin our work. In the 1930s, diesel pioneer Clessie Cummins became aware of a problem involving braking big trucks and buses; in 1957 he lay awake one night and came up with the solution, and the Jake Brake went into production in 1961. Though your dreams may not take that long to come to fruition, they probably won't happen overnight if they are dreams worth achieving.

The most fundamental skill of the curious person is the ability to look, to observe. Though we all need to read and to absorb books and magazines, the greatest source of our knowledge is our own eyes and ears in the real world. Even after we begin to build toward our goal, we need to keep scanning the world around us, observing and learning.

We sometimes confuse education with schooling, but most truly educated people receive only a small part of their education in the classroom. Two of the most successful entrepreneurs in my town of Austin, Texas—Michael Dell, of Dell Computers, and John Mackey, of Whole Foods Market—dropped out of college; they found the slow pace boring. Harvard, Oxford, and the local public schools are critical parts of our educational system. But so are PBS, Amazon, Barnes & Noble, Borders, our wonderful museums, and the ability to travel anywhere in the world at reasonable prices.

Exercising the Mind

Before we begin to explore and understand the world around us, we need to prepare our minds. We will grow stronger trees of wisdom if we first till the fertile soil of our mind. We must make sure it is clear and ready to accept the many seeds we will discover.

When people have extra money, they tend to pamper themselves—stay in luxury hotel suites, fly first class. But what about pampering our eyes and minds with images and ideas? Our culture puts great emphasis on getting rich, looking good, and being famous. But what usually makes people rich, and sometimes famous, is what's in their heads. We spend enormous amounts of time, money, and energy on making our bodies look good, exercising, watching our diet, eating supplements, and working out—but how much time do we spend exercising our eyes—our ability to look? Or exercising our minds—our ability to truly see?

Like our muscles, the eye and the mind can be exercised. We can make them better and stronger with practice. In his book *Living to 100,* Harvard researcher Thomas Perls reports on what he has learned from people who have lived a century. He stresses the importance of mental exercise, of working the brain. Beautiful bodies are fine, but beautiful minds are equally fine, and they too can be developed and strengthened.

The Sense of Wonder

"Wisdom begins in wonder."
—SOCRATES

Watch what children do when they are brought into a new environment. Notice how curious they are. Nothing escapes their attention. They become absorbed in things adults consider commonplace. The world is new, a landscape without limits, full of wonderful sights and sounds and ideas.

Once upon a time, we were like that. What happened? Maybe it was our school, our parents; maybe we've seen too much, listened to too many news stories; maybe it's having to work, or just living in the world. We are perilously close to a perpetual state of "can't be impressed," "seen it all," "been there, done that"—a condition that can be fatal to the mind.

The first thing we need to do is get back our childlike sense of wonder. In order to understand the present and the future, to see the opportunities that lie all around us, we must recapture the ability and the *willingness* to be amazed.

When was the last time some new bit of knowledge took your breath away?

- Just west of Java, in what we know today as Indonesia, there was once a volcanic island known as Krakatau. In 1883 Krakatau obliterated itself in the fiercest volcanic explosion of modern times. The sound was heard twenty-eight hundred miles away. The tide shifted in the English Channel, nearly the opposite point on the globe.

- Baby blue whales gain two hundred pounds a day for the first seven months of life.

- The arctic tern, a bird that weighs less than two pounds, follows the summer from pole to pole, spending most of its life in daylight, almost never landing. It migrates more than eighteen thousand miles each year—over its twenty-year life span, more than the distance to the moon and back.

Nature is not the only source of wonder. Humans can accomplish amazing feats, and the results are all around us:

- A fully loaded Boeing 747 weighs more than seven hundred thousand pounds when it takes off. One hundred years ago we couldn't have lifted one pound into the air using wing technology—unless we had a carrier pigeon nearby.

- Today, in your neighborhood, a supermarket brings you the best of the world's produce, the freshest and safest products, at low prices, often twenty-four hours a day. No one gives this a second thought; no one ever seeks out and thanks the manager.

- Last night, a huge team of people looked at all the developments in the world in the last twenty-four hours, summarized them, printed them in a newspaper, then rolled it up and put it on your doorstep—for less than a dollar.

If you cannot be amazed by facts like these, if you cannot say, "Oh, wow!" then you probably should put this book down and go on to something else. With an underdeveloped sense of wonder, you can't be amazed at human enterprise. You won't be able to create or lead such an enterprise, because you won't have adequate respect for its tremendous power.

Ponder First, Act Later

After opening (or reopening) our minds to wonder, the next thing we have to do is ponder. That is, we need to think before we speak, before we act, and—most important—before we conclude. Our lives move so fast that we've become hooked on urgency. We always want to "Go, go, go!" But there is also a time to stop and think, to contemplate, to ponder.

In a century that began with the Wright Flyer, we've grown blasé about traveling five hundred miles per hour six miles up in the sky. But maybe you've wondered what it's like to spend every day piloting one of those big 747s. If so, read Stanley Stewart's book *Flying the Big Jets*. In one of its most interesting passages, Stewart talks about what you do when the emergency lights are flashing, recorded voices are blaring with instructions, and it looks as if your world is coming to an end. What does the good pilot do? She stops and thinks. She knows she may have to act quickly, but she also knows she should take time to consider all the possibilities and options so that she can act with confidence.

Cultivate the skills of contemplation. The next time you go to a museum, don't just rush through it. Stop and think about each exhibit. Think about the people who were involved: what led them to create this art, explore this place, invent this thing? Why is the museum featuring this story? How does it all relate to what you are doing with your life? Your enterprise? Sit down at a table in the snack bar, linger over a cup of coffee, and make notes about what you've seen, heard, and thought.

Don't confuse pondering with indecision—becoming so paralyzed with thought and internal debate that you never act. There is a time to think and a time to act. If we picture passionate action as an exclamation point that follows the question mark, a life of searching, thinking, and planning followed by action might read like this:

?! ???! !!! ?! ?! ??? ?!!!

If we skip the period of exploration, of study and uncertainty, if we don't take the time to piece it all together in our heads, if we don't knit our knowledge into whole cloth, then our exclamations will only bring disappointment and failure.

Getting into the Information Flow

Sometimes it seems as if our thoughts just rattle around inside our heads. But that is not the way to really get your mind around a subject. We are at our best when information flows through us. We want to be a channel for the river—not a pond (or a puddle).

If your ideas flow—through your pen to the page, through your fingers to the keyboard, out your mouth over the phone or in casual conversation—they will become so much more vivid, more practiced, more tested. The more we think about our ideas, the more we bounce them off people, the stronger the ideas become—even if we find that everyone disagrees with us. Because we will interpret why they disagree, and we will either change our mind or be strengthened by their opposition.

The role of transcribing information can be a rush. We all know what it feels like to "break the news" to someone, to be the first to tell them something of major importance. Even when listening to a speech or sitting in a seminar, if we let the ideas flow into our head and down onto a note pad, they will have a more lasting effect on our mind. The more we can touch, feel, and see ideas, the better we become at handling them.

It's a good idea to set aside a few hours each week to take in new information—whether by reading or by exploring on your own. But even better is to use those hours to flow information. When you read something, pass it on to at least one person who would find it interesting; e-mail your insights and discoveries to a friend; do your exploring with others.

Great university teachers will tell you that in order for them to be satisfied they must have great students. It is the ongoing conversation with passionate students that helps teachers' ideas take form, that helps them articulate and better understand their own discoveries. And students are at their best if they are in turn teaching other students, discussing and debating their ideas intensely and frequently.

One of the fastest and most effective ways to learn is to become a two-way information conduit. If you have two friends who strongly disagree on some topic, try sitting between them and moderating the debate. If you can serve as a translator, helping each side to understand the other, then your understanding of the issues and passions involved will grow, too.

Information is a unique commodity: we can give it away and not only still possess it, but actually come out ahead. We are at our strongest when we are always learning and at the same time sharing what we know.

TRY THIS

Seek out the eccentrics around you. The folks in school or at the office who are a little different—who are obsessed with physics, with steam engines, with the tribes of New Guinea, with rugby, with the violin. Find out what drives their passion. When you run into someone like this, take them out to lunch.

GATEWAYS

Further Readings for the Open Mind

Read the *Wall Street Journal* or the *New York Times* as often as you can. These papers provide a broader perspective on life than most other dailies. *What Are the Seven Wonders of the Ancient World?* is a great book by Peter D'Epiro and Mary Desmond Pinkowish that has brief entries on lots of different topics throughout history. Each can serve as a springboard to further research and thinking. Other books that are great for spurring curiosity and exploration are *How to Think Like Leonardo DaVinci*, by Michael J. Gelb, and *Flatland*, by A. E. Abbott.

2

Complexity, Gathering Information, and Asking Questions

Once our mind is open and ready to receive, we can begin to absorb information.

But sometimes the world seems a hard place to figure out. Now and then we hear a simple explanation for everything, but when we examine the ideas, we can think of many circumstances where the explanation doesn't work. Oliver Wendell Holmes, Jr., said, "I would not give a fig for the simplicity this side of complexity, but I would give my life for the simplicity on the other side of complexity." Simple explanations arrived at without study, without a deep understanding of the underlying complexity of an issue, are meaningless.

The first task of the thinking person is to separate out what is mean-ing*ful* from what is mean*ingless*.

Virtually everyone has the capacity to better understand the world about them, even to be visionary with respect to one or more aspects of the world, if they learn the basic techniques presented in this book. The first step is to sort out all the information, to be comfortable with the intensity of the flow.

Every person, no matter how "smart" on any standardized test, remembers millions of pieces of data. What we remember depends on what we find interesting. And a corollary is that we remember things when they are connected in our heads. Most everything in our head, at least everything that stays there very long, is related to one or more other pieces of data. One of the great ways in which our minds really outpower even the biggest and fastest computers is the way in which we can rapidly link data, including linking it through different dimensions. In other words, in a single instant, our heads can do a mental dance that goes something like this: "Magic Johnson — Lakers — L.A. — Hollywood — John Travolta — Liberal Politics — Conservative Politics — Charlton Heston — Moses — Church — the Bake Sale Saturday."

In short, we all have tremendous power to see and to remember. But we can achieve understanding only if we are interested in what is important, if we link it together with other information in our heads, and if we keep our eyes open for it.

One of the things that scares a lot of people is information overload. The rise of the Internet has even increased the flow of information and placed it at our fingertips. How do we keep this avalanche of knowledge from crashing our brain?

First, relax and take pleasure in not knowing everything. A wine lover would be depressed if she felt she had tried every wine and there was nothing new to experience. No great athlete looks forward to the day when all the races have been run. If you love learning, then you have no problem with not knowing everything. You look forward to your future education.

Knowing everything is not the key. The key is to know five things:

1. Know what matters; rise above the clutter.

2. Know how it ties together; create a structure on which you can hang new information and link it to information you already have.

3. Know where to look for information; how to research and learn more.

4. Know how to analyze information; how to think about it.

5. Know how this information relates to your job, project, or personal goals—for example, how the information you gather might help you do your job well, understand how your car works, learn how to invest, or develop your life philosophy.

The first step in gaining wisdom is to sort out the meaningful from the meaningless. There are plenty of people trying to "edit" our information for us—newspapers, TV networks, cable news, magazines, radio, our friends, our family, our bosses, our employees. Having the *Wall Street Journal* or the *New York Times* show up on our doorstep each morning has spoiled us. Watching CNN and network anchors has spoiled us. We forget the huge effort behind these results. The critical process of editing, screening, sorting, and analyzing the flood of information is labor intensive and time consuming. But in fact we must ultimately take responsibility for editing our own information. And this often means undoing the editing done by others.

TRYTHIS

Owning over forty thousand nonfiction books, I could never assimilate their lessons if I read every page. Here are the steps I usually use:

1. Read the covers and inside jacket.
2. Look at the copyright page (usually right after the title page) to see when the book was published.
3. Read the "About the Author" to see where he or she is coming from.
4. Read the table of contents and think about what it says about the book.
5. Read the first paragraphs of the first chapter and the last paragraphs of the last. If this is not enough to understand the premise of the book, read the first paragraph of each chapter.
6. Look through the book for tables, charts, maps, and graphs.

Study each one and see what conclusions you can draw from it; then read what the author says about it.

7. Scan the index for people, places, and subjects that you already know something about, and which will therefore help you weave this book into your mind.

Asking Questions

"The master key to knowledge is to keep asking questions."
—ABELARD

Of course, there's no better way to draw information into our minds than to ask questions. It's hard to beat starting with the old-fashioned who, what, when, where, why, how much, and how.

Knowing our context always pays off. When I began working as a book buyer for a department store chain, I had the chance to sit down with the sales representatives of each major publisher. For years they had called on accounts and heard the same questions:

- What are your leading titles this season?

- How many copies are you printing?

- What's your advertising budget on this book?

- Is the author doing a publicity tour?

But I did not ask these questions—at least not right away. There would be plenty of time for these questions later. Instead, I asked:

- How big is your company?

- Do you publish in any specialty?

- What are your company's strengths and weaknesses?

- What's your market share?

- What are the most successful books you've ever published?

- What is the personality of your company?

- Who runs your company?

- What are they like?

- Are they new to the business, or veterans?

- Who's your boss, and what are they like?

- Where is your company based?

- Are the offices fancy or simple?

- How long have you worked for this company?

- Do you like it?

- What could your company do better?

That may sound like a lot of questions, but it took me only fifteen to thirty minutes to get the answers. They are questions you don't have to ask every time you meet. Gathering and comparing this information from all our suppliers gave me a huge advantage in understanding the industry and how it worked. When it came time to say, "Yes, I want to order a thousand copies of this book, but I want to have the author sign them in our store," I was better prepared to know what the answer would be and how to respond to it. Being familiar with the abilities, needs, and tendencies of my suppliers, I knew what to ask them for and how to get a creative advantage over the competition.

Remember the Pan American Airlines pilots who lost their jobs when the original Pan Am went broke? Many of them went to work for the airline in the 1970s and early '80s. They bemoaned the death of the company and blamed a million factors. Many were totally surprised by its demise. If these folks had only taken the time to study the airline industry before going to work in it, they could have seen that the future lie with Southwest, not with Pan Am, which had been troubled for many years. Southwest was hiring pilots all through these years, and the people who went to work for Southwest are glad they did. It is a tragedy to see people make bad decisions when the information to avoid them is often readily available.

Be curious about the world around you. It is the context for everything you do and everything that happens to you. No matter what your position or your enterprise, the more you understand your context, the more successful you'll be.

TRYTHIS

Every evening, ask yourself, "What have I learned today?"

3

Seeing the Whole:
Comprehensive Thinking Using
Concepts, Clusters, Patterns, and Chains

"Order and simplification are the first steps toward the mastery of a subject."
—THOMAS MANN

One trait that distinguishes successful leaders is their ability to get their minds around important concepts. When they look at an opportunity or a changing industry, they see not just details but the whole picture. It's like designing an airplane. Engineers concern themselves with whether the wing-fuselage joint is strong enough and where to run the hydraulic lines. The chief designer concentrates on the fundamental question: Will it fly?

Before we begin looking around the world, keep in mind that our ultimate goal is to bring together everything we learn into a unified body of understanding. This is known as comprehensive thinking. In the last chapter we talked about asking questions. We can ask a lot of questions, but if we cannot make sense of all that information, we will get no closer to our goals. The first step in such big-picture thinking is thinking in concepts instead of (or in addition to) words.

Conceptual Thinking: Using Word Clusters

Conceptual thinking starts with freeing ourselves from thinking one word at a time. We sometimes assume that words are exact representations of their meanings. But words are just symbols, no different from the little @ sign. They stand for ideas, concepts, and emotions. The meaning of most words is subjective and contextual. When an eight-year-old says she is in love with her favorite movie star, and I say I love pinball machines, and you say you love your spouse, the word "love" is in each case an approximation of the emotion we are trying to describe. Most conversation goes like this: we convert our ideas into words that approximate what we are thinking or feeling; we speak the words; the listener hears the words; the listener converts the words back into underlying meaning.

Each word carries certain baggage with it, and that baggage varies from one person to the next.

We can waste a lot of time and energy trying to force our thinking into little boxes, or trying to deal with other people's favorite words. Therefore, one of the best things we can do is to think in word clusters—groups of words which have overlapping, related meanings. For example, to describe the level of commitment and dedication that it takes to be a successful entrepreneur and avoid people thinking it just means hard work and long hours, it's best to lay down a whole string of ideas: dedicated, committed, obsessed, focused, single-minded, unwavering, driven, unstoppable, self-invested, all on the line, with all your heart.

Thinking in word clusters is made much easier by the fact that a doctor named Roget gave us an index of thoughts called the thesaurus. There are lots of good ones, but make sure and get one that is organized by ideas, not alphabetically (that is, avoid those that are dictionary-style). In other words, we don't want to see "politician" next to "poison."

We want to see (hopefully) "politician" next to "leader." Roget went to great lengths to put all our words into a logical structure, and it is a shame to waste his (or his successors') efforts toward that end. Anytime you are thinking about an idea or concept, pick up a thesaurus and drift around the pages near your word.

Network Thinking: Connecting What You Learn

Every piece of information you collect is probably meaningless unless you can connect it to the web that you are always building inside your head. Even if you have to stretch your thinking, connect it to something. If you hear that General Motors laid off a number of workers, connect it with the fact that Kodak laid off workers yesterday, or with the quality of the last GM product you purchased or rented, or with the news that GM is opening a plant in Mexico next month. Sometimes you will find an odd pattern linking the new piece of information with something that at first seemed irrelevant.

Once you begin to build information structures in your head, it will come easier. You should always assume that every fact you learn somehow relates to your own mission, your own enterprise. Many times the connection will be hidden, a mystery to figure out. Perhaps 10 percent of the time the connection is obvious; maybe another 40 percent of the time there is no connection at all. But buried in the 50 percent of the time that there is a less-than-obvious connection, there is a gold mine of understanding. If you don't see any connection immediately, assume there is one and keep mulling it over.

Every article about a successful business, no matter what industry, probably has a lesson for your enterprise. If you run a toy company and hear that teenage boys have a rising interest in reading, somewhere there may be a connection, a lesson, or an opportunity. Don't worry if you don't see it right away—but at least give it a try.

We are generally pretty good at looking at building blocks. We can understand bricks and other hard assets. But we are less good at understanding the value of the intangibles and of the linkages. No bricks stand without mortar; nothing moves without joints and tendons. No transactions take place without pipelines, phone lines, and wireless networks. Business dies without networks of people and relationships. Look at Coca-Cola's stock market value of more than $120 billion and compare that with its hard asset (book) value of less than $30 billion. That $90 billion gap is what Coca-Cola's brand name and its relationship with its distributors and customers (its "network") is worth.

As we form our understanding of a subject or part of the world, we begin to see how things relate to one another. One way to do this is to think of your industry—whether education, religion, or making pencils—as a game. In your industry, what are the "chance" cards? What are the penalties? Who are the players? How can they help you or hurt you? What are the defining moves, the moves that determine the outcome of the game? What is a "full house" in your industry? What is "Boardwalk" on your industry's Monopoly board?

If you're in the movie business, you acquire scripts and sign actors and other talent. You go through cycles of production, marketing, and distribution, and you end up playing your videocassette and international distribution cards. If you're in the oil business, three assets matter: oil reserves, refineries, and filling stations. Japan is on the game board as a destination; Kuwait as a source.

If you can think of your business as a game, you can begin to understand it as a whole. Even if you don't think through a complete game, at least diagram your business on a piece of paper. (Please note that I am *not* saying business is *only a game*—it is much more important to people's lives and aspirations than that.)

Looking for Patterns

In a TV ad, basketball great Bill Russell says he usually "made" the rebound before the other player even made the shot. Whenever you discuss any subject or any event, think like the chess player who sees three moves ahead while his competition sees only two—get on the elevator and take it to another level. Whenever you see A take action B, the first questions that come to mind should be next-level questions:

- What did A do yesterday? What will A do tomorrow?

- What are A's peers (the other A's) doing?

- Who else does B?

Note that this is different from looking for hidden agendas, a favorite hobby of the cynic. It is about looking at the plain, obvious facts and taking them to a higher level.

If we see that Prudential is going to acquire Aetna, the headlines will be talking about the two companies' press releases, about how much the stocks went up or down, and about who gets to run the new company. But we also need to ask:

- Who else was considering buying Aetna?

- Who else might those companies be thinking of buying, since they didn't get Aetna?

- Who else might Prudential be looking at buying?

- How will owning Aetna change Prudential?

- What are the cultures (personalities) of the two enterprises? Will it be a hard marriage or an easy one?

- What are the things that could go wrong?

- Who will benefit most if they go wrong?

- Who outside the companies involved will benefit most if they go right?

- What does this mean for my company?

Every year, I watch the TV stations do a story about the decline of the family farm and how sad it is. I have never once seen a broadcaster take

this story to the next level, to examine the pattern that is the real story—
the decline of small family businesses in general. Rare is the story about
the slow extinction of the family pharmacy, the family shoe store, the
family grocery store, or even the solo practitioner doctor. And yet there
is no way we can understand the whys, wherefores, and "solutions" for
the family farm without this broader understanding.

When a big corporation gets a new CEO, we are told the bio of the
new person. As to the previous CEO, we know only when he or she is
stepping down. But we need to be looking for patterns:

- What kind of people has this company hired as the last three or
  four CEOs? Is the new CEO the same, or different?

- How does the new person's age, gender, and years of service compare with historical patterns? Compared with the other companies
  in this industry?

- How does this person's background compare with that of his or
  her predecessors and peers? Is this the only marketer in an industry run by lawyers? Is this the first finance person to run the company after years of engineers?

Then, for each answer to the questions above:

- What does it mean, or what might it mean, for this company and
  for other companies in the industry? For your company?

- What can be learned from this event?

There's always another level you can take your thinking to. We hear
that people are migrating to city X because of jobs. But many other cities
have jobs available, too. What else about this city makes it the city of
choice? What can we tell from knowing which cities people are moving
away from? Are they coming from somewhere with a higher crime rate?

In everything you see, look for patterns. Look for the essence. Sometimes it's hard to see, sometimes not.

One of the most striking things everyone notices about Austin is its low voter participation. We have some bond referenda and other votes on which well under 20 percent of the people vote. But no one notices that state, national, and local elections and primaries are scattered throughout the year. It is not unheard of to have an election for a major race, then a bond election sixty to ninety days later. The real issue is not so much the voters' lack of interest as is the inconvenience and complexity of the process. Moving elections to two days per year might do more good than additional "get out the vote" campaigns.

Is the frequent-flyer mileage system really that different (in concept) from S&H Green Stamps? We think of one idea as the hottest thing going and the other as ancient history, but they are of the same essence—giving customers an incentive to be loyal.

Old ideas come back again and again. Scooters are back after a twenty-year absence. Ted Turner and his people had a great idea when they started the CNN airport channel—little snippets of relevant news just the right length for people waiting on airplanes. But it wasn't new—in the 1930s the New York City airline terminal showed newsreels to waiting passengers. Not only is the CNN idea not an invention of the late twentieth century, but maybe we've even regressed: that 1930s airline terminal was conveniently located in mid-Manhattan and had shuttle cars that took you directly to your plane at the airport just in time for departure. Maybe this is another idea worth bringing back.

Chains

One way to start connecting things is by understanding the chain (or chains) that the thing you are studying is a part of. If you own a bookstore, your chain starts with trees and ends up as a book someone is reading in bed. If you are a scientist, your chain goes from subatomic particles through atoms, molecules, cells, organisms, species or communities, planets, solar systems, galaxies, and the universe. Scientists who study the brain are finding it increasingly more difficult to separate physics, chemistry, biology, and medicine—another chain, with new con-

necting links being discovered every week. If you are a social scientist, your chain starts in the mind, then goes through the individual to the family or household unit, to the community, the city, the region, the state, the nation, the world. When I am writing this book, I am working on the "word chain": letter•word•sentence•paragraph•page•chapter• book•library•universal thought.

In this chain, each item is part of the next one. Starting at any point on the chain, you ask, "What is this a part of or an example of?" to go up the chain, and you ask, "What are the parts or examples of this?" to go down the chain.

The chain may be a time chain: baby•child•teenager•adult•senior citizen. The chain may branch: book goes to both bookstore and to online bookseller and maybe even a big corporation will buy thousands of copies for its employees.

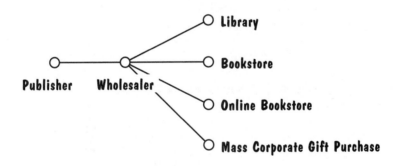

Loose Ends

Often the most interesting questions arise at the two "loose ends" of a chain. In physics, much of our energy goes to the tiny end (nuclear physics) and the big end (cosmology). In economics, the most interesting problems are often at the small end (why did I buy this book from Barnes & Noble instead of Amazon?) and the big end (how can we save the Brazilian rainforests?).

If you go to museums that feature history, the greatest growth of our understanding is at the two ends. That is, if you went to the museum twenty years ago and then go again today, much of the "new stuff" will either be about the last twenty years or it will reflect a better understanding of the distant past—new discoveries about Egypt, Mesopotamia, pre-Columbian America.

In human relations, the biggest challenges are often at the husband-wife level and at the Bosnia-UN level.

Multiple Dimensions

It is also important to realize that every entity is a part of multiple groups or chains. I am a part of Austin, of Hoosiers (people from Indiana), whites, males, students of retailing, music lovers, and Hoover's stockholders. We all play many games at the same time. General Motors is a carmaker and a giant financial company. We are each a crossroads of multiple dimensions. For example, here is another chain that this book is on.

The Book Is Somewhere on This Chain

2nd Reader
Used Bookstore
Reader
Book Retailer—Online or Store
Book Wholesaler
Publisher
Agent
Author

In reality, though, the book is on several chains. With a little reflection, you may dream up other possible chains. The more of them you can see or imagine, the stronger your vision.

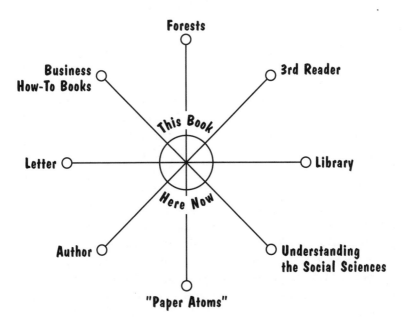

Common chains to keep an eye out for include these:

- Time—from past to future.

- Age—from old to young.

- Path—from the source to the destination.

- Price—from low to high.

- Hierarchy—from chief to subordinate, from king to vassal.

- Classification—from the specific to the general, from all living things through animals and carnivores to your dog Spot.

- Quality—from low to high. Any attribute that can be put on a scale—length, width, depth, durability, style, efficiency, maintenance costs, colorfulness, service level, convenience, customization level.

Take a moment to think about your business (or your idea for a new business). Dream up all the chains it might be on. Sketch out your web and think about the implications.

GATEWAYS

Further Readings on Conceptual Thinking

My favorite thesaurus is the *Bloomsbury Thesaurus,* edited by
Betty Kirkpatrick. Unfortunately, it is not sold in the U.S. but it
can be ordered online at www.waterstones.co.uk. Of the
thesauruses readily available in the U.S., the ones most similar to
Bloomsbury are *Roget's Bartlett's Thesaurus* and the classic bestseller
Roget's International Thesaurus (edited by Robert L. Chapman).

There are several computer programs available to boost your
creative thinking. Idea Fisher (www.ideafisher.com) is a computer
thesaurus that will readily give you lots of ideas. If you have your
own ideas and want to diagram them, one of the most interesting
pieces of software is Inspiration (www.inspiration.com). A very
advanced "idea processor" called Axon 2002 contains elements of
both and is available at web.singnet.com.sg/~axon2000/
index.htm.

4

First Step for Innovation:
Redefining and Reclassifying Your World

Quick, what is the largest stringed instrument in a typical orchestra?

Did you think only of instruments shaped like violins, such as the cello, viola, and bass? Or did you think of the piano, the correct answer?

Our thinking usually starts with a set of definitions and classifications. Often, we are so familiar with these definitions that we don't even think about them. "Major" sports means baseball, basketball, and football. "The networks" means ABC, NBC, and CBS. Whoops—now we have to include Rupert Murdoch's Fox. But our definitions sometimes go astray. Companies are often held back from innovative thinking by using worn-out definitions. So we should start by checking our definitions before proceeding.

Here are examples of definitions that have gone astray or become bent out of shape:

- We have been told all our lives that Europe is a continent. But by any rational definition of a continent (a large hunk of land surrounded by water), Europe is not a continent. It is a peninsula on the continent of Asia.

- If you go to a bookstore and pick up a guide to North American mammals, it will almost never include dogs, cats, or cows, and certainly not humans. Are we not mammals? The reality is that these books are not guides to mammals, they are guides to *wild* mammals.

- In the 1950s, one of the biggest figures on the world stage was Soviet "dictator" Nikita Khrushchev. He was supposed to have the same kind of "job" as Hitler and Stalin. Then all of sudden Khrushchev was sent to live incommunicado in his country cottage outside Moscow. If he could be fired, then what did this word "dictator" really mean?

- Go to the history section of a bookstore, or sit in a history class. When academics and authors say "history," much of the time they mean military and political history. But real history includes more: the history of General Motors, of Microsoft, of restaurants, of salads, of pets, of sports, of aviation, of churches, and of movies.

Great minds break through definitions that aren't right. For years, most of the work done in economics was restricted to money and business. But anyone who really understands the power of the economic way of thinking realizes that it is the study of the allocation of scarce goods. These "goods" can include religion, love, and many other intangibles. If the only reason we did things was to maximize the amount of money we had in the bank, why would anyone (except a farmer) ever have kids? It took Gary Becker at the University of Chicago to begin to apply economic logic to family and marriages, to racism and discrimination, even to crime and punishment. Eventually he won a Nobel Prize for his work, which changed the way we define "economics."

My first job out of college was working for Citibank. At the time, Citibank was led by a great thinker named Walter Wriston. While the other banks considered Citibank the competition to watch, Wriston told us that we were not just a bank, we were a financial services company, and that we should watch not just the other banks, but companies like Sears, Merrill Lynch, and Household Finance.

Lessons from Retail Definitions

Later in my career, I got to know the people who ran one of the best supermarket chains in the U.S. They were talking about how disappointed they were in their sales of greeting cards. They asked my advice. I looked at their organization chart to see how they classified their world. It read: "MEAT, PRODUCE, CANNED GOODS, DAIRY, BAKED GOODS, NONFOODS." That was all I needed to know. In their world, all those "nonfoods" combined—magazines and pots and pans and cookbooks and school tablets and garden sprays and greeting cards—got no more attention than baked goods. To this day, it is amazing that I can walk into the office-supply section of that supermarket chain and find no inkjet printer cartridges, no Zip disks. But the truth is that they are limited by their own classification system, by their own definition, by the structure they have put on their world.

The big department stores I worked for, companies like Macy's and May, were equally off-center in their own way: they saw their world as young women's clothes, teenagers' clothes, jeans, ready-to-wear, designer clothes, menswear, and the home store (appliances, furniture, books, stationery, records, sporting goods, pet supplies, toys, hardware, auto parts, tires, and bath and kitchen linens). Apparel is where these companies made their money and their reputation. The apparel department was also where most of the top executives came from. The long collapse of many of these "home store" departments in the 1980s and '90s could have been foreseen by studying a 1975 organization chart. Many of these categories were the fastest growing, allowing the creation of such companies as Toys "R" Us, Barnes & Noble, Office Depot, Tower Records, and Home Depot. The department stores that really flourished, such as Wal-Mart and Target, did not run away from these categories, but they also did not start out by thinking of them as stepchildren in an apparel-centered map of the world.

Today booksellers continue to define themselves as "booksellers." But customers often may be indifferent about the format in which "content" is delivered to them. They may want business information in an online subscription service; they may want electronic bird guides with sound and pictures in their pocket; they may want novels in paperback. The two things that booksellers really sell—information (or education) and entertainment (stories and visuals)—have a great future. But books in themselves may not have such a great future. In the coming years, I expect that books' share of total information and entertainment sales will decline (although I believe the total sales of books will continue to grow, just not as fast as other "information delivery" formats).

I have been talking to grocers who are in charge of meat departments. If they continue to define themselves as "meat departments," they may miss out on the great opportunity called "meals" or "dinners." That is, shouldn't hot dog buns be sold next to hot dogs? And if I want a vegetarian meal for a change of pace, might such meals be most successfully marketed as an alternative in the same "department"?

More Mis-Definitions

A famous article by Theodore Levitt, "Marketing Myopia," tells how the railroads lost out to the truckers because they saw themselves as railroads rather than as freight transportation companies. Today there are articles about the education industry that go on and on about universities and schools. But the strongest "competitors" in the education industry may include the A&E channel, the Public Broadcasting System, Barnes & Noble and Borders bookstores, Amazon.com, the public library network, and DeVry Technical Institute. Articles about health care focus on hospitals, HMOs, and doctors, but aren't Whole Foods Market, GNC, fitness centers, Johnson & Johnson, and Walgreen's an equally important part of our health infrastructure?

When you use the phrase "making my investments," do you mean just investing cash, or do you also value your time and energy? When I form new enterprises, my investment in time and effort is several times as great as my investment in money, no matter how much money I put in. When I borrow from the bank to take a trip overseas, I believe that I may be earning the highest "return on investment" of anything I could do with these funds.

Every time we stick a label on something or someone, we are classifying them. Some retailers call their customers "guests." This may lead them to a positive mindset about their customers. At the other extreme, a friend told me about a large "power and light" utility that refers to its customers as "ratepayers." It is unlikely such a company is prepared for a deregulated world in which customers have real power, in addition to some new light on the rates they'll pay.

One of the most misleading classification systems that we grow up with is the division of the world into politicians, lawyers, doctors, dentists, writers, ministers, educators, gardeners, and businesspeople. If you study the greatest businesspeople, they were often people with a very specific craft. Allen Neuharth, who created *USA Today*, was a newspaperman, one of many greats in that industry. Walt Disney was an animator-turned-dreamer. Lee Iacocca was a car guy through and through. Bill Gates was a nerd. These people are no more or no less "businesspeople" than the lawyer who runs a giant law firm, the doctor who runs a medical clinic, or a university president. They are leaders of people, trying to get things going in the same direction, trying to build their enterprises, trying to make their dream of the future become real. Walt Disney could no more have run a bank than Madonna. Yes, there are people who are purely "great managers"—Harold Geneen and Jack Welch come to mind—but they do not outnumber history's great merchants, inventors, marketers, broadcasters, and engineers.

Another of our current mis-definitions is the way we look at the Internet. We have this wonderful new technology that lets us network easily with everyone else on the planet. The Internet promises to bring us multimedia interactivity, twenty-four hours a day, seven days a week. It is perhaps the most powerful communication and transaction tool in history. But that's all it is—a tool. Just as the automobile, the airplane, the television set, the movie screen, and the microprocessor have changed our lives, the Internet is changing our lives again—perhaps more than any of these other tools, perhaps not. But this fact does not make every company that uses the Internet an "Internet company," to be studied by "Internet analysts." Amazon was a "mail-order" book retailer, one of the best-run retailers ever. Today it has evolved into a mail-order shopping mall, using this new technology to deliver information and services that old-fashioned mail order could never have done. Amazon may go on to greater and greater things, but it is no more an "Internet company" than Lands' End was a telephone company back when it got all its orders by phone. We cannot properly understand the business components and economics upon whose success or failure Amazon relies unless we understand the company's true industry and its direct competitors—Barnes & Noble, Borders, and every other seller of competitive merchandise.

eBay is not an Internet company; it is a wonderful clearinghouse for collectibles and other items—a great business model that can transcend any single technology such as the Internet. eBay could not have existed without the technology of the Internet, but eBay may be even more powerful when it adopts the next technology.

People are today so enamored of technology that we forget its transient nature. My town of Austin proudly calls itself "Silicon Hills." But the high-tech center of America in 1880 was Pittsburgh; in 1920, Cleveland or Detroit. Technology will by definition move on. Brands and customer relationships, however, have proven more durable over the years. When I began studying the top companies, Xerox and Digital Equipment were high-tech success stories, vying with Coca-Cola and Procter & Gamble for investor attention. Thirty years later, Coke and P&G still stand, but Xerox is weak and Digital is gone.

It is just as bad to lie to ourselves about the definition of our own enterprise. If you are an insurance company but call yourself a "financial services company," you'd better not be just an insurance company. Are you cashing checks, taking deposits, paying interest, trading stocks, or helping with taxes and accounting? Those are all financial services. If you're not providing at least some of those services, you're misleading yourself.

If you start your search for understanding with bad definitions and classifications, you will not learn what you hope to learn. When you first begin to think about any subject, take a hard look at how it is defined. Study the generally accepted categories, the way people normally divide things up. Is it a logical system? Is it an inclusive system that takes into account all of the players? If the definition other people are using is wrong, if it is not robust enough, discard it and think up a better one. You cannot afford to build your whole structure of understanding on weak foundations. And you may not be able to afford to see the world in the same light as everyone else.

If you have a strong foundation in place, if your mind is ready to absorb and connect new information, then its time to get out and start looking—in the oddest of places and in the most unexpected ways.

5

The Expected World
and the Role of Serendipity

Aristotle Onassis, the Greek shipping magnate who became Jacqueline Kennedy's second husband, once said, "The secret of success is knowing something nobody else knows." He was right, but it could be worded more broadly: "The secret of success is *seeing something nobody else sees.*"

In order to creatively explore the world around us and the opportunities it holds, we must first open our eyes and minds to these opportunities. There are probably a million ways to see such opportunities. In this chapter and the three that follow, we'll look at some of the most useful techniques. We'll first look at how to ditch our expectations and then at how to see what others do not see.

The Expected World

It's amazing how much of our time we spend in ruts. This is "the expected world," because it is exactly what we expect.

In the 1970s, in the process of developing my first enterprise, BOOKSTOP, it became clear that one of the most significant retail trends for the next twenty years would be the rise of the superstore—the "category killer." The idea, invented by Charles Lazarus and his colleagues at Toys "R" Us, was to sell a wide range of merchandise in a specialty category, at competitive prices, and in large, well-organized stores. Instead of scattering fifteen little stores around a city, build five monster stores.

Large stores have economies of scale. Retailers like Kmart and Sears already understood this, but most specialty stores of the time did not. By operating a large store, superstores reduced real estate, payroll, and other costs as a percentage of sales. Anyone observing Toys "R" Us (and watching its profit statements) saw a company that made millions of customers happy, created thousands of interesting jobs, lowered prices, and made exceptional profits. I believed that this powerful new concept would sweep through retailing. This was the mid-1970s, when Toys "R" Us was going strong but few other superstores had started up. Home Depot, which ultimately built the largest superstore company, did not open its first store until 1979. In later years, these companies were followed by other entrepreneurs who created more superstores, including Circuit City, Best Buy, Bed Bath and Beyond, PETsMART, Office Depot, Staples, and Virgin Megastores.

Thus my study of the retailing industry indicated that my odds of success would be improved if I applied this new technology—the superstore—to some category of merchandise. But what kind of merchandise should I sell? The answer to that question came from studying people. If I could link into some growing or accelerating demographic trend, my odds of success would increase.

The most important trend among consumers was the rise of the baby boom, which I define as the surge of children born between the end of World War II and the next low point in births—1973. People of this generation were better educated and more active than their parents, had broader interests, were committed to continuing self-education, and were raised in the television age. They included the Woodstock generation, but in the latter part of the twentieth century, they would be getting raises, buying houses or renting bigger apartments, raising kids, and living in the suburbs. As longshoreman-philosopher Eric Hoffer said, today's protestors are tomorrow's insurance salesmen. Given these trends, I believed that this huge population group would increase their spending as they aged, and that they would in particular spend more on toys, recorded music, sporting goods, home improvement, auto parts, and books.

If I could bring the superstore concept to one of these categories, I would take advantage of both current trends in the retail industry and long-term trends among consumers. Since I love books and bookstores, I chose the book business.

Early in the process of planning BOOKSTOP, I attended the 1981 annual bookstore-industry convention, held that year in Atlanta. I went to a workshop titled "The Future of Bookselling," expecting a discussion of the coming of the superstore. But all I heard was talk of factors that were already at work—such as the competition from book clubs and from wholesale clubs like Sam's and Costco. The superstore was never mentioned. It was as though the booksellers had never been to a Toys "R" Us. Certainly they had never looked at the superstore chain's annual report, which contained the numbers that proved the concept. When talk turned to customers, the primary observation voiced was, "No one is reading anymore." This was the opposite of what was actually happening, and would continue to happen into the 1980s and '90s.

Why did no one in the industry see what was coming? The people in the bookselling business were (and are) a very bright, well-read lot, but a little parochial—they never got out of their stores, they never looked at other types of retailing or studied successful retailers outside of the bookstore business.

All of us tend to think in familiar channels. We all get into ruts. We never venture outside of our own industries. Doctors don't go to lawyers' conventions; hardware store owners don't go to restaurant conventions. Heck, brain surgeons don't even go to heart surgeons' conventions! It can be very difficult to see beyond the four walls of your store, your office, your sanctuary. If you're not looking around, you're not likely to see much.

Lots of folks would like to become rich. Some of them go to get-rich seminars. When they're eighty years old, they won't be rich—they'll just be experts on get-rich seminars. Why? Because *the basic rule of discovery is that nothing has ever been discovered by looking in the same place and in the same way as everyone else.*

If you *must* look at the same things as everyone else, at least look at them in a different way—wear colored glasses or stand on your head.

Jump the Track

Every day when we get out of bed, most of us are on a track—our old habits, our usual way of thinking, our comfortable routine. We follow that track wherever it leads.

Even the most creative people often get stuck in their ruts, not being truly creative in the broadest sense of the word:

- Rock music has been going strong for fifty years now. Yet most of the top recording groups are generally locked into the use of two or three guitars, a drum kit, a keyboard, and the human voice. Every few years, someone jumps the track and adds some horns.

- Writers produce novel after novel, but they usually stay within rigid rules. For example, few are illustrated, and not many novellas are produced.

- The genius of the great classical composers remained within tightly structured rules of point and counterpoint, of harmony and orchestration. You may have to listen to music from the other side of the world—for example, Balinese or Javanese Gamelan music—if you want to really get outside the box.

- Most architects in America and Europe do not use color or organic curved shapes. Go look at the architecture of Mexico, at the architecture of Shanghai, or at Gaudí's architecture in Barcelona to dramatically expand your vision of creativity in architecture.

- We write book after book about our technologically driven era. But most of these books are about computers and electronics, occasionally biotech. Rare is the book that mentions what Milton Friedman thought was one of the most important technological innovations of the postwar world: the ability to raise chickens en masse. Detergent, the superstore, and the cable television system were all important technological innovations, yet we rarely think of them that way.

I am not disparaging all those rock groups that use only guitars, keyboard, and drums—my life would be much diminished if Eric Clapton and his two friends had not formed Cream. Nor am I saying we should boycott architects who don't use color on their buildings. But if we occasionally take a step sideways, if we take the path less traveled 5 percent of the time, if we at least glance around us as we make our way through life, then we have a dramatically improved shot at making breakthroughs—a shot at discovering great things, at leading great enterprises, at turning dreams into reality. Only by thinking about the unexpected, by looking for the undone thing, can we really jump the track and create a whole new vision.

We all get into ruts. This book is about exploring, about getting out of ruts. I recommend that we all take more classes and learn every day. But if you are already going to night classes and have been doing so for years, then that is your rut. Skip some classes and drive through Alabama or Montana—or a unique neighborhood like New York's Harlem. You'll learn something surprising.

Charles Kettering was the engineering wizard at General Motors before World War II. He did more inventing than any American except Edison. Kettering started a company called Dayton Engineering Laboratories Company (DELCO) in his hometown of Dayton, Ohio, then sold it to GM. His new boss, Alfred Sloan, made him head of science at GM and wanted him to move to an office in Detroit. Kettering wouldn't move, so every week he drove U.S. Highway 25 between Dayton and Detroit. Others who drove the same stretch marveled at how Kettering made the trip hours faster than they did. When they asked him how he did it, he admitted that he detoured around small towns. He spent most of his time on country roads, not the main road. "You never get anywhere going the obvious way," he said.

We usually only consider a tiny fraction of the possibilities available to us. At any given moment, you could be doing any one of *millions* of different things. You could be sailing the Nile, reading Dickens, watching sports on TV, painting a picture of your dog, or praying. Open your mind to the possibilities. Most of the excuses about why we can't do this or that—not enough time, not enough money, not enough skill—are silly and can be overcome if the desire is strong enough.

TRYTHIS

- Go to a large newsstand and select fifty dollars' worth of magazines you've never heard of—the more diverse and the more unappealing to you the better. Take them home and scan them. Think about the people who read these magazines. What are they interested in? Why? What are the similarities and differences—between audiences and between magazines? Who advertises in these magazines, and what does that tell you?

- Do the same exercise with books in a bookstore or a library. Find the section that you are least likely to visit.

- Focus on a subject that you have superficially touched upon—something you don't know much about but think you might like to know more about. Maybe it's something you saw in a movie, a magazine, or a museum—World War II history, steam locomotives, dinosaurs. Go deeper into this subject; start perhaps with an encyclopedia, find references to three or four books, then read or scan them. Search the Internet. Write a summary of what you learn. Always seek links to other things you know.

- Do the same exercise with some famous person in history. You can start by looking through a biographical dictionary until you find someone who seems interesting. Find out who his friends were, his enemies, his competition, his students, his teachers, his passions.

- Contact some living famous person in an area that interests you. Many are more accessible than you might think. I had never done this, but thought I should follow my own advice, so I called up Stanley Marcus, the visionary retailer who built Neiman Marcus. I ended up visiting him in his office and learning a great deal.

- Pick something unusual that is of potential interest to you and include it in your next trip to New York or another major city. It could be anything—a collectible, unusual cameras, old maps, retro dresses—but it should *not* be something you can find at the mall. When you go to the city, ferret out places that sell the item. This exercise may take you to a neighborhood you've never even heard of.

The Ultimate Radar: Your Mind

To extend our horizons, we must get up on the highest hill around and look out as far as we can. We should look east, west, north, and south. We should look up. But we must also look down—at our village, at our own house, at our friends and family. All are potential sources of ideas and information. The more landscapes we know, the more scenery we see, the stronger our vision will be. We should try to travel as far as we can in every direction—into our own souls, backward through time, and physically to neighboring towns, states, and countries.

As we look, travel, and explore, we should try to leave our emotions and biases behind. Every person on earth has his own favorite hobbies, interests, and passions. But if we momentarily suspend our own tastes, maybe we will discover new ones; maybe we will see things in a new light. The human mind is a powerful antenna, maybe the best radar ever created. It is capable of receiving and processing vast quantities of information. It can handle a lot more than we ever ask of it. Keep your antenna turned on.

The Power of Serendipity and Browsing

Remember, in your search for answers, the answer is almost never where you expect it to be or where you are looking for it. The history books and the company profiles at Hoover's are full of stories of accidental discoveries that gave rise to great innovations—and often created great fortunes. It is difficult to exaggerate the power of serendipity:

- In the early 1950s, George de Mestral went for walk in the Swiss woods and came home with burrs in his socks. He invented Velcro.

- Percy Spencer was working in the microwave labs at Raytheon in 1946 when the Hershey's bar in his pocket melted. He invented the microwave oven.

- Pierre Omidyar's fiancée collected and traded Pez candy dispensers. In 1995 this led him to start a website called Auction Web. Today that company is eBay.

Having an open mind means always exploring—everywhere, all the time, and in multiple dimensions. Listen to every kind of music. Try every type of food. Go to a variety of movies. Read books from every shelf in your local bookstore or library. Go to another industry's convention. Don't say, "I'm not interested in going there," if you haven't been there.

One of the great risks of the Internet Age is the fact we can do our research with surgical precision. Online service providers offer customized services—such as a newspaper personalized to cover only your hobbies, your sports, your stocks, your news. But how did we ever discover our hobbies, our sports, our stocks, and our interests, except by stumbling across them? We did not know to look for them when we first found them. How much have we discovered by browsing an old-fashioned ink-on-paper newspaper and glimpsing a headline about some subject we had never heard of?

Today's automated dictionaries let us look up a word like "scone" without wasting time on other words. But flipping the pages in a traditional dictionary might also lead us to discover the meanings of "sclaff" (to strike the ground with the golf club before contacting the ball), "scoliosis" (curvature of the spine), and "sconce" (a decorative wall bracket for candles).

I love buying books on Amazon. The Web site suggests other books I might like, sometimes as perceptively as an intelligent bookstore clerk. But if I bought my books only through Amazon, I would miss that bargain table at my local bookstore's front door, the tables devoted to James Dean's birthday, the anniversary of the invention of aspirin, and African-American history. I'd miss all those books that I need, but that I had no idea I needed—all those ideas that I might otherwise never have stumbled across.

Of course, we must use the latest tools and take advantage of their power. But if we put our minds on cruise control all the time, we have no reason to expect they will remember how to work. Southwest Airlines, among the safest in the airline industry, is one of the few that requires pilots to land planes manually; most airlines use automated landing systems. They have the right idea: We must stay in touch. We must keep our minds, our eyes, and our mental muscles toned up. We must be strong enough "mental swimmers" to resist the tides of thought that sweep away all around us (or at least their minds).

TRYTHIS

Play a game with yourself—I call it "Toss It Up"—in which you break out of your normal patterns of living and thinking. Here are some ways to get started:

- If you always eat out, try eating frozen dinners at home for a week. If you usually eat at home, eat out every day for a week.
- When you eat out, try restaurants that are radically different from the ones where you usually go.
- If you go to church but not night clubs, or vice versa, reverse them.
- If you usually stay at Hiltons or Hyatts, try a Days Inn.

- Go three days with no TV, or watch TV several hours in a row.
- Explore performing arts you've never experienced before—opera, symphony, ballet, country music, polka dancing, or a gospel choir.
- Hang out at the mall or a hotel lobby on a Saturday afternoon, or at a downtown intersection from five to six P.M. Watch people.
- If you like the Rolling Stones, sample another musical revolutionary: Stravinsky.
- If you like Barbra Streisand, try another great set of female lungs: *Le Mystere des Voix Bulgare* (Bulgarian Female Vocal Choir).
- Daydream.

6

Seeing What Others Do Not

Be Skeptical

As we consume information, we first need to cultivate a healthy skepticism. Don't trust or believe something just because you've read it in a book, saw it on television, or heard it from an expert who tosses out statistics. Take a few seconds to compare what you hear with what you know. When it comes to data, official statements, assertions, and opinions, it's hard to beat that old Missouri slogan, "Show me."

Don't confuse skepticism with cynicism. I have friends who believe that everything that comes from the major networks is filled with liberal bias, and other friends who think the media is full of "corporate bias." None of these people are likely to gain a deep understanding of the world around them. If you suspect hidden agendas and dark motives in everything you hear, you're probably assuming way too much about our information providers.

In my experience, most of the bad information we get comes from people who are inexperienced, are innumerate, or are just poor observers.

Look Behind the Headlines

Although I believe our free American press is one of our country's greatest assets—in fact, one of the world's greatest assets—it has one inherent problem as a source of ideas and information. Journalists are normally focused on news, and news is often not very important.

A central truth in the life of a news editor is something called the "news hole." There are so many pages of newsprint that have to be filled with news each day, so many minutes of radio time, so many hours of television time. No matter what happens in the world, *the news hole must be filled.* If nothing of note happens, the newspapers and airwaves still have to be filled.

If you watch CNN Headline News (one of my favorite sources of leads for information), you know that it used to place state headlines at the bottom of the screen, rotating through all fifty states. I'm confident that the CNN editors were working hard to pick the most important stories. But on some days, nothing much happens. Consider these headlines, all taken from CNN on the same day (February 21, 2000):

- Ohio: SPRINGFIELD AUTO DEALER USES CANNON TO DEAL WITH PESKY CROW PROBLEM

- Illinois: PROPOSED HOOTERS RESTAURANT STIRS CONTROVERSY AT PEORIA WATERFRONT

- Tennessee: STATE EQUINE POPULATION THIRD IN NATION, AFTER TEXAS AND CALIFORNIA

- North Dakota: AGRICULTURE COMMISSIONER TO LAUNCH HIS REELECTION CAMPAIGN TODAY

- Texas: NEW VIDEO CAMERAS INSTALLED IN 214 CRUISERS USED BY LUBBOCK POLICE

- Indiana: EVANSVILLE TO GET DOPPLER RADAR TWO YEARS EARLY

- Alabama: BIRMINGHAM MAN'S UNWANTED COFFIN IS GOODWILL'S STRANGEST DONATION

Even when the headlines really are important, like "VICENTE FOX WINS MEXICAN PRESIDENTIAL ELECTION," the big news is often not what follows the page-one headline but the story that ran a year earlier, probably buried on page fifteen: "FORMER COKE EXECUTIVE MAKES BID FOR MEXICAN PRESIDENCY." The people who write the news, who live by the daily headlines, naturally tend to focus on the most recent event, when the real story includes events that happened at many times and in many places. It's often left up to us to piece it together.

When headlines reading "GREYHOUND DECLARES BANKRUPTCY" appeared some years ago, the real story occurred several years before: "CONGRESS DEREGULATES AIRLINES." When Boeing took over arch-competitor McDonnell Douglas in the 1990s, much of the real story dated from forty years earlier, when Boeing got its first passenger jet (the 707) into service a year before Douglas launched the DC–8.

Why is some information so hard to find in this age of superabundant information? It's not conspiracy; it's just another reflection of our tendency to follow others blindly, to march en masse down well-traveled streets. Book publishers do it, moviemakers do it, network executives do it. We all do it—unless we make a determined effort not to.

Perhaps we need our skepticism most when we read pessimistic stories. It's natural to take things that go right for granted. No one remarks over the dinner table or at the office water cooler, "Isn't it great that the occurrence of home fires in the U.S. has dropped significantly in recent years?" even though this is true. We're a nation of problem-solvers, so we go looking for trouble.

At the extreme, it has become an intellectual vogue to believe that things are bad and are getting worse. Arthur Herman has written a fascinating book, *The Idea of Decline in Western History*, which tells the intellectual and philosophical history of the doomsayers. Fortunately, the doomsayers have rarely been right and are not likely to be so in the future. They habitually underestimate the adaptability, intelligence, and power of people to make their world better—particularly people working together in voluntary enterprise to realize shared goals.

In a society inundated with significant and not-so-significant information, every thinking person needs to ask:

- Is this headline the right headline? Is it really the big story?

- What prior headlines led to this one?

- Are the numbers in this story correct? Do they make sense? Are they the ones we need to be looking at?

- How does this story relate to other things I know?

- Does this journalist's interpretation agree with, contradict, or add to my perspective on this subject?

- How much of this story is spin, opinion, or conjecture, and how much is hard fact?

We cannot delegate our responsibility to understand, even to the finest and most accurate of journalists, interpreters, and commentators, or even to the greatest of experts.

Looking Where Others Don't

Here's a good question to ask: What's *not* in the headlines? If you can think of some subject or industry that has not been written up in years, you may be onto something that's important and overlooked. The wholesale air-conditioning industry, President Rutherford B. Hayes, and the source of the Manoogian family's wealth can go years without being mentioned in the press. The Manoogian family? You'll find their name in the National Gallery of Art in Washington as major donors. They made their money from single-handle (Delta brand) faucets.

It's not enough just to look behind the headlines—you need to look where there are *no* headlines, where other people *aren't* looking. Headlines, whether on target or off, direct your attention to what everybody else is thinking about. To gain a broader perspective on the world, you need to spend some of your time looking at things no one else seems concerned with, thinking in ways other people aren't thinking.

When we started BOOKSTOP, we thought about how best to design our circulation—the aisles and paths that lead people through a store.

In the 1950s, when I was little, my dad owned small grocery stores. Among his books was one about supermarket design. It told how the inventors of the supermarket had discovered something interesting back in the 1930s: that people automatically turn right when they enter a store. And, if you put the high-traffic items—meat, bread, milk—on the perimeter of the store, customers will go all the way around the store to pick them up. In the process, they'll see the other items and probably buy some of them.

No one in the bookselling business had ever looked at store design the way the supermarket guys had. So when we opened our BOOKSTOP stores, we had a "raceway" aisle system that ran around the store in the shape of a baseball diamond. The three big traffic generators in bookstores—bestsellers, the newsstand, and children's books—were at the bases of the diamond, and home plate was the cash register. The results were impressive. In an industry where the average bookstore did under $500,000 per year in sales, our average soon surpassed $2.5 million. One of the keys was that we did not think like booksellers. In laying out our aisles, we thought like supermarket operators.

At Citibank, I covered retail stocks working for one of the top retail analysts, Pete Wetzel. One company I studied was Tandy (now Radio-Shack), one of the best retail chains ever. At its peak, it was spending close to 10 percent of its sales on advertising. With the help of that big ad budget, Tandy obliterated its competition.

Another very profitable retailer of the time was Petrie Stores, which operated clothing stores for young women under the names Marianne and Stuart's. Petrie spent *zero* on advertising. It put stores in regional malls and let Macy's and Sears bring in the traffic. Tandy and Petrie showed me that there is a wide range of marketing strategies that can work.

A few years later, I worked in the department store industry, which at the time still had some creative energy in it. But even then I would sit in planning meetings in which people would endlessly debate what percentage of sales to spend on advertising. All agreed that the figure had to be between 2 and 4 percent. Anyone who suggested any outside-the-box amount—1.5 percent or 5 percent—would get laughed out of the room. Yet none of those department store companies ever matched the profitability of Tandy or Petrie.

Jack Welch of General Electric calls this phenomenon "pushing the peanut." If you've budgeted 6.9 percent of sales for customer service for the last five years, you'll probably consider going to 6.6 percent or 7.2 percent in next year's budget, pushing the peanut a little bit this way or that way. You'll spend hours debating which way to go. You'll think of all the implications. You might get radical and consider going to 6.0 percent or 8.0 percent. But you will never, ever think about what would happen to your business if you slashed service spending to 3 percent, or raised it to 12 percent. Really good ruts are so powerful that we don't even know we are in them.

Several years ago, the press and the futurists were saying that the price of oil would skyrocket to $100 a barrel. Gas would cost Americans $5 a gallon at the pump. The oil companies based their business forecasts on this common wisdom—except Shell. Shell asked, "What if oil prices collapse?" They didn't *predict* a collapse; they simply planned what they would do if all the experts turned out wrong. In fact, the experts *were* wrong, and Shell was able to adjust quickly in a period of falling oil prices. The fact that Shell outsmarted its competitors was no surprise to anyone who has studied the long history of this fine Dutch-British company.

Unconventional thinking can and should be applied to every area of your business. As I go around talking to people about being an entrepreneur, I hear a lot of talk about how to raise money. The experts always mention venture capital, banks, angel investors, and strategic partners (big corporate investors). But your best sources of financing are often your customers and your suppliers. If you can get your customers to pay in advance or join a club, if you can get your suppliers to either buy stock or extend credit terms, that money is just as good as any other. No one has as much to gain from your success as your customers and vendors. But this is not inside-the-box thinking, not part of the standard textbook approach to financing.

Look for lessons you can transplant from one industry to another. Where are things being done right, and where are they being done wrong?

Sometimes thinking creatively is just a matter of taking something we are all familiar with and turning it on its head. We've all been told since childhood, "Don't play with your food." But it took the creativity of Joost Elffers to come up with clever "Play with Your Food" books and calendars.

Even people with opposing points of view are often locked into the same perspective. We can debate all day about whether General Motors or Ford uses better management techniques, until an outsider comes along and points out that DaimlerChrysler makes better-looking cars. For years, IBM and Unisys battled for the large mainframe market while Bill Gates and Steve Jobs were talking another language. If you can get out of the channel everyone else is in and look at things from a different angle, you can often gain fresh insights.

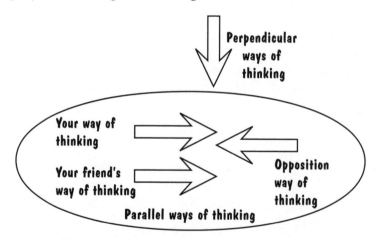

Finding the Strangeness in the Familiar

It's hard to get far enough out of our familiar patterns to see what is truly odd in our everyday lives. Yet there are things that we would view as strange if we came from another planet. I've always thought that extraterrestrials would be amazed at the way we ritually gather in our dwellings, alone or in groups, every evening between seven and eleven, and gaze silently at little boxes of flickering light. Visitors from afar might think these boxes were altars to some deity.

What would someone from another planet think of the Western sport of rodeo? We train the bull to throw the rider; we train the rider to stay on the bull. To quote a rodeo announcer on TV, "If you land on your feet, then things didn't go well at all!" Meanwhile, the participant at greatest risk is the one dressed like a circus clown. If this doesn't fit the definition of strange, I don't know what does. But every region and country has sports that appear odd from the outside (check out curling, or golf).

Would our intergalactic visitors find it odd that grain alcohol is legally available and acceptable throughout most of America, but that people who smoke marijuana are supposed to go to jail? Or that our government's way of showing it is wrong to kill is . . . to kill? Or that many powerful leaders of business and government organizations tremble at the idea of appearing in public without a knotted piece of silk dangling from their necks?

I am not suggesting that we stop wearing ties. What I am saying is that it's worth stepping outside our own world and looking at what might be odd from other points of view.

Learning from and Living with Paradoxes

"The paradox is the source of the thinker's passion."
—SOREN KIERKEGAARD

If you can get to the point at which half of you is asking "Why?" and half of you is saying "Why not?" then you may achieve new insights. For example, in the 1960s, you might have asked, "Why does it take me so long to get in and out of supermarkets?" But the next day, you might be in one of first 7-Eleven stores saying, "Why do people pay so much for these items when they could buy them for a lot less at the supermarket?" If you had put the two thoughts together, you might have answered your own questions.

Look at the paradoxes that you will find throughout this book if you read between the lines:

- One of the most important things is understanding the future, being a visionary in some way, large or small. But understanding the future first and foremost comes from looking at the past.

- Understanding the world, the key changes going on around the globe, depends on understanding our own town and neighborhood. Putting our own culture in perspective requires looking outward at other cultures. The foreign is understood through the familiar, the familiar better understood through the foreign.

- The best teachers are also scholars, always learning. Learning is enhanced through teaching and discussing what you know.

- To succeed, you must be obsessed with observing others and serving them. You must go out of your way to see things as others see them, to put yourself in other people's shoes. But you will not succeed unless you look deeply within yourself, at your own goals and desires, understanding and developing your own unique style and personality.

- To understand the world, you must be continually "grazing," eyes wide open and interested in everything. But to be successful you must be extremely focused, figuring out what things are most important to achieving your goals and putting your energy into them.

- Successful enterprises are successful because they have a consistent essence, which they hold true to, through thick and thin. Successful enterprises adapt on a daily basis to the shifting needs of their customers and to new technologies. Knowing what to change and what not to change are at the core of leadership.

Resolution of such conflicts is *not* what we seek. We don't want to pick "either–or." Remember that a string stretched taut is made stronger by the tension of being pulled from both ends. The interwoven nature of all these ideas will become clear throughout this book. It is above all else intended to be a challenge to your thinking, a springboard from which you can create you own success.

TRY THIS

Here are some things that will help you think in unusual ways:

- Art by Rene Magritte, Salvador Dali, M. C. Escher, and Jeffrey Smart
- Music by John Adams, Afro Celt Sound System, Astor Piazzolla
- Movies by Terry Gilliam, Werner Herzog, Errol Morris
- Nonfiction films *Koyaanisqatsi* and *Microcosmos*
- When in Chicago, visit the Seminary Co-Op bookstore at 58th Street and University Avenue near the University of Chicago and browse the books, most of which you will not find in other bookstores. The store also has one of the most unusual entrances of the world's great bookstores.

7

Looking Through Different Lenses:
The Renaissance Mind

The three words that people with new ideas hear most often are "Can't be done." People told us that BOOKSTOP could not both discount books and carry a big selection. When we started Hoover's, we were told that we could not provide great company information at a reasonable price. People thought Ted Turner's idea of an all-news network, in a world dominated by Walter Cronkite and the other big-network anchors, would never fly. When Allen Neuharth dreamed that America needed a national daily newspaper, especially one in color, they all laughed. Every day, entrepreneurs and other dreamers confront the impossible.

The most powerful tool for accomplishing the impossible is the ability to look at a problem—call it a challenge—in different ways. If you can see things only from the point of view of the marketing person, or if you can think only like an accountant, then you probably cannot lead a great enterprise to success. But if you can look at a problem with the passion of a preacher or of a salesperson, then turn the problem around in your mind and look at it with the precision of a physicist or of an accountant, then turn it once more and look at it with the eyes of an economist or of a psychologist, you're much more likely to figure out a creative answer. The more arrows you have in your quiver, the more likely you are to hit your target.

Even a cursory understanding of the way some other profession sees the world can be invaluable. The worldview of an accountant is a powerful one. So is that of a marketing professional. The perspectives of the biologist, the theologian, the auto mechanic, and the historian all have their power. You don't have to study each of these fields for years and become a professional, but the more points of view you can bring to bear on the world around you, the better.

A great way to sense the viewpoint of others is to read a book of interviews with workers. The classic is Studs Terkel's *Working*. Even broader and more current is *Gig*, a collection of interviews and articles edited by John Bowe and others. Both books let you sample how people from varied walks of life see the world—an eye-opening experience.

Work has become more specialized. In academics, in medicine, even in corporate environments, most workers tend to become more narrowly focused every day. A professor is no longer simply an historian, he is an expert in the Spanish monarchy. A computer person is no longer just a programmer, she is a Java applications specialist. This narrowing is an inevitable result of society's increasing complexity and a natural evolution of the division of labor, a powerful concept first fully understood by the great economist Adam Smith.

But the more specialized we become, the greater our need for leaders who can help bring unity to our efforts. We need people who can think, write, and speak with clarity and conviction, people who can relate to and motivate accountants and salespeople, nurses and electrical engineers, systems analysts and social workers.

Certainly we should not stop specializing. But if we devote just a small part of our time to learning other disciplines, other points of view, and other ways of seeing the world, we and the world would be better off. Of course, the ideal time to do this is during the four years many of us spend in college. It's called a liberal arts education. Maybe you went to college but didn't get much of a liberal arts education, because you got a specialized undergraduate degree, because you took liberal arts courses but didn't understand their importance at the time, or because you were too preoccupied elsewhere on campus. But it's never too late to start.

Entrepreneurs in Singapore have told me that their government prefers that the brightest students study science and math in college, while lesser students are directed toward the arts and humanities. I hope this is an exaggeration, but it's symptomatic of worldwide trends. On its website (www.compete.org), you will see that the American Council on Competitiveness has carefully studied the science and math scores of eighth- and twelfth-graders around the world, recognizing that these skills will be crucial to our future success. This is a good thing for the council to do, but it is unwise not to also look at skills like writing, reading comprehension, and awareness of history and the arts. The Council on Competitiveness frets that too few of our young people get science and engineering degrees, especially compared with Asia. So why is it that most of the world's entrepreneurs and inventions have come from America, not from Asia?

Two of the kings of the technological world, Steve Ballmer of Microsoft and Steve Case of America Online, both worked at marketing training ground Procter & Gamble before their rise to power. These are sociologists in charge, not scientists. The people of Singapore are concerned that they are not creative enough, not entrepreneurial enough. If all of their kids get science degrees, this is not going to change. Where is Michael Dell's Ph.D. in science, where is Bill Gate's E.E. degree? These fellows have a broad perspective on life, much of it gained in the real world rather than in the classroom.

I'm not knocking science. Many of my heroes are great scientists, and much of this book is devoted to seeing things scientifically. But many of the great scientists were people who also studied history and literature, music and psychology. Look at Benjamin Franklin, Leonardo Da Vinci, and Albert Einstein.

If you study the great enterprise builders, the people who have made a difference, you find that breakthroughs are usually made by people with a broad view of the world. They make use of the tools of science alongside the tools of social studies and the humanities. We need jacks-of-all-trades, renaissance men and women who can make sense of our incredibly complex and rapidly changing world, people who can weave many strands together into a clear vision of the future.

The World from Upside Down

We are all different. It is the variety of our viewpoints, our personalities, our life experiences, that makes the world an interesting place. We should take great pride in our differences, and we should go to great lengths to put ourselves in the shoes of others, to see things with different eyes. The visionary leader has the capacity to understand many perspectives, to see the world from many views.

We all have things we like to do and skills we are secure about using. We also have tasks we dislike, areas where we tread with fear. Some of my friends, when they need to add sound cards and other peripherals to their computers, hire technicians. I think, "How silly! Anyone can open up a computer and add these things!" But when I take my car to the Jiffy Lube to have the oil changed, some of my friends probably think, "I can't believe how stupid [or lazy] Gary is."

When I arrived at college, I met a fellow from Tarrytown, New York, where there was a General Motors plant, just as there was in my hometown of Anderson. He told me about his town: "The middle-income people live up on the hill; the poor people who work at the GM plant live in the valley." Talk about differing perspectives—in my world, the affluent people worked at the GM plants and the poor people were trying to get on at GM.

Sergio Zyman, former marketing master of Coca-Cola and author of *The End of Marketing As We Know It,* points out that marketing success is really about studying people—why they do what they do and how you or your enterprise fits into that. Study people's jokes, see what movies they line up for, check out what music they listen to, what they wear, what they eat, what they drive, what kinds of pets they have. Stop and think about how these things have changed over time.

Crossing Boundaries

Understanding the world around us means understanding people—lots of people. Not just ourselves, not just our friends and family, not just people who think like us. It means putting ourselves in the shoes of as many different kinds of people as we can discover.

One thing that holds many people back is that they hang out only with people who agree with them. It's easy to talk to people who share your religion, your politics, your racial background, or your club membership. That's not the challenge. Can you hold a conversation with a trucker, a member of the Communist Party, an evangelical Christian, or a hip-hop artist? Can you enjoy chatting with a divorce lawyer, a plumbing fixtures salesman, an Avon lady, a dance instructor? You may be asking, "Why would I want to?" But understanding the world comes from crossing boundaries like these.

It's equally important to study ideas you disagree with strongly. When I was in college, I had the privilege of being taught by Milton Friedman, the Nobel Prize–winning economist. It was the early 1970s, a turbulent time on college campuses. Some of the students in the class were ardent socialists and would argue the merits of Marxism with Friedman. These were bright kids, totally committed to their socialism. And yet, every time, Friedman would demolish their arguments in short order. Over time, it became apparent that he won these arguments because he knew more about socialism than anyone he ever ran into. He had read every book; he had taken Marx and Engels very seriously; he had studied all the nuances of socialist theory. In short, he understood the "enemy" better than they understood themselves—a pretty tough position to attack.

When you study a subject, whether socialism or management techniques, abortion or the environment, do you look only at the books and magazines and websites that agree with you, or do you try to look at the issue from different angles? Do you make an honest effort to see the world through the eyes of others, including the eyes of your opponents?

Beyond the Executive View

Last year, I came home late one night from a grueling business trip. At the airport, I realized I didn't have enough cash to get my car out of the parking lot. Spying an ATM machine across the airport, I trudged over to it, lugging my bags (which, as always, were full of books). After the usual pause, the machine flashed a message: "OUT OF SERVICE." As it happened, a passing security guard pointed out another machine some distance away. From where I was, I could see the glow of its well-lit screen, and it looked as if that machine was working. So I lugged my bags and tried again. No luck.

By now, I was not in a good mood. I thought, why should the next poor fool have to walk all the way across the airport only to discover that this machine isn't working? I reached down and unplugged it from the wall, darkening the screen.

But this story is not about a malfunctioning machine—it's about malfunctioning management. When I came back through the airport several days later, I checked the machine once more. Lo and behold, not only was it not fixed, it was still unplugged! I know that many of the bank's executives pass through that airport daily. But would it ever occur to any of them to check their ATMs? No, that would not be their department.

How many managers at a big bank cash their own checks? How often do they wait in the drive-up lane? Do their assistants always take care of these things for them? Are their paychecks on automatic deposit? If you're in the insurance industry, do you really know what it's like for the typical customer to deal with your industry and with your company? If you work for a university, do you know what it feels like to be a high school senior filling out applications or a grad student looking for a grant?

When the CEO of one retail chain I worked for—I'll call him Jack—finally talked his board of directors into getting him a corporate jet, I felt it was the beginning of the end for his "connectedness." When Jack flew on commercial airlines, even in first class, he at least ran into a *few* customers and had to sit there and listen to their comments: "What I don't like about your stores is . . ." But that era ended when Jack got into the company jet. A corporate pilot isn't likely to come back to the cabin and say, "My wife hates your stores because . . ."

Putting yourself in the shoes of an average customer sometimes takes work. Travel agents, especially the high-volume producers, receive perks from the airlines and hotel chains. Thus, when these high-achieving agents travel, they usually stay in plush hotels and resorts and pay reduced rates—from one-third off to free. A side effect is that you will almost never meet a travel agent (except a beginner) who has stayed in a Motel 6, or who has actually paid $300 of their own money to stay in a luxury room. Travel agents avoid coach-class seats like the plague. As a result, relatively few of them really know what it is like to be a typical traveler.

Seeing Things in Their Normal Context

Another important exercise is something I call "contextual observation"—seeing things the way others will see them, in the same order and environment. For example, if you're a typical company executive and your company has just produced a new TV ad, the standard way to see the finished ad is in a viewing room—a comfortable room at the ad agency or video production center with giant, high-quality monitors. Everyone is very quiet, there's a "Ten, nine, eight . . ." countdown, and you see your ad in all its glory. Then everyone reacts—either by getting upset, by saying it's great, or by saying nothing.

But no viewer of your TV ad will ever see it this way. She may see it in a house with kids running around, she may see it on a hotel TV, or she may see it while relaxing in front of a big-screen TV in her family room.

In any case, she will certainly see your wonderful creation sandwiched between a million-dollar Nike ad and a "Sam's The-Devil-Made-Me-Do-It Low-Priced Car Lot Next to the Giant Chicken" ad. These surroundings impact how the viewer will experience your ad.

When retail executives travel around looking at their stores, they usually go from one location to the next—from Circuit City #312 to Circuit City #499 to Circuit City #800. But most of their customers experience the stores in a very different way. When comparison-shopping for a new stereo, they go from Circuit City #312 to Best Buy #499 to Mom & Pop #1 to electronics.com to the Sharper Image catalog.

If we try to understand things out of their natural context, we may never understand them the way our customers do.

The more we can see things the way others see them—our work associates, our community, and, most important, our customers—the more we can build a comprehensive view of what matters.

8

Right Under Your Nose
and All Around You

Life all around us has texture, a feel. Some of that texture is chrome and glass and silk, but more of it is cobblestone and brick, burlap and wool. In seeking new ideas and opportunities, it's important to reach out and touch everything around us—especially the world that's right at our feet. We look around, we look straight ahead, sometimes we look up, but rarely do we look down. We miss so much that is right under our nose.

There are streets that you drive again and again, on the way to work or to the grocery store or to the restaurant. Get out of your car and stroll one of those blocks. See what you've never seen before. Every block tells stories—of people, their needs, their wants, their dreams. Every statue in every yard, every half-restored old car, every tricycle, every picture in every window, tells a story.

When we travel, we go to a new city, we eat at the best restaurant, we go to the observation deck atop the skyscraper, we *oooh* and *aaah*. But do we stop in the corner deli or diner? Do we sit with the people who keep the city running? You can learn as much from the local workers in one hour at a breakfast counter as you can learn in a year of nice meals at the trendiest restaurant with your best friends. Great politicians know this. So do great leaders of enterprise.

We are naturally fascinated by the rare, the unusual, the near-extinct. But we ignore the everyday. If you go to the bird section in a bookstore or to a "birds of prey" Web site, you'll see lots of information about the California condor, the nearly extinct raptor, but very little about the turkey vulture, which has thrived in much of the U.S. by adapting to a changing world. You will find more books about wolves than about coyotes, more information on sports cars than minivans, more research on rare diseases than on headaches and colds.

No detail around us is too small to be noticed—and, in the right hands, used. As a retailer, I know that the most valuable real estate on earth is the ten square feet that surrounds the supermarket checkout stand. If I have something great to sell, I can make a fortune if I can just get it next to the cash register in every supermarket or every convenience store. So I am always studying how the world economy uses this most valuable of real estate, how its highest and best use changes from one visit to the next, from one season to the next, from one fad to the next.

You can learn about family structure by walking the aisles of a supermarket—how many people are in the average household, how many kids, how many elderly folks, how many pets. You can learn how people are organizing their lives, how their priorities are shifting, by walking through a Container Store (one of America's most exciting specialty store chains). When was the last time you *really* absorbed all the information a mall has to offer? Such information may be the most valuable thing (and the least expensive) in the mall.

When you go to a Chrysler dealership to check out the Chrysler 300 or the even hotter PT Cruiser, pick up a brochure about the minivan to see what is important to people today.

One of the greatest retailers of all time was a fellow named Harry Gordon Selfridge. Starting with nothing, he rose by the turn of the last century to be the great manager, innovator, and promoter at Marshall Field's in Chicago. He finally decided to strike out on his own and opened the biggest store in Britain, Selfridge's, which you can still visit

today in London's Oxford Street. No detail escaped his eye. When one of
his people disparaged the hundreds of city buses that clogged the
street in front of the store, Selfridge remarked about how frequently the
buses came by (he had timed them), how many people got off each one
(he had counted them), and what share of the store's business came
from these people (he had tracked it). Selfridge subsequently ran a newspaper ad thanking the employees of the bus system.

Coca-Cola marketer Sergio Zyman talks about how much time and
energy (and millions of dollars) Coca-Cola invests in its TV ads. But he
also points out that the sides of the thousands of Coca-Cola trucks
around the world are a more important part of its advertising than television. Look closely and you'll see that the company's vending machines
have evolved from being merely dispensing devices to powerful visual
appeals.

I had a speaking engagement in Brisbane, Australia. I got there a day
early so I could look around. Brisbane was wonderful from the start and
kept getting better. After I had toured the downtown botanical garden,
I went to the bus station, where the Australian long-distance buses came
and went. I am sure I was the only American businessman in the building. The first business my college friends and I started was a charter bus
business. I've never lost my interest in the industry. In the 1960s, the
largest carrier of passengers in the world was the Greyhound Bus System. After the 1979 deregulation of airlines, that era came to an end in
the U.S.

So I am standing there watching the Aussie long-distance busses
come and go, and I realize two things: they are frequent and they are
packed with people. And this is a country that has lots of long distances
to cover. My first reaction was one of melancholy, for the old days when
U.S. bus stations would have been buzzing with activity like this. But my
second reaction was more instructive: airline ticket prices in Australia
were too high. I knew this from what I saw in the bus station. I did not
have to study the airline industry; I did not have to look up airfares. The
evidence was right in front of me. Forty-eight hours later, even before I
left Australia, Virgin's Richard Branson announced he was going to start

a low-cost no-frills Southwest-like airline in Australia. Qantas's shares dropped 25 percent. I guess Richard must have stopped in the bus station, too.

Motivational speaker Bertice Berry says she doesn't believe in networking, where you're always trying to link up with people who have power and influence. She believes in quiltworking, in which every patch has its place, every stitch matters. It is critically important that we look at every thread. You never know which one may be the starting point for your next great idea. The credo of the learning person is: *There is no one on earth who I cannot learn something from—the rich, the poor; the bosses, the workers; the young, the old—no one.*

Looking for Gaps and Vacancies

As we've discussed, in order to see opportunity, we must be open to it. We must be ready for new ideas.

If you wish to start an enterprise but have not yet figured out exactly what you want to do, the most important thought in your mind should be a simple one: *Find a need and fill it.* I've looked at hundreds and hundreds of business plans. Many use cutting-edge technology in intriguing ways. Others meet the needs of the inventor and no one else. Still others are designed to look good to venture capitalists and other investors. But the business plans that are likely to succeed are the ones that address the real needs of real people.

Ultimately, the opportunity to create significant new enterprises from scratch, as well as the ability of existing enterprises to embark on bold new initiatives, depends on the ability to see unmet needs and unseen desires. Successful enterprises and their leaders continually search for new ways to serve people better.

Many times this starts with asking why and why not; with looking around at how things are done today and imagining how they could be done better; with thinking about an ideal world. Look for things that are not working, look for problems, for opportunities. Look at things that are working, that are popular. Think about how to take those ideas and adapt them to other industries. Look at things that need tweaking, where a small shift in style, operations, or attitude would create a new opportunity. *Observe every transaction and think about its implications.* Why is this person buying what he is buying? Why is the seller selling what she is selling? What else is the buyer likely to want to buy? Might the young man driving off the lot with a new Camaro be going straight to the custom stereo shop? Might the old gal looking for hot dogs in aisle 16 be looking for hot dog buns in a few minutes?

Last year I worked with a very bright group of young software engineers. Their goal was to dream up new business ideas. They met every week in wonderful brainstorming rooms—the walls were covered with whiteboards; their technological tools were the best. They talked and surmised and dreamed together. I pointed out to them that if the best way to come up with great business ideas was to get a bunch of bright people in a room talking to one another, then all of our great companies would have been formed at Harvard and Oxford and Yale. But most of our great enterprises were not formed in those places. I told my young friends to get out of their isolated tower as quickly as possible and *run* to the mall—or to the cafeteria of a giant company, or to an airport, anywhere that they could find and watch real people having and talking about real problems. Get out of the strategy room and onto the battlefield.

Back in 1951, Memphis building contractor Kemmons Wilson was driving across the country with his wife and five kids. He couldn't find a decent place to stay that he could afford—every little motel charged $2 per child, TV was extra, and there was usually a key deposit. Wilson told his wife that they should build four hundred new places to stay, enough to cover the country. She laughed. But when Wilson got back to work, he had a draftsman draw up a concept for a chain of such motels. The night before, the draftsman had watched a Bing Crosby movie called *Holiday Inn*, and he stuck that name on the drawing.

The idea of the motel chain and the larger concept of franchising took a giant leap forward. The old lodging-industry leaders like Hilton and Sheraton took years to realize what had hit them. Twenty-eight years later, when founder Kemmons Wilson retired from the company, there were 1,759 Holiday Inns all around the world.

Looking at the Best

Every day we encounter examples of high quality and low quality, good industries and bad. And in those experiences lie hidden insights. In the worst-run industries lie opportunities through which an innovator can succeed, and in the best-run industries are found the ways to do so.

When we fail, we point fingers, assign blame, and even form high-level committees and task forces to look into the causes of failure. But when we succeed, we tend to pat one another on the back and head straight for the celebration. We waste an awful lot of time crying over spilled milk but often spend too little time studying our successes.

In nature, we should be at least as interested in the world's longest-surviving species as we are in the endangered species. Study cockroaches if you want to understand durability and adaptability. Study coyotes and turkey vultures.

In politics, too, success is often overlooked. People in one party may try to make something of their successes, but the opposition and the media rarely grant them any credibility. People examine failures with a fine-toothed comb.

To overcome this tendency, we need to seek out success and study it. Almost every organization, whether it's a corporation, a church, a college, a hospital, or a government agency, does something right. The more we understand about success, the better.

Stop and look around. Look at your town, your company, your industry. What are the most successful organizations? Who are the most successful people? Who does the most to make the world a better place? Who does the most to help other people? What can we learn from them?

Of course, we can learn from failure. But we don't have to go out of our way to study it—the press will see to that. On the other hand, it is usually up to us to recognize and understand the greatness that is all around us.

GATEWAY

Further Readings on the Everyday Things Around Us

People are writing more books about the history of the things that are all around us. Some of my favorites include any book by John Jakle and colleagues. They include *The Motel in America*, *The Gas Station in America*, and *Fast Food: Roadside Restaurants in the Automobile Age*. Other good books include *Crabgrass Frontier: The Suburbanization of the United States*, by Kenneth T. Jackson; *Ranches, Row Houses, and Railroad Flats: American Homes—How They Shape Our Landscape and Neighborhoods*, by Christine Hunter; *The Way Things Work* and *The New Way Things Work*, by David Macaulay (now available on CD-ROM); *The Design of Everyday Things*, by Donald A. Norman, and two out-of-print classics, *The Americans: A Social History of the United States, 1587–1914* and *Great Times: An Informal Social History of the United States, 1914–1929*, both by J. Furnas. (My favorite source for out-of-print books is www.abebooks.com.)

EXPLORATION II
History: The Study of Change Through Time

9

Why History Matters:
The Importance of Watching Trends

"In every affair, consider what precedes and follows, then undertake it."
—Epictetus

Once our curiosity is in place, how do we use it? What do we pay attention to? We can and should ask questions like, How much? Why? and Why not? But often we fail to ask, What came before? How are things changing through time? My study of business has led me to believe that one of the most common causes of failure is the inability of leaders to see the most important underlying trends—trends that emerge from the past to create the present and shape the future.

For example, one of the most important developments for retailing and marketing since World War II has been the entry of women into the workforce. In 1940, 25.8 percent of American women had full-time jobs. As of 1999, that figure was up to 60.0 percent. This shift has had huge implications for our society, affecting everything from the demand for child care to car design. But one of the resulting changes is that people no longer shop Monday through Friday from 9 to 5; they primarily shop in the evenings, on weekends, and during lunch hours.

The entry of women into the workforce is a big, slow-moving, almost glacial trend. It was never an event, never the kind of "news" that journalists (or the rest of us) could readily get their hands around. There was never a morning when the *New York Times* ran a headline declaring, "50.1 PERCENT OF U.S. WOMEN AT WORK THIS MORNING." Since this development was never "news," many people missed it, including many who could not afford to miss it. The U.S. Post Office, which hired a lot of those women, never noticed that their customers might need to pick up a package on a Thursday night or to drop one off on a Sunday afternoon. But competitor Federal Express didn't miss the change. Unlike the Post Office, they adopted extended work hours.

U.S. banks, which hired large numbers of those working women, never noticed that their customers might need to be able to apply for a car loan on a Saturday afternoon or a Friday night. The travel agency industry, which employed 64 percent women the last time I checked, even today is not available to sell cruises or package tours on nights and weekends in most cities. Travel agencies that stay open until 2 P.M. on Saturdays pride themselves on their "long hours." My retail experience tells me that the peak of the retail week is from 2 to 4 P.M. on Saturday. The "long hour" travel agencies are closing down just as people are starting to spend their money! The next busiest times for retailers are Friday nights, Sunday afternoons, and Thursday nights.

Of course, not everyone missed this huge trend. Supermarkets, book superstores, and even the older department stores have now extended their hours. The ultimate in round-the-clock shopping has become available with the rise of the Internet. Today, trapped-in-the-ways-of-the-past service companies which have ignored their changing customers, like banks and travel agencies, have set themselves up to be especially vulnerable to the rise of Web-based businesses, which provide service twenty-four hours a day, seven days a week.

Large, slow-moving trends are easy to miss. But missing them can spell the end of your enterprise. Fortunes are lost this way. On the other hand, alert observers create new fortunes by seeing where things are going, by recognizing trends at work a little quicker than the competition.

Early in the twentieth century, a young American soldier named Wood was stationed in Panama. He came down with a fever and was sent to the infirmary for an extended period. The only way to kill time during his recovery was to read the handful of books the army had placed there—including some compilations of census data.

In his shoes, most people would complain bitterly: "Stuck here in bed with nothing to read but columns of figures! What could be more boring?" But young Wood became a student of demographics.

Years later, the same fellow—now called General Wood—found himself at the head of the great merchandising giant Sears, Roebuck. After World War II, Wood's interest in demographic trends helped him recognize that the suburbs would soon rise to prominence. He built as many stores in suburban locations as possible, offering new homeowners tools, appliances, and lawn mowers.

Meanwhile, Sewell Avery, who ran Sears's arch-competitor Montgomery Ward, believed that the U.S. was sure to experience a recession with the end of the war. Fearing the effects on business, he held Ward's construction of new stores to a minimum. The bankruptcy of Ward's in 2001 was in part a long-delayed reaction to the strategic error Avery made (and Wood did not make) fifty years earlier.

Sears won the battle because it was run by a fellow who took the time to study where people were going and why. The Sears-Ward retailing war may have been decided in an army ward in Panama many years earlier.

Major trends are often much easier to forecast than the daily indicators we watch so closely. No one can know where the Dow Jones average will close today or what the prime interest rate will be in twelve months, but demographers can tell you will great precision how many sixty-five-year-olds there will be in the U.S. in forty years. We even have a pretty good idea about where they will live, how much spending money they'll have, and what their health will be like.

In the following pages, we'll review some of the biggest trends at work today. The great leader watches trends to see things that others do not see, to seize opportunities where others only see confusion. *Applying these ideas in unique ways to your own unique enterprise and your own unique goals in life is what will set you apart from the crowd.*

GATEWAYS

Further Readings to Thinking and Learning About History

Two books that will make you think are *Nonzero: The Logic of Human Destiny,* by Robert Wright, and *The Modern Mind: An Intellectual History of the Twentieth Century,* by Peter Watson. For basic reference, or browsing, try the *Oxford Companion to United States History,* edited by Paul S. Boyer. Finally, be prepared to think about the "big picture" if you pick up *The Collapse of Complex Societies,* by Joseph A. Tainter. Other fascinating historians who have tackled the big picture include Fernand Braudel and Will and Ariel Durant.

10

The Biggest Trend:
The Implications of an Aging Baby Boom

The single most important trend for most of us, especially in the U.S., is the aging of the baby boom generation. This trend is critically important because of three things:

1. The baby boom generation is the largest single bulge in population in U.S. history.

2. The years in which the members of this boom will reach particular stages of their lives are precisely predictable.

3. People do many important things at predictable points in their lives.

First, the size of the baby boom: After World War II, the number of babies born in the U.S. began to accelerate. The figure rose from 2.8 million babies in 1945 to a peak of 4.25 to 4.3 million in each year from 1957 through 1961. Then a decline started, with a trough at 3.1 million births in 1973. By 1977 the number of births began to rise again as the oldest baby boomers began to have babies of their own.

While different observers use different definitions, I consider the population of the baby boom to include all of those born during the bulge from 1946 through 1973. During these years, 107.5 million people were born in the U.S. This number was equal to 50.7 percent of the 211.9 million Americans alive in 1973. Today's baby boom generation is reduced by the number who have died and increased by net immigration. But the bottom line is that the size of this population bulge is huge and, in fact, unprecedented in history.

The baby boom is so huge that as the baby boomers have children, they are producing a so-called echo boom that is also quite large. As a result, the number of annual births today is almost as high as it was at the peak of the baby boom.

This huge population bubble has had enormous effects on our society. This generation grew up with TV, interstate highways, air travel, and the automobile-based suburb—things that came late in life to their parents. This generation helped end the Vietnam War, accelerated the demand for civil rights, and made the Beatles wealthy. Books have been written about these folks, and books will continue to be written. Not all of the baby boomers have the same social, political, cultural, and economic characteristics. Many baby boomers born before 1951 were not exposed to the drug era. Boomers born after 1960 were not the ones who bought Beatles albums. But now all these various boomers are getting older.

So what are some of the things that usually change as people age? While any individual—you or me—might not fit the mold, here are some general conclusions that hold true when you aggregate a large number of people—like 107 million. In general, people tend to:

1. Commit crimes in their teens and twenties.

2. Experiment with drugs and various "alternative lifestyles" in their twenties.

3. Complete their formal schooling in their teens and twenties.

4. Get their first jobs in their teens and twenties.

5. Get married in their twenties and thirties.

6. Move to a new city in their twenties and thirties.

7. Rent apartments in their twenties.

8. Buy their first home in their thirties.

9. Have their first child in their twenties and thirties.

10. Pay for their kids' upbringing and education in their thirties and forties.

11. Spend heavily on consumer items in their thirties and forties.

12. Begin to invest in their thirties but don't get serious about it until their forties and fifties.

13. Achieve their greatest wealth in their fifties or sixties.

14. Steadily increase their skills and job productivity until their fifties.

15. Launch their kids (and therefore stop spending so much on them) in their forties and fifties.

16. Begin to spend heavily on travel in their late forties and into their fifties and sixties.

17. Spend more time and money on hobbies and leisure pursuits in their fifties and beyond.

18. Give away more money in their sixties and beyond.

19. Gradually increase political participation, especially voting, from a very low level in their twenties to a peak in their seventies or even eighties.

20. Increase their power (corporate, community, political) through their fifties and possibly sixties.

21. Begin to retire in their fifties, with a peak of retirement in their sixties.

22. Begin to establish second or retirement homes in their fifties and sixties.

23. Move into nursing homes and assisted-living facilities in their seventies and eighties.

24. Increase their concern with health and nutrition in their fifties and sixties.

25. Die in their seventies and eighties, supporting enterprises even with their last breath.

Starting with the near-peak birth year of 1960, the "typical" baby boomer was twenty-five in 1985, thirty-five in 1995, will be forty-five in 2005, fifty-five in 2015, and sixty-five in 2025. So there will be lots of interesting developments in the years ahead.

Obviously, there are millions of exceptions to each of these generalizations. But there are even more millions of cases in which the generalizations hold true. And each generalization amounts to a trend. When millions of people take up (or drop) a particular activity, it produces much more than a blip on the social and economic radar screen. In fact, each of these shifts produces changes that affect almost every enterprise.

The implications of the aging of the baby boom are many. Every aspect of life, from cars to stores, will change. Retailers currently dependent on customers driving twenty minutes to shop in their stores (called "trade area radius") may find their reach shrinking as aging people are less willing to drive. The demand for taxis and tour busses could increase significantly. Buttons and zippers may go the way of the slide rule as arthritic hands reach for Velcro.

Some sports will die off, others will rise in prominence. Shuffleboard, anyone? Less-physically-intense activities like card playing and stamp collecting may return to favor. The American Association of Retired Persons (AARP) will continue to grow in influence, ultimately becoming a political force as powerful as the AFL-CIO was in the 1950s. If changes are to be made to the Social Security system, they need to be made today, before the aging baby boom becomes a totally politicized, entrenched recipient of transfer funds rather than the tax-paying generation they are today. Levels of charitable contributions will skyrocket.

In particular, I believe the aging of the baby boom will result in dramatic expansion of four key industries: health, education, travel, and financial services. The next fifty years will be golden years for these industries.

In all of these trends lie major opportunities for enterprises old and new, both for-profit and not-for-profit.

In the "Gateways" section of this chapter are listed some books that study the aging of the population in depth. While many Wall Street observers ignore the importance of demographic factors in forecasting corporate profits, other experts believe that demographics alone explain every social and economic trend. I believe a careful analysis of the facts and how they apply to your industry and company will probably put you somewhere in the middle. *For most enterprises, there is no single factor as important as the demographics of the customer and how they are changing over time. But there are other factors at work, and to ignore them would be a mistake.*

In weighing the social and economic impact of the baby boom, I would list four caveats.

First, the aging of the baby boom is not a single-point trend. Placing the baby boom at age forty is not like placing the Dow Jones average at 10,000. In the above analysis, we've assumed that the baby boomers were born in 1960 and therefore that they turned forty in the year 2000. But millions of baby boomers were younger and older in 2000—as young as twenty-seven and as old as fifty-four. That's a big spread.

Similarly, while the average age at which people first marry may be twenty-six, the range is from the teens to the nineties, with millions married before and after age twenty-six. So when you build up the whole curve, the first baby boom marriage occurred in the early 1960s, while the last one—a ninety-year-old honeymooning on Viagra—won't occur until about 2060. Furthermore, there were and will be millions of baby boomers getting married for the first time every year between (say) 1968 and 2006. (Statistics show that the annual number of marriages remained at about 2.4 million throughout the 1980s and '90s.) That's a long time for a peak.

The fact that the baby boom is not a one-year phenomenon means you must interpret its influence with care. Nonetheless, the influence of the boom is still enormous. You may not be able to use the boomers as a guide to the exact year when you should get into the bridal business and when you should get out. But 2008 is probably not the best year to get in.

Second, be careful not to confuse age-related trends with generation-related trends. When I was a stock analyst on Wall Street in the mid-1970s, common wisdom was that it was time to start selling Coca-Cola stock and start buying General Foods. The logic was, "Soft drinks were for kids, but adults drink coffee." And with an aging baby boom generation, people reasoned, General Foods, the largest coffee maker (including the Maxwell House brand) was surely poised for a long-term rise.

The prediction turned out to be wrong. People thought that drinking preference was an age thing. But it wasn't—it was a generational thing. The baby boomers kept right on drinking soft drinks, and never made the anticipated en masse switch to coffee. Thus coffee lost share while soft drinks stayed strong.

Today the phenomenal marketing power of Starbucks and the rise in coffee popularity among members of Generation X have turned coffee consumption up from its 1995 low. Even so, per capita 1997 U.S. consumption of coffee is down 12 percent from 1980, while per capita soft drink consumption has risen 51 percent in the same time frame. Soft drinks were the right place to put your bet twenty-five years ago.

Similarly, when I was a teenager, movies and music were for kids. My parents and most of their friends did not go to the movies very often, and they certainly didn't buy many record albums or cassette tapes. Today, my baby boom friends and I, all *well* past thirty, are going to movies in droves and buying CDs like crazy. While the peak years for movies and music are still the teens and twenties, baby boomers remain an important part of the market. Baby boomers have also demonstrated a lifelong interest in learning. Unlike their parents, they kept on reading books *after* they graduated from school.

The bottom line is that for each age-related trend, you need to ask yourself, "To what degree is this something that will pass as these people age, and to what degree is this going to stay with them for life?" Who knows—maybe the members of Gen X will be buying $5,000 Sony PlayStations when they are fifty. Weirder things have happened.

Third, historical age-related consumption patterns can change. Today the peak for spending on motorcycles is by people in their forties and fifties. This was not true forty years ago. Long-distance cruisers popularized by Japanese makers and brilliant history-aware manufacturing and marketing by Harley-Davidson have changed the shape of demand.

Many other patterns have shifted in similar ways. Over time, as more people have pursued more degrees, people have started working later, and the age of first marriage has risen. For decades, the average retirement age fell; now it may rise again as Social Security evolves and as more people opt for second or third careers in later life. Demand for expensive trips and resorts has historically peaked among people in their fifties and sixties, but today more and more people are able to buy these things when they are younger.

The sheer size of the aging baby boom generation may change some basic assumptions. They will be healthier and live longer, maintaining more varied interests than the senior citizens of prior times. I believe that we will see a significant rise in demand for college and other educational services by senior citizens. We think of suburban apartments as starter homes for people in their twenties. But if there are not enough people in their twenties to fill them, landlords and developers may figure out ways to make them attractive to senior citizens—like hiring an on-call nurse for every twenty units, or providing pickup services for groceries.

In coming years, the number of people over eighty will grow faster than any other age group. Whole new industries will be born to serve these people. In the past, few marketers have studied how people in their nineties differed from people in their seventies. Such analyses will become very important to enterprises everywhere. Author Ken Dychtwald thinks the average life span could hit ninety-five to one hundred by midcentury, with many people living beyond the age of one hundred and twenty.

Fourth, the aging of the baby boom is a phenomenon of the developed world. As the world becomes more globally integrated, this one is the real kicker. The U.S. age structure described above, with a huge bulge of people born in the years after World War II, is also present to one degree or another in Japan, Canada, Australia, New Zealand, and most of Europe. But this bulge, with a decline in births afterward, is not true in the Middle East, Asia outside of Japan, Latin America, and Africa. The rest of the world ranges between two extremes:

- Those nations that had a higher birth rate after the mid-1970s, and so have a younger population than the "first world," but later put the brakes on their population growth. Today such nations have more younger people than the "first world," but their populations are no longer growing quickly. This list of countries is led by China and includes such other large nations as Brazil and Indonesia.

- Those nations that have not significantly slowed their population growth and are still having lots and lots of babies right up to the present. Their populations continue to boom. This description applies to many nations in Africa and the Middle East.

This division of the world into young countries and aging countries will result in a newly defined "new world" (or "young world") and "old world." While the U.S., Japan, and Europe will be great places to sell Viagra, wheelchairs, golf clubs, and museum passes, most of the world—from India to Brazil—will still be consuming diapers, bicycles, video games, and condoms. If you are running BMG (Bertelsmann Music Group), Warner Music, or Sony Music, you cannot focus on the aging baby boom alone; you will have half your market waxing nostalgic over Sinatra, Elvis, and Led Zep while the other half (or more) wants hip-hop and the latest techno tunes. Brand management—determining who you are and who you serve—will become a major challenge for any global company, from DaimlerChrysler to Hilton, from Coke to Sony. A nightmare for some, an opportunity for others.

These population curves will intersect in millions of ways, and at each intersection there will be both risks and rewards. Americans will be stock-owning sixty-five-year-olds when Mexicans will be consuming twenty-five-year-olds. Will U.S. mutual funds seize the opportunity to invest in Mexican consumer product companies? One country may be at the perfect age to create and market animated cartoons while a neighbor is old enough only to watch them. Americans too old to drive Harleys and Corvettes may find ready markets for their used vehicles in other nations.

You need to know the population and age structure of any nation you do business in, be it producing or selling. And you need to think about how that structure is going to change and how your enterprise will need to change in response. What can we predict about the future of younger countries from the patterns demonstrated in the "old world" countries like the U.S.?

The aging of the baby boom is not the only important long-term change under way in the world today.

GATEWAYS

Further Readings on the Impact of the Aging Baby Boom

The key books here are *Age Power: How the Twenty-first Century Will be Ruled by the New Old* and *Age Wave: How the Most Important Trend of Our Time Will Change Your Future,* by Ken Dychtwald, as well as *The Roaring 2000s: Building the Wealth and Lifestyle You Desire in the Greatest Boom in History* and *The Roaring 2000s Investor: Strategies for the Life You Want,* by Harry S. Dent, Jr. But read my comments about the aging baby boom before you buy into these ideas 100 percent.

11

Other Big Trends to Watch, from Diversity to Individualization

The Increasing Diversity of the People of the United States

Many leaders of enterprise understand that the aging of the baby boom will affect them in one way or another, even if they have not thought through exactly *how* they will be affected. But many leaders do not think about the huge impact that America's increasing racial, ethnic, and religious diversity will have on them. In the nineteenth and early twentieth centuries, the U.S. experienced massive waves of immigration. Most Americans had ample opportunities to meet and do business with newcomers to these shores—people who looked "different" and spoke English with an accent, often immigrants from Europe: Romanians, Czechs, Italians, Irish, Greeks, Russians, Ukrainians, Poles. By the 1950s, this had become much more rare. Today we are in the midst of a new rise in the number (and power) of Americans who come from afar.

The first and most significant component of this trend is the increasing Latinization of North America. As recently as 1980, people of Hispanic origin, as defined by the Census Bureau, represented only 6.4 percent of the U.S. population. By the 2000 census, this statistic was up to 12.5 percent, almost double. By comparison, in the same period, the percentage of Americans who are African-American has only risen from 11.8 percent to 12.9 percent. By 2005 the number of Hispanics will exceed that of African-Americans. By 2025 more than 18 percent of the American population will be of Hispanic origin. In the second half of the twentieth century, the number of Hispanics is expected to rise toward 30 percent, twice the number of African-Americans. This is the greatest demographic and ethnic shift in the history of our nation.

The Latinization of the U.S. is pervasive, affecting most states, but the effect is greatest in some of our largest states. California (according to the 2000 Census) was 32.4 percent Hispanic. The second-largest state, Texas, was 32.0 percent Hispanic. The figure for third-ranking New York was 15.1 percent, while Florida (which will grow larger than New York in the next ten to fifteen years) is 16.8 percent Hispanic. These four states contain about two-thirds (more than 23 million) of America's 35 million Hispanics. The Los Angeles metropolitan area (as of 1999) included 6 million (38.5 percent of L.A.'s total population), New York 3.5 million (17.4 percent), and Miami 1.4 million (38.5 percent). Other cities with more than a million Latinos are San Francisco, Chicago, and Houston. Just below the million line is San Antonio, our "most Latin" major metro area, at 53.5 percent.

But Latinization is not only a trend in big cities and big states—the fastest-growing group in Iowa is the Hispanic population. Go to small towns in northern Illinois like Elgin and Belvidere and you'll be surprised to see how many *taquerías* you find.

This trend will have an enormous effect on the United States of the future. Large cities have a disproportionate effect on television and other media. California, Texas, and Florida tend to be trend-setters in mass culture, from retailing to restaurants. Today we can already see the effect of Latinization in our food (at home and at restaurants) and in our popular culture (from music to movies to books). But this is just the beginning. Alert enterprises will pay notice to the following implications of this shift in our society:

- *Language.* Words from Spanish (and eventually Portuguese, the language of Brazil) will increasingly become part of American English.

- *Color and design.* When you see a fountain in a courtyard, you're looking at vestiges of the Spanish Moors, whose influences have found their way to us through Mexico. Go to Latin America today and you will see a much more colorful world than "Anglo America." The impact of this on American style is inevitable.

- *Religion.* The vibrancy and role of Roman Catholicism in the U.S. is going to change.

- *Family attitudes.* In large part due to the influence of Roman Catholicism, we will likely see changes in family size, in birth rates, and in the roles of mothers and fathers.

- *Politics.* Whether the topic is abortion, education, or relations with Latin America (for example, the expansion of NAFTA), people of Latin descent in the United States will play a more active role in setting our national agenda.

It is difficult to anticipate every result of America's Latinization. But it will be worth the effort for those enterprises that try. One crucial truth is that Latinization is not a single monolithic trend. "Hispanics" is a loose term; some prefer "Latino"; others, "Chicano." The Spanish-heritage segment of the U.S. population includes Mexicans, Cubans, Dominicans, Puerto Ricans, Haitians, Colombians, and the people from other nations in the Caribbean, Central America, and South America. In a cultural sense, it includes many people from Spain, Portugal, and the Philippines. The first mistake many observers will make will be to lump all these people together, making assumptions that they are all alike, sharing the same music, language, and beliefs. Close observation will often show important differences. For example, third-generation Mexican-Americans are likely to have different viewpoints from new arrivals, and the younger generation (as in most cultures) may not see things as their parents do.

The first people to understand the subtleties and significance of these trends are what I call the "close-to-the-ground marketers"—those enterprises who deal with the vast scope of our population on an intimate daily basis: supermarkets, tobacco companies, beer and soft drink companies, food companies. Philip Morris had Spanish-language billboards in San Antonio twenty years ago. At the other extreme, those enterprises furthest removed from the ground are often the slowest to see and interpret these shifts. It may be a long time before Fifth Avenue stores offer Spanish-language customer service representatives and store directories.

The rise of Hispanic North America is just the largest of many cultural waves currently at work. People of many backgrounds are coming into our country and reshaping it. We use the term "Asian-American" to denote immigrants and descendants of immigrants from countries covering a huge swath of the globe, from India to China, Japan to Cambodia, Pakistan to Singapore. Their percentage of the U.S. population has risen from 1.6 percent in 1980 to 4.2 percent in 2000. This number is expected to cross 10 percent in the second half of the twenty-first century.

Their economic influence is large and growing. It has been stated that 40 percent of all Korean immigrants own their own businesses, the highest percentage ever recorded for any ethnic group. However, Asian-Americans have not yet begun to penetrate U.S. national politics in a significant way. That will change. Today Asian-Americans make up more than 40 percent of the enrollment at many big California universities. Their influence in our politics, language, and culture will rise dramatically. And we will begin to understand their diversity and importance. For example, Islam (much of it from Asia) is already one of the fastest-growing religions in the U.S., with estimates ranging from 4 to 7 million adherents. There *will* be a Mosque in your neighborhood—if there isn't one already. The only question is when.

Taking all of these groups together, America will become a much more diverse nation in the twenty-first century. I believe we will see a dramatic increase in intermarriage between these groups. Only twenty years ago, an interracial couple was a very rare sight in all but the very largest cities. The WASP family of the 1950s sitcom is a shrinking portion of the United States and the world. Before the present century is out, less than half of all Americans will be "white folks" as classically defined.

The Changing Role of Women

The percentage of our population that is female is not changing in a significant way. Since 1970 it has been stable, between 51.0 percent and 51.5 percent. But the importance of women in our economy, in politics, in the media, and in other seats of power continues to increase rapidly by historical standards. This trend is first seen in the labor force participation rates discussed at the beginning of this chapter. While some nations like New Zealand (which first gave women the vote), Canada, the Scandinavian countries, and the old Communist-bloc nations are even further up the curve of placing women in positions of power, the U.S. is very high by world standards. Most of Asia, Africa, and Latin America are well behind. According to 1990 estimates, 36 to 42 percent of women in the U.S. and Northern Europe are "economically active." This compares with 24 to 30 percent in India and most of Latin America, and just 6 to 12 percent in the Middle East and North Africa. But all the statistics show the same upward trend. In every profession, in every graduate school, in every legislature, the number of women is increasing over the long term.

When I went to work on Wall Street fresh out of school in 1973, the early waves of women MBA's were just getting their feet wet. They were testing the boundaries and struggling with their roles. The men around them were often uncomfortable; those who were enlightened enough to drop their familiar locker-room humor were unsure what to replace it with. A common debating point among working men was, "Could you ever work for a woman boss?" (I soon moved on to the department-store industry, in which the question was moot—you'd work for a woman sooner or later if you stayed in that business.)

As a student of business, I believe a critical milestone was passed with the selection of a woman to head one of the nation's largest companies. It (finally) happened in 1999 when the Hewlett-Packard Board of Directors selected Carly Fiorina as the firm's new CEO. Ms. Fiorina will not be alone at the top for long. Thousands of key women execs are coming into their prime leadership years—their fifties—and will soon be taking the reigns of enterprises large and small. This will also hold true in our universities, in our churches and hospitals, and in the capitals of the world. The shift in this century will be dramatic.

The Increasing Diversity of Avocations and Interests

As a member of the baby boom, I was born into a world in which three newsmagazines told us everything we needed to know. Three TV networks were enough—entrepreneurs repeatedly launched independent fourth stations, but only the most populous cities provided audiences big enough to support them. On any given weekend, you had a handful of movies to choose from. You read either the morning paper or the evening paper; you shopped at Sears or at one of two or three local department stores. And, perhaps most remarkably, no one sat around griping that they had too few choices.

Today, one hundred cable channels don't provide enough TV for us. Thousands of movies are available for sale, rent, on cable, or at theaters. Hundreds of thousands of Web pages are created every day. Our choices in almost every aspect of life have exploded.

When we were building the BOOKSTOP chain, I was often asked, "Won't the rise of cable television with its immense variety of information and entertainment hurt demand for books?" But the truth was that the rise of huge bookstores with hundreds of diverse subjects was a response to the *same trend* as that which supported cable and now supports the Internet: the increased individualization of the consumer. As time passes, we Americans become more diverse in our passions.

Our diversity of enthusiasms is incredible and continually increasing. Everyone is becoming a specialist and an expert in something, from beekeeping to Barbie dolls, *feng shui* to rock climbing, Thai cooking to German opera, acupuncture to stockcar racing. More and more people are collectors; more and more things are collectibles. The real power of eBay is based in its ability to link together thousands of very tiny groups of people all over the world. As these groups, defined by passionate interests, continue to proliferate, the complexity and fascination of our population keeps expanding.

All of the trends examined in the preceding pages have global implications, and all have compounding effects. For example, an aging population with time and money on its hands and a propensity for philanthropy is likely to devote itself to supporting an increasing diversity of interests: the baby boom will fund everything from pinball museums to Tibetan cultural centers.

Making sense of these trends and thousands of others like them, which affect your industry and your customers, requires a fundamental understanding of how to look at trends through time and how to put history to use. We'll discuss these topics in the pages that follow.

GATEWAYS

Further Readings on Trends and Americans

The Clustered World: How We Live, What We Buy, and What It All Means About Who We Are, by Michael J. Weiss, one of the best writers about the consumer. Clustering is a system for grouping people according to their lifestyles—very insightful. *Time for Life: The Surprising Ways Americans Use Their Time,* by John P. Robinson and Geoffrey Godbey—*the* experts on time studies, an under-emphasized aspect of knowing the customer. One of the *very few* people who looks at the long-term trends is Stanley Lebergott; his key title is *Pursuing Happiness: American Consumers in the Twentieth Century.* To look at where people stand today, try *Myths of Rich and Poor: Why We're Better Off Than We Think,* by W. Michael Cox and Richard Alm, which contains lots of upbeat data about the U.S. and its people; and *The Social Health of the Nation: How America Is Really Doing,* by Marc Miringoff and Marque-Luisa Miringoff—a more "pros and cons" view of where America stands, but, again, based on looking at hard facts. Three very visual books, full of great graphs, are *It's Getting Better All the Time: Greatest Trends of the Last 100 Years,* by Stephen Moore and Julian L. Simon; *The Illustrated Guide to the American Economy,* by Herbert Stein and Murray Foss; and *The First Measured Century: An Illustrated Guide to Trends in America, 1900–2000,* by Theodore Caplow, Louis Hicks, and Ben J. Wattenberg—a wonderful book, linked to a PBS series. To understand more about minorities in and immigrants to the U.S., the best source is a textbook: *Strangers to These Shores: Race and Ethnic Relations in the United States,* by Vincent N. Parrillo.

12

Watching History Unfold and Looking at Curves

"The further backward you look, the further forward you can see."
—WINSTON CHURCHILL

In the previous chapter, we looked at some of the key trends currently at work in the world. But understanding change through time is most helpful when you get in the habit of doing it every day, when you look at each event and try to put it in historical perspective, when you look at your own company, nonprofit organization, or industry with your "time-sensitivity" turned on. The following pages contain techniques you may be able to use in developing your own time-sensitivity.

First, remember that you cannot know where you are going unless you know where you are coming from. It is as important to be *retro*spective as it is to be *prospective* and *intro*spective. We must seek balance, looking before us and behind us as well as inside of us. I have seen many Wall Street analysts' reports that show sales and profit projections for the next five years but show only one year of history. Such analyses are likely to be seriously flawed. An image that may help you in remembering to maintain your "time balance" is shown below. The present is the fulcrum of the seesaw of time.

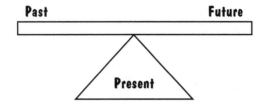

The Evolutionary Mindset:
Watching Change Through Time

"History may be divided into three movements: what moves rapidly, what moves slowly, and what appears not to move at all."
—FERNAND BRAUDEL

Of course, history is easier to recognize and analyze in retrospect than while it is happening all around us. Hence the expression, "20/20 hindsight." But there are ways of observing history in the making and thereby gain a quicker and more accurate understanding of change than most people enjoy.

The first step in watching history as we live it is to separate what is changing from what is not changing. Experience suggests that most aspects of human nature change very little: the need for food, shelter, and other basic requirements of life; the desire to make a better life for the next generation; the importance of honor and reputation; the wish to love and to be loved. On the other hand, technologies and artifacts of civilization—from cars and music to houses and clothing—are changing all the time. There are also human attitudes that are changing over the long term—not all at once, but gradually, one society or subgroup at a time. In general terms, we can say that the human race has changed its attitudes and practices in regard to such topics as slavery, education for the masses, the rights of women, the importance of freedom and democracy. In each of these categories, the dominant worldview held today is significantly different (and most would say improved) from that of five hundred years ago.

Sometimes unchanging human nature intersects with ever-changing artifacts. My grandfather thought my dad was nuts for liking Louis Armstrong; my dad thought I was nuts for liking Mick Jagger. I suspect that, if I had a son, he would like Eminem—and I'd think he was nuts. Yes, styles of music have changed, but the fact that dads think their sons are crazy has not.

The leader of an enterprise must deal with all of these aspects of human culture: artifacts, technologies, customs, attitudes, beliefs, preferences, and much more. Most of the "things" that an enterprise deals with are changing, some slowly, some quickly. We humans are naturally good at noticing things that move fast—action movies, horse races, basketball games. It takes more work to watch things that move slowly—clouds, demographics, long-term trends in industry, history, or culture.

Yet most things are evolving. Seeing things as evolutionary is an important change-watching skill, one that applies even to things that seem not to move at all—in fact, *especially* to things that seem not to move at all.

One excellent example is language. You may assume that the English (or other language) you learned at your mother's knee is the same English you use today and will use until the day you die. But our language evolves every day. Try communicating in business today and not using words like "dotcom," "Internet," or "cell phone." Young people are especially adept at integrating new words into the language, from "rad" to "phat." No matter what your personal tastes in music may be, you know what words like "rap" and "hip-hop" refer to. And as our world becomes smaller and our culture more diverse, languages increasingly intermingle. You probably know the names of a dozen popular Mexican foods and can understand *"hasta la vista"* and *"Cinco de Mayo"* without thinking about them. Asian-American terms are sure to blossom in coming years.

Over the very long term, the changes in language are enormous. Englishmen who spoke the language of Shakespeare would have difficulty understanding the English our great-great-grandchildren will use. There was a time (only some fifteen centuries ago) when English did not exist, and there may be a time in the future when it no longer exists, a dead language like Sanskrit or Sumerian, preserved only in whatever books or other written artifacts survive.

Sometimes you have to work hard to see evolutionary change. My parents made their first trip to New York when they drove from Indiana to attend the World's Fair of 1939. I made my first trip to New York when my parents drove our family from Indiana to attend the World's Fair of 1964. The tradition of enormous world's fairs started in Europe and peaked with the turn-of-the-century fairs in Chicago (1893) and St. Louis (1904). At these fairs, millions of Americans were introduced to cultures from around the world, to "foreign" religions, and to the newest marvels of science. Even some of our favorite foods, from the ice-cream cone to iced tea, were first popularized at world's fairs. Enterprises used them to showcase their visions of the future.

A world's fair visit was an eye-opening experience for a thirteen-year-old kid. But over the years, the power and popularity of world's fairs has declined. While cities occasionally still hold fairs in an effort to draw tourists, no recent fairs have enjoyed the attendance or success of the great fairs of the past. With my fond memories of 1964, I began to mope about their decline. But then I realized that the fairs were not gone. They had just morphed into other forms. What is Epcot at Disney World but a permanent world's fair? Our society had become rich enough that we could afford not just one fair every five to twenty years, but an ongoing fair, open all year round. This trend is further manifested in the world-wide growth of science, technology, and natural history museums. But seeing the link between world's fairs and Disney World was not obvious. One had to look behind their structure to recognize their underlying function, their essence.

It is important to take an evolutionary viewpoint, whether we are looking at something as fundamental as the English language or as specific as the fate of world's fairs. Every industry, every company, every nonprofit enterprise, is evolving. Every consumer need or desire, from the need for food to the desire for entertainment, from insurance to transportation, is unfolding over time. We are aware of the latest startup company, we know the hottest trend. But are we looking for how things have changed over a ten-, twenty-, fifty-, or even one-hundred-year time horizon? And therefore how they might change when we look that far into the future?

Seeking Patterns Through Time

Our understanding of how things are changing starts with answering three questions:

1. In what *direction* is the change taking place?

2. At what *rate* is the change taking place?

3. Is the rate of change constant, accelerating, or slowing down?

If we can answer, even approximately, these three questions, then we have some chance of knowing where current changes are taking us.

The best way to start is by charting change. Take anything that is quantifiable—the percent of households that are online, the size of your industry, the reliability of cars made by U.S. manufacturers, the number of video-rental stores in your town, the average number of children in a family—and chart it over time. Often this process is as simple as plotting a collection of dots against two axes on a piece of graph paper, as shown in the following figure.

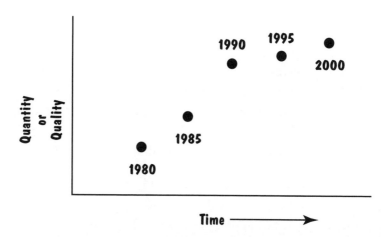

The next step is to connect the dots. While you can actually connect the dots in sequence, this will often give you a jagged pattern of peaks and valleys, emphasizing all the little up-and-down variations that are less important than the broader trend over time. This is what statisticians call "noise." It is usually more informative to draw the straightest line you can among the dots, or a curve that reflects the general trend, as shown in the following figure.

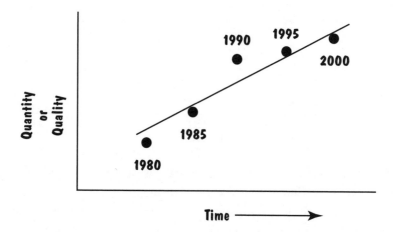

The way statisticians draw the "best" line to capture the overall direction of a trend is by using a mathematical process called a *least squares*

regression. You can perform this easily using most spreadsheet programs and even on some pocket calculators. The overall field of studying trends is called *time series analysis.* While specialists in statistics spend their lives working to perfect these systems and using them for forecasting, you can do your own lines by hand as a matter of course, simply by eyeballing the numbers and drawing a trend line that seems to fit the movement of history correctly. The results may not be precise, but they suffice to give you some general idea about where things are heading.

Most trends involve the relationship between two quantities or factors. Very often one of these quantities is time: as time passes, the other quantity (population, income, industry size, et cetera) will increase or decrease. In other instances, a factor other than time may be involved. For example, a graph relating the two quantities of height and weight for a group of individual people would probably show that, as height increases, weight *generally* increases as well.

When you plot quantitative relationships like these onto a graph, you will sometimes get a straight line connecting your data points. For obvious reasons, this is referred to as a *linear relationship* (see below).

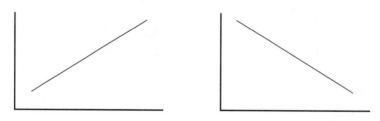

Linear

Sometimes you will see that things are not changing in a linear direction over time, they are just cycling—moving up and down in a more-or-less regular fashion, as shown in the following figure. Temperatures tend to cycle, of course—higher in the summer, lower in the winter.

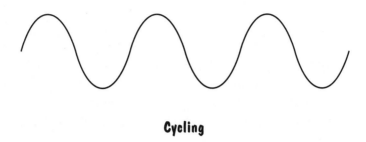

Cycling

One of the most talked-about curves is the S-curve. A good example is the "women in the U.S. workforce" curve (see below).

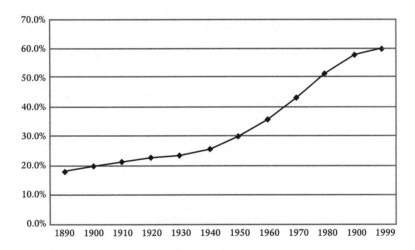

Of course, an S-curve doesn't really look exactly like an S. The idea of the S-curve, also called the logistic curve or the Gompertz curve, started in biology and population studies. If you have a particular ecosystem—say, a pond—with plenty of plant life in it, and introduce a new species—let's say, a particular species of fish—you will find that at first the fish reproduce slowly. Then they multiply faster and faster, consuming the available food. Finally, because the amount of available food eventually runs low (and sometimes because new species arrive to compete for resources), the growth in the number of this species of fish begins to slow. Finally, the growth stops, and the curve flattens out.

It turns out that the S-curve is also descriptive of many other phenomena. For example, it describes the way most technologies take hold: rapid increase up to a point at which the population is basically "saturated" with the technology, then a flattening out of the rate of growth. If you graph the increase in the number of U.S. households with electricity, television, or the Internet, you get an S-curve.

Also note that S-curves in real life can play out over a few months or over decades. And they can take on many shapes (see below).

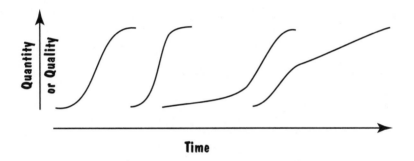

Of course, in real life what we usually see are compound curves—that is, curves in combination or multiplied on top of one another (below).

Real Life: Compound Curves

For example, the stock market tends to look like one of the first two curves over a period of years. These are linear patterns with cycles over the short term. Thus, the stock market has its daily, weekly, and annual ups and downs, but over the long term it steadily trends upward.

The percentage of the vote going Democratic (or Republican) tends to look like the third curve. This is a long-term cycle with little cycles within it.

In this context, let me mention one other curve. This one is not one you will normally see when studying change over time. But it often describes how a given collection of things will break down into categories at a single point in time. It's called the *normal distribution* or the *bell curve* (see below).

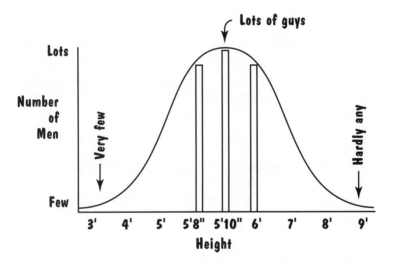

If you are looking at how tall people are (as shown above), how many wear size S, M, L, XL, and XXL T-shirts, or the distribution of income among a group of people, you are going to get a bell curve. That is, most people will be of "medium" height, while a few are very short and a few are very tall.

Once in a while, as shown in Figure 12-10, you will get a so-called *bimodal distribution*, with large numbers of individuals at each extreme and almost no one in the middle. For example, a graph of the voting patterns of legislators, or of the voters themselves, usually reveals a bimodal distribution.

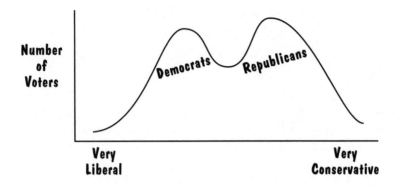

I believe that a basic understanding of these fundamental curves can be a powerful tool for analyzing the world around you. If your eye is trained to watch for these curves, you will gain a significant advantage in understanding the world and how it changes.

Thinking About Change Through Time

When comparing today with yesterday, start by asking:

- What's different?

- What's the same?

- How did we get where we are today?

- Can we get any good ideas from the past?

Here are some examples of how you can use these ways of looking at today and at the past. They aren't based on research, but rather on observation and thought. They illustrate how considering change methodically can yield interesting, often useful insights.

What are the biggest changes in the typical CEO of a Fortune 500 company today versus in 1963 (when I started studying business)? Here is a starter list:

Today's CEO is more likely:

- to be able to type

- to be younger

- to have an advanced degree in business

- to have worked for more than one company during his career

- to have lived and worked outside the United States

- to be a woman or member of a minority

At the same time, ask "What has *not* changed?" A great deal is written in the business press about the life of today's road warrior, about frequent flyer programs and hotel amenities. Technology has altered the life of the traveling businessperson, of course. But the lifestyle of the road warrior is not fundamentally new. If you study the hotels and railroads of the 1930s, you find a multitude of references to traveling salesmen and other businesspeople who spent most of their working lives traveling from city to city.

Many of us were born into a world where a reference to "The Big Three" in the automotive industry meant GM, Ford, and Chrysler. They were all headquartered within a few miles of one another. When we leave this world, there will probably still be a big three—but one may be in Detroit, one in Tokyo, one in Stuttgart.

Think about your own life. What changes, innovations, and trends did you grow up with? I am old enough to remember the construction of the Interstate Highway system in the 1950s. If you are only ten years younger than I am, you are unlikely to remember a world without Interstates. On the other hand, I was born just as railroads were retiring their old steam locomotives, and all my memories are of diesels. As a railroad aficionado, I sometimes wish I'd been born just five years earlier! Do you remember a world without cassette tapes? Without CDs? Without airport security scans? A world *with* TV repairmen and their boxes of tubes?

If you market products or services to customers of different ages, understanding these kinds of differences is critical. It is even more challenging in the nations that are booming. In Thailand, Malaysia, Brazil, and Korea, today's young people are growing up in an entirely different country from the one their parents grew up in.

Think about changes that are *not* in the headlines. How has your life or that of your enterprise been affected by the decline in fires in the U.S.? By the worldwide decline in accidental deaths? By the decline in airline accidents? All of these are beneficial long-term trends that rarely make the headlines. There may be dozens of factors like this that affect your industry.

When Encyclopedia Britannica tried to sell their books door-to-door in the late twentieth century (as they'd been doing for decades), they eventually discovered two things: half the women had gone to work and weren't at home any longer, and the ones who were at home were so nervous about increasing crime rates that they often wouldn't answer the door. Did these trends affect Britannica?

Think about the future in the broadest possible terms. To the managers and engineers at NASA, whose work was severely curtailed in the 1980s and 1990s by sharp budget cuts, it probably appeared that humankind's effort at space exploration had peaked with Neil Armstrong's walk on the moon in 1969. But the recent decline in interest in space is more likely just noise in the long-term trend. The odds remain high that our descendants will in fact colonize space.

Think about a world in which the United States is no longer the world's most powerful nation. Think about a world in which power, while widely dispersed, is increasingly centered in China. Demographic, economic, political, and cultural trends all point to this as a highly likely scenario for our future. In later chapters, we will consider the state of the world, and its future, in greater depth.

Avoiding Chronocentricity

One of the biggest risks in thinking about the past and the future is that we become "chronocentric"—that is, obsessed with our own era, considering it the most important or most dynamic time ever. This is probably a natural function of our human ego, and I am sure that generations before us felt the same way. But our understanding of our times will be clearer if we do not fall victim to this trap.

Chronocentricity is especially common in the business world. We see the explosive overnight growth of technology companies—Microsoft, Dell, AOL, Cisco, and others—and we think, "How '90s." But PCs and the Net are only the latest wave of technological innovation to spawn a host of new enterprises. In their day, technologies like steam power, electricity, the railroads, the automobile, the airplane, and the transistor led to similar economic revolutions. When Charles Kettering started DELCO in the early twentieth century, he went from zero employees to twelve hundred in eighteen months.

Look at the last ten to twenty years. It is often said that this is the time of greatest change in our history. The period of 1980 to 2000 saw the birth and rapid spread of the personal computer, the video cassette recorder, the compact disc, cable TV, and, of course, the Internet. Admittedly these are great innovations. But look at the data in the following chart (which could also easily be plotted as a series of S-curves) and think for a moment what it was like to live in the 1920s. In only ten years, America crossed the magic 50 percent participation line in cars, electric lighting, and indoor plumbing. Just one year later (1931), radio crossed the same line.

Percent Penetration of U.S. Households by Selected Technologies

	1910	1920	1930	1940	1990
Cars	1	26	60	high 50's	84
Radios	0	0	46	81	99
Electric Lights	15	35	68	79	100
Indoor Toilets	17	20	51	60	99+

Watching history and studying trends depends on thinking clearly and objectively about where we stand today, how it compares with where we (or our grandparents) stood yesterday, and how it compares with how we (and our descendants) will stand in the future.

13

A Useable Past:
Learning from History

As we've seen, looking backward can help us to understand the present and to forecast the future. But looking at history also has a value in itself. It can strengthen our understanding of our human nature and help us to tackle the challenges we face today with greater insight and wisdom. Unfortunately, most people in the world of business have little or no appreciation of business history. We are totally focused on the present and the future, to the neglect of the past. Students in law school have to study legal precedents and understand the heritage of Roman jurisprudence and English common law. Musicians in training study the works of Bach and Beethoven and listen to CDs of the greatest performers of the past. But very few business schools require any study of business history. It's a serious omission, in my view.

At Hoover's, we have a staff of editors who research companies around the world. Sometimes when they call a company headquarters with a basic question about the firm's history—the name of the founder, for example—no one at the company knows the answer. When I mentioned to our writers that we should point out that telecommunications giant Sprint derived the "SP" in its name from the formerly great Southern Pacific Railroad, they were hesitant to do so because even the canned company history at Sprint's Web site said no such thing. It's true, though—whether many at Sprint know it or not!

Many people writing about business history get lazy. Unfortunately, few people seem to care about it enough to get it right. When GE bought out RCA in 1986, the press coverage was extensive. But almost no one picked up on the fact that GE had been one of the original founding parent companies when RCA was launched.

The widespread ignorance of business history is a real shame, because those who study business history have a heightened appreciation of the importance of what today's business leaders are doing and can accomplish. While millions read with fascination about the exploits of our famous explorers and great generals or the breakthroughs of our leading scientists and thinkers, we give short shrift to the role played by entrepreneurs, industrialists, and managerial geniuses in our history.

Furthermore, business history can also be a fountain of great ideas and insights for enterprises of the present and future. Let me make my point by telling a few stories from the treasure trove that is business history.

The Art of Branch Management

Two men owned a successful business and decided to open a branch in another city. They gave the manager of that office "sweat equity"—ownership of 25 percent of the branch. After a period of time, it turned out that the manager was "cooking the books," falsifying the profits, and stealing money. The owners went to court to get back the money the manager had stolen, but the owners had no success. However, they did not give up. They got rid of the first manager and brought in a new fellow, who did a great job and increased the profits of the branch. The branch did so well that it became, according to one source, "a nursery of future branch managers."

The owners were the Medici family of Florence, the branch office (of their trading and banking company) was Venice, and the time period was A.D. 1402 to 1440. If you look back at this story and say, "What has changed?" you realize that many of the challenges of business have remained the same—finding and keeping dedicated employees, developing accounting systems that are reliable and accurate, dealing with risks and new challenges.

Empire Building

In 1916 U.S. railroads were among the most important, powerful, and massive enterprises in world history. They had accumulated investments exceeding $21 billion. Their employment rolls totaled 1.7 million workers. The entire system had been built and managed without the kind of resources modern enterprises take for granted, such as Federal Express, the Internet, NASDAQ, or Excel.

Industry leader Pennsylvania Railroad called itself "the standard railroad of the world." It was to turn-of-the-century America what IBM was to the business world in the 1960s and '70s, or what Microsoft is today—in fact, relatively speaking, the Pennsylvania was probably much more important in its day than either of those great computing companies.

From its founding in 1846, the Pennsylvania had competed with railroads from other coastal cities for the lucrative trade to the west. Industry pioneer Baltimore and Ohio reached out from its namesake city, while Vanderbilt's New York Central empire had the best lines directly into New York, which was emerging as the most important port on the East Coast. The Pennsylvania's New York passengers and freight had to be ferried across the Hudson River from New Jersey in order to reach Manhattan, a severe competitive advantage in comparison with the Vanderbilt line.

After years of study, the Pennsylvania under President Alexander Cassatt in 1900 boldly decided to build tunnels under the Hudson and a giant new terminal in Manhattan. The project took until 1917 to complete. It cost the Pennsylvania $160 million, at the time the largest private investment in history. The Pennsylvania remained a blue chip until after World War II, and even after the late 1960s demise of successor Penn Central, its New York real estate holdings remained valuable. Today the Norfolk Southern Railroad profitably operates much of its original route.

Despite the enormous importance of his leadership role as the head of one of America's greatest enterprises, Cassatt today is far less famous than his impressionist painter sister, Mary Cassatt. His grand neo-classic Pennsylvania Station was thoughtlessly demolished in 1963, perhaps our nation's single greatest architectural loss.

If you were Alexander Cassatt, would you have had the nerve to bet the company on the Hudson tunnels and Penn Station?

Grand Hotels

Ralph Hitz was born in Vienna in 1891. He ran away from home to work as an elevator boy at the Hotel Sacher. (Ever hear of a Sacher torte? Yes, it's the same Sacher.) But Ralph's father, a horse dealer, lured him home by promising to take the boy to New York on his next business trip. (Sounds odd? Not really—New York was a great place to buy cavalry horses.)

In 1906, at the age of fifteen, Ralph again ran away, this time to become a busboy at a hash house on New York's Broadway. He subsequently worked his way through kitchens across America—Oklahoma City, Houston, Galveston, and Cleveland. He gradually learned English but never lost his thick accent.

By 1928 Hitz was the manager of the Gibson Hotel in Cincinnati. His results were so phenomenal that he was able to start his own company, National Hotel Management, which operated (for a share of the profits) such famous hotels as the Book-Cadillac in Detroit, the Netherland Plaza in Cincinnati, the Nicollet in Minneapolis, the Congress in Chicago, and the Adolphus in Dallas.

His crowning achievement was the opening of the Hotel New Yorker—Manhattan's largest hotel, with twenty-five hundred rooms— ten weeks after the stock market crash of 1929. Does the date sound inauspicious? Not necessarily. By the Depression year of 1936, the New Yorker was making a profit of $1.5 million on revenues of $5.5 million. Note that this hotel was not for rich people; it was a large-volume hotel for the masses of road warriors—at $3.50 a night.

How did Hitz do it? Check out the May 1937 issue of Fortune to learn all the details, but I'll mention a couple. Hitz's team tracked every regular customer. If they didn't hear from a particular patron for a few months, they'd send a letter asking if anything was wrong. If a bellhop saw a little boy with his parents in the elevator, he'd ask the little boy what his birthday was. A birthday card would follow. Hotel management knew the preferences of every regular guest. Teams of clerks kept track of all this information in the days before computerized databases. The New Yorker's positioning line was "The Big Hotel That Remembers the Little Things."

In a thousand ways, from marketing to telephone operators to kitchen management, Ralph Hitz perfected the operation of his hotels. Today Ralph Hitz is long gone, but the New Yorker is still in business at Eighth Avenue and Thirty-fourth Street.

What lessons might we learn from Ralph Hitz? Looking back, I see that he could afford to capture customer histories and to send out birthday cards and other messages because he had access to cheap Depression-era labor. By the 1950s and '60s, labor costs had risen dramatically, and these labor-intensive marketing techniques may have seemed impossible. By the 1990s, top-end hotel chains like the Four Seasons and the Ritz-Carlton prided themselves on knowing these kinds of details about their customers.

But I believe that if Ralph Hitz were alive today, he would be operating inns with one-hundred-dollar rooms and he would know *everything* about his customers. Of course, he would take advantage of today's low-cost computers and database management software, and he would probably use the Internet as a super-efficient tool for communication and management. Hitz would care about every detail and he would act on it, just as he did seventy years ago.

A Little Publishing Story

In 1924 two young fellows pooled their $4,000 in savings and rented a one-room office at 37 West Fifty-seventh Street in New York. They wanted to publish books. But with no authors in their stable, their future looked bleak. Their phone rang only when someone dialed a wrong number. They decided they must come up with their own book ideas. They started to write possibilities on index cards. Finally they picked one—the creation of an inexpensive crossword puzzle book. They asked others what they thought about the plan, and nearly everyone told them they were crazy. The leading distributor of books thought so little of the idea that he told them, "If you must publish it, keep your name off it, or you're dead in the publishing business." Publishing such an insignificant title was sure to lead to a permanently scarred reputation in literary circles.

But in the next ten years, Richard Simon and Lincoln Schuster sold 1.5 million crossword puzzle books. Would you have listened to the experts or would you, like Simon and Schuster, have plowed ahead?

Using History in Business

From stories like these, we can draw not only inspiration but also some good ideas. And every industry, every company, every nonprofit, has stories like this in its past, if we just take the time to dig them up.

A glance at the history of the airline industry reveals it to be one of the most fascinating of all industries. The bravery of the pioneers—heck, the bravery of the early customers—is amazing. Airline advertising of the 1930s speaks to the adventure, romance, and excitement of high-speed, long-distance travel. And yet today most of our airlines have no sense of history. Their marketing is an extension of corporate America, with the same muted blues and subdued grays of life at the Fortune 500. If they looked back to the railroads even for a moment, they might give key flights evocative names like "The "California Zephyr" or "The Houston Rocket." Would rekindling the romance of travel be a winning business proposition? Who knows? Could it be any worse than the boring marketing of most airlines today?

If the hotel industry took a few moments to look back fifty years, they'd see how hotels advertised themselves with beautiful luggage labels, which today are collector's items. An idea worth reviving? Why not?

Any study of history and of changing consumer preferences indicates that many ideas of old recycle back to us. Hewlett-Packard is running TV ads that hark back to its beginnings in a garage in Palo Alto. Chrysler is beginning to find design inspiration in the past—look at the best-selling PT Cruiser. I believe it is only a matter of time before we see fins on cars again, and perhaps even the return of the full-sized traditional station wagon. Convertibles have already come back in force.

I understand that Procter & Gamble is one of the few companies that actively looks backward at its own history and even reviews decisions of old to see what can be learned from them. Disney perhaps understands the recycling of history best of all, as it brings back classics like *Snow White* every few years. Bravo!

What was your industry like in the 1930s? What products did your company make fifty years ago—or ten years ago? When was the last time you scanned your old ads or catalogs? Could you even lay your hands on your company's first annual report, or the marketing strategies that made your company famous in the 1960s? What did the founders of your museum, college, hospital, or candy company have in mind? What can be learned from them? Can they help us differentiate in today's market?

Look backward first, then look forward. But now it is time to look North, South, East, and West.

GATEWAYS

Further Readings About Business History

For understanding business history over the long pull—from 3500 B.C. to Yahoo, I like *Foundations of Corporate Empire: Is History Repeating Itself?*, by Karl Moore and David Lewis. In *Worldly Goods: A New History of the Renaissance*, Lisa Jardine tells how trade and commerce led the way for art and thought. Produced in conjunction with a PBS series, *Money and Power: The History of Business*, by Howard Means, covers everyone from the Medicis to Bill Gates. You cannot beat reading old business periodicals for providing new insights, especially *Fortune* and *Forbes*.

The senior statesman of business historians, Alfred D. Chandler, focuses on the history of management and organization in such classics as *The Visible Hand: The Managerial Revolution in American Business* and *Scale and Scope: The Dynamics of Industrial Capitalism*. Other favorite business history books include *Brand New: How Entrepreneurs Earned Consumers' Trust, from Wedgwood to Dell*, by Nancy F. Koehn; *Masters of Enterprise: Giants of American Business from John Jacob Astor and J. P. Morgan to Bill Gates and Oprah Winfrey*, by H. W. Brands; and *The History of Black Business in America: Capitalism, Race, Entrepreneurship*, by Juliet E. K. Walker. The best overall business history surveys are two college texts with identical titles, *A History of American Business*, by C. Joseph Pusateri and *A History of American Business*, by Keith L. Bryant, Jr., and

Henry C. Dethloff. The best history of American business, though forty years old and out of print, is *The Enterprising Americans* by John Chamberlain.

Histories of Specific Companies and Industries

Perhaps the best business book ever is *My Years with General Motors,* by Alfred P. Sloan, Jr.—how enthusiasm and common sense took over an industry and revolutionized management practice, by the man who did it. My favorite book on Disney is *The Magic Kingdom: Walt Disney and the American Way of Life,* by Steven Watts. *Sony: The Private Life,* by John Nathan, is a story as amazing as that of any U.S. business. One of my favorite business autobiographies is *Be My Guest,* by Conrad Hilton. Also recommended are *Wall Street: A History,* by Charles R. Geisst; *A Nation of Steel: The Making of Modern America 1865–1925,* by Thomas J. Misa; and *The Hollywood Studio System,* by Douglas Gomery.

The railroad industry probably has more lessons to teach us than any other industry—it was America's first big industry, a pioneer in everything from investment bubbles to technology application. It proceeded to become a mature industry, then a near-dead one, then reborn. It has seen it all. So much to be learned. The best place to start is with *American Railroads* and *The Routledge Historical Atlas of the American Railroads,* by John F. Stover. And the story of an enterprise, a construction project, and a man: *The Baldwin Locomotive Works, 1831–1915: A Study in American Industrial Practice,* by John K. Brown; *Nothing Like It in the World: The Men Who Built the Transcontinental Railroad,* by Stephen E. Ambrose (a master historian tells what is probably the single most dramatic story in the annals of the American railroads); and *The Life and Legend of E. H. Harriman,* by Maury Klein (in a field full of dreamers, Harriman stood above the crowd).

For more business history sources, see our website at www.hooversvision.com.

TRYTHIS

- Look around in your organization or industry for the person who knows its history. Often, he (or she) may be weird, nerdish, old, or eccentric. But you can learn from him. Pump them for all they know (they'll love it). Use them as a resource for your own growth.
- Look at old copies of *Fortune* magazine. In each issue, try to find at least one great but forgotten business idea. How could this idea be recycled in a new form for today's business world?
- Study some aspect of your local history. Pick a thread and follow it. Learn about one or more of the following: the history of the most prominent local hotel or park; the biography of the person your city is named after; who owned the land 100 years ago where your house is located, and what it was used for; who decided where the local airport would be; the story of the first radio station in your town.
- Who were the largest companies in your industry thirty years ago? Which ones are the largest today? What happened to those that faded? How did the new leaders rise to prominence? Are there lessons they could learn from the leaders of the past?
- You may have heard of Lambert Field (an airport) in St. Louis. You have almost certainly heard of former pharmaceutical giant Warner Lambert. Did you ever wonder if there was a link? What was the basis of the company's success? Listerine! Find another such link in your life and learn all you can about it.

EXPLORATION III
Geography: The Study of the World Around Us

14

A Sense of Place:
Why Geography Matters

Pick up an old *Fortune* magazine. It doesn't matter how old it is—it could be from the 1930s or the 1960s. As it still is today, *Fortune* was then a primary showcase for institutional corporate advertising, a place where the giants of world commerce tell their story in expensive full-page or multipage ads. But there's a curious difference. In 90 percent of these old ads, you will find a reference to the headquarters location of the company. A Coca-Cola ad will name Atlanta; Ford mentions Dearborn; Cunard, London. But pick up the most recent issue of *Fortune*, scan through those same beautiful full-page ads, and geography is nowhere to be found. By my own count, today fewer than 15 percent of the ads mention the home base of the advertiser.

The word is out: this is the Internet Age, we are all one click away from one another, everything is global, and geography doesn't matter anymore. Marketing professionals are telling these companies that the sense of place is no longer important.

Yes, we have gone global; and, yes, we are all just a click away from one another. But the real truth is that, *because* of these things, not in spite of them, geography *does* matter. It matters more than ever. For we humans are still creatures of place. We were all born somewhere, we were all raised somewhere, we all live somewhere now. And each of us is shaped by our geography.

I am a product of central Indiana in the 1950s—cars and car racing, basketball, factories, and big labor, but no foreign languages, no classical music, no crime, no divorce. When I hear a basketball game on TV, I cannot help but turn my head. It is not up to me; it comes from Indiana. We are shaped by our place of origin, whether it was a small town in the deep South, an inner-city neighborhood in the Northeast, a suburb in California, a village in India, or a ranch in Argentina. We carry our places with us wherever we go. Whenever I meet someone new, my first two questions remain two of the most significant—Where are you from? Where did you grow up?

We even name industries after places. Hollywood means movies. Detroit means cars. Specific streets in New York City designate businesses: Wall Street (finance), Madison Avenue (advertising), Seventh Avenue (fashion), Broadway (theater). Silicon Valley (and its successors, the Silicon Alleys, Highways, and byways that have sprouted around the world) will not be the last time that we name a part of our economy, perhaps even a lifestyle, after a place.

So geography is much more than a physical place. It is culture, history, ethnicity, a way of life. Those who ignore geography do so at their peril. For example, let's say you have put together a startup company. You are growing fast from your base in Mountain View, California, and now have offices in Milan, Italy, and Melbourne, Australia. You are planning to hold the most critical business meeting of the year, using an advanced videoconferencing system. When the Milan office says, "The date you propose won't work—we have to go to a football game," you will be clueless unless you realize that, in Milan, "football" means soccer, and that soccer in Milan is even bigger than the Super Bowl in the U.S. Then when the folks in Melbourne object to a different date, this time because they have to go to a test, you will be lost again unless you know that a test is a cricket match—which can last up to five days.

The world was not always so closely linked. As I watched the huge millennium fireworks show televised from Beijing and Shanghai on December 31, 1999, I reflected that the Chinese did not participate in the last millennium observation. It was not because they were culturally or technologically backward—by most accounts, they were well ahead of Europe at the time—and it was not because there was no such observation. It was because China followed its own calendar, and December 31, 1999, did not even exist in their minds. No one had told them that "the world" reset the calendar when Christ was born (give or take a few years). Will we all be on the same calendar when the next millennium rolls around? Whose calendar might it be?

The Internet, the jumbo jet, world culture, and globalized production make it more important than ever to understand geography. Knowing "where other folks are coming from" is critical—where they are coming from historically, culturally, commercially, artistically, musically, and in every other way.

Everything happens in time and space. In the last two chapters, we discussed the importance of history—how things change through time. Geography is how things change through space, how things differ at different points on the globe or at different points in your city. In fact, time and space are inextricably intertwined. New York is eight hundred miles from Chicago, but it is also three hours from Chicago (in a Boeing 737). A particular village in rural China is one hundred miles outside of Shanghai, but it may also be thirty years behind Shanghai (measured in terms of economic, political, and cultural change). In 1850, New York was a month away from San Francisco; today, it is milliseconds away (measured by the flow of information on the Internet).

Physical Geography and Human Geography

Human geography is rooted in physical geography—mountains, deserts, lakes, forests, climate, minerals, and all the other elements that comprise the "geography" we all studied in school. This first level of geography is critically important, and we must not forget it. My home city of Austin, Texas, has been enjoying an economic boom for many years. People usually explain that boom in terms of the University of Texas and the high-tech industries it spawned. Too often they forget the sunny hills that were here long before mankind; they forget the chain of lakes deliberately constructed here by politicians like Sam Rayburn and Lyndon Johnson. Without the picturesque hills and the opportunities for water sports provided by the lakes, Austin would not have attracted so many migrants. The modern Austin, high-tech capital, has been built upon an advantageous physical base.

At the same time, Austin would have never made it without a critical technological innovation—not the computer chip, but air-conditioning. It's no coincidence that the American sunbelt was an economically underdeveloped region until well into the twentieth century, and that it has blossomed as a home to industry, technology, and academia only since the arrival of "refrigerated air."

But while not ignoring physical geography, most of the geography that leaders of enterprises need to be aware of is the geography of people—human geography. Where did the blues come from? What sports are played where? What products are made where? Where do people talk fast and walk fast? Why do people, industries, and enterprises reside where they do, where are they moving from and moving to? Where are the customers? What languages are spoken there, and how is all of this changing over time?

Americans Weak on Geography

Although geography is a more important subject than it ever has been, our knowledge of geography has gotten worse—especially here in the U.S. Our ignorance of geography puts Americans at a competitive disadvantage. Go into a U.S. bookstore and try to find a geography section. Other than a few books about oceans and volcanoes, you'll probably come up empty. Compare this to the bookstores of Canada and

Britain, where (perhaps as a vestige of their once-proud empire) they still care about geography.

Most Americans know very little about faraway places. Take China as an example. In 1830 China represented an estimated 30 percent of the world's economy. Under Mao, that fell to only 5 percent. Today the figure is closer to 10 percent. Yet it's clear that, in the new century, nothing will stop the rise of China from becoming the world's largest economy. Even their government can only accelerate or retard the process. If you are starting a company today that has a long growth curve, your most successful period may be ten to twenty years in the future. Within that time frame, the importance of China will rise dramatically. It will change the lives of many of us. It will certainly change our travel patterns. And yet we know so little about this giant nation.

The most populated state in the U.S. is California, with a population of 33.9 million people (based on the 2000 Census). But if California were a province in China, it would rank *nineteenth* in population. Do you know the names of the eighteen larger provinces? I certainly don't. And yet millions of Chinese know the names of our states; they've heard of New York, California, and Texas. They even know one of our zip codes—90210. This one-directional understanding isn't sufficient, and it will not survive. Trade connects us with the rest of the world, and awareness and understanding must rise in parallel.

As Americans, we have to work harder than others around the world in order to achieve good geographical understanding. There are many reasons. We're isolated from much of the world by two large oceans that serve as buffers. We have our own huge country that is wonderful for traveling, with the result that fewer than 10 percent of Americans have a passport to see the rest of the world. Our newspapers and broadcast news sources overflow with domestic news; we cover the rest of the world only when there is an earth-shattering event or a dramatic catastrophe. Anything less than three thousand people killed in a flood in India is considered unimportant compared to one child stuck in a well in our own state.

A good place to begin a better understanding is by looking at our two closest neighbors. In 2000 Mexico held a presidential election that may well have been the most important North American election in fifty years. Yet few in the U.S. paid much attention. The night before the voting, *Larry King Live*, one of our nation's most important political-interview TV programs, featured yet another discussion of the Jon Benet Ramsay murder case. Most Americans think of Mexico as a beach resort. That may be adequate—unless you are leading an enterprise in the twenty-first century, looking for new ideas, new employees, new customers.

Americans tend to think of Canada as our economic "little brother," rather than as one of the world's most advanced urban cultures with a remarkably high level of successful cultural diversity and integration. Canada is one of the world's largest and most powerful economies, and Mexico has the chance to become another. Few things would be better for the United States.

An enterprise must be built with an awareness of what is going on in the world. The following pages will offer tips on how to view our changing world, what the major trends are, and where they are taking place. We'll examine the concept of globalization—what it really means, and what it may mean for local cultures around the world. We'll also take a look at the cities of the world.

GATEWAYS

Further Readings About Geography

Since there are so few popular books written on geography, especially human and economic geography, the best books are often textbooks. They are full of maps and important insights not readily found elsewhere. You should look for the one that has most recently been updated, as most of them are updated every few years (but rarely annually) with the latest data. Two excellent textbooks are *Human Geography: Cultures, Connections, and Landscapes*, by Edward F. Bergman, and *Human Geography: Culture,*

Society, and Space, by H. J. de Blij. My favorite overall geography
textbook, breaking the world into rational "continents," is
Geography: Realms, Regions, and Concepts, by H. J. de Blij and Peter O.
Muller. You can sometimes order this book in a package with a
great atlas for leaders—*Goode's Atlas,* (Rand McNally, editor
John G. Hudson). This is the best U.S.-produced atlas for issues of
concern to enterprises—issues like people and the economy. A
good pocket atlas to travel with is the *Haack Pocket Atlas of the
World,* from Barron's.

A great book for understanding Europe is *The New Superregions
of Europe,* by Darrell Delamaide, which does for Europe what Joel
Garreau did for the U.S. and Canada in *The Nine Nations of North
America.* A good introductory book is *The European Culture Area,* by
Terry G. Jordan, which is helpful if you need to understand the
varied parts of Europe. I would also recommend *A Geography of the
European Union,* by John Cole and Francis Cole, which is a good
look at emerging Europe. My favorite book on Asia is *Video Night
in Kathmandu: And Other Reports from the Not-So-Far East,* by Pico
Iyer. Australian journalist Greg Sheridan may have the best
handle on Asia of any non-Asian observer in his excellent book
Asian Values, Western Dreams: Understanding the New Asia. In *The River
at the Center of the World: A Journey Up the Yangtze and Back in Chinese
Time,* by Simon Winchester, storytelling, history, and travel are
beautifully combined.

Historical atlases are often the most pleasurable way to
learn geography and history simultaneously. But one needs to
get into the habit of stopping on each map and thinking,
"What does this map tell me?" The *Hammond Atlas of the
Twentieth Century* is a beautiful atlas that covers (in words and
maps) the major events of the century, from the fall of the
Ottoman Empire to the rise of AIDS. The much larger
Hammond Atlas of World History, edited by Richard Overy and
part of the *Times* series, is excellent. Every continent, every era, is
well covered. If you want to save a little money—or carry a few
less pounds—*The Harper Atlas of World History* is a good medium-
sized historical atlas.

15

Seeing the World Through Foreign Eyes

We are all foreigners somewhere. Foreignness is a reciprocal quality. Maybe you've seen the message on a trucker's rearview mirror: "I can't see you if you can't see me." Foreignness is the same way: If you are a foreigner to me, I am a foreigner to you. If your language is strange to me, then my language is strange to you.

It's a worthwhile experience to spend time looking at the world through the eyes of a foreigner. The most effective way to do this is to go abroad. When you travel, it is important to use of all the looking and seeing techniques covered earlier in this book. We tend to travel to sit by the beach, to see a famous museum or two, or to attend business meetings. But if that is all we do, we are not making the best use of our mileage. Exploratory travel means traveling with your eyes glued to the window, asking questions everywhere you go, noticing everything, from local sports and music to architecture and billboards.

The greatest opportunities for our minds to absorb new ideas often come while we are far from home. For many of us, just the experience of being outside our normal environment is stimulating, creating a rush of new ideas and insights. To me, nothing is more exciting than my first arrival in a new city or a new country.

I have devoted a fair share of my time and energy trying to convince people to explore the world. Frequent, affordable air travel makes this possible to a greater degree than at any time in history. Travel can be greatly enhanced by studying history, geography, and culture in books, but there is ultimately no substitute for walking the streets, eating the food, meeting the people—for *being there*.

Whenever I meet a high school senior planning on college, I am tempted to suggest that they would learn more if they went to college for two or three years, then traveled the world for another year or two. Many Europeans, Australians, and some Americans do just that, although they usually finish their four years of college as well. This is one of the best investments a young person can make—if they really travel with an open mind, ready to absorb all that they see.

A key concept in exploratory travel is "making a place your own." If you go to New York City and take the same tours, go to the same skyscraper observation decks and the same museums as everyone else, you'll come home with "the standard New York"—the same city that everyone else sees. To really get your arms around a city like New York, you need to reach further, to create a New York City that is your own. Find the restaurant or diner that is not in all the tour books. Find the quiet neighborhood that has no tourists. Visit the bubbling ethnic caldron of Flushing in Queens or the nineteenth-century enclave of Brooklyn Heights. If you go to France, don't limit yourself to Paris and the Riviera; see Lyon or Bordeaux. Every city has neighborhoods that are off the beaten path, every country has cities and regions that are unknown to most tourists. If you can approach a new city, a new state, or a new nation and make it your own, you will gain a deeper understanding and usually retain more vivid, more personal memories.

Another important aspect of travel is coming home. When I go to another country, I try to notice everything—how the stoplights look, how the banks work, how the food tastes, how the playgrounds are different. But when I land back in my familiar United States, I always try at first to see my homeland in a new light, through foreign eyes. When I get home from Hong Kong and land in Texas, I ask myself, "If I had never known anything but Hong Kong, what would be the most striking thing about Texas?" How would it seem odd to me? How would it seem the same? When I first turn on the radio or TV I ask, "What would this sound like to Hong Kong ears?"

Stereotypes

In all of our travels, we should seek to understand similarities and differences. Above all else, we should seek to understand people. For better or worse, most of those understandings start with preconceptions, with stereotypes. Try as we might, we can never completely get common wisdom, wives' tales, and Hollywood imagery out of our heads. When we meet and get to know someone from another part of the world, most of those stereotypes quickly fade. But if we don't run into a Korean every day, if we don't live next door to an Iranian, stereotypes about those nationalities are likely to dominate our thinking.

Stereotypes are not by definition evil: they are natural, human tools that we use to try to make sense of the world around us. I have sat on airplanes and listened to a Dane tell me all about the idiosyncrasies of the Norwegians and Swedes; I have listened to a Panamanian tell me how weird the Nicaraguans are; I have heard Hoosiers from Indiana explain what hicks Kentuckians are. In almost every case, there are some facts or historical experiences that gave rise to these stereotypes. They are not usually complete fiction. You and I harbor plenty of similar stereotypes about people. But always remember three things about stereotypes:

1. Stereotypes change.

If you are my age, you will remember an America in which many thought of Asians only in terms of ethnic slurs. Our understanding of China was sometimes limited to clichés like "There are so many people over there, they place no value on human life." Today the more common stereotype of Asians is "good at math and science," and the basic image of China that many businesspeople subscribe to is, "There are so many people over there—and someday they all might drink Coca-Cola."

2. Relying on stereotypes is dangerous.

I remember working with a shopping center developer from small-town Missouri who had begun his career as a plasterer and built his business from nothing. He had no M.B.A. He made the most of his easy, folksy style. I would sit in meetings in which he was negotiating with the "suits" from Wall Street, and you could tell that they thought they were taking advantage of him. He'd say, "Howdy," and they'd draw out their HP calculators like dueling pistols. But his understanding of the implications of every clause in the contract was always three steps ahead of theirs. It gave me great pleasure (especially since I was on his side) to see the slickers realize, usually several days later, that they had been had.

If you are dealing with anyone and assume you are smarter than they are, you may already have begun to fail.

3. It's unfair to apply a stereotype to anyone.

No matter how "true" a stereotype may be, it will never be true for every member of the group. There are Asian students who can write novels but are bad at math. Many people used to assume that only white people could play golf. Then Tiger Woods came along.

When you get on that plane heading to a new city or a new country, own up to your own stereotypes—try listing them on a sheet of paper. Then prepare to dismantle them, prepare to grow into a broader understanding. Look hard for the real similarities and differences that all people exhibit.

In my travels around the world, meeting people of all types, it strikes me that there are some major and important similarities that cross borders and cultures. The most striking thing that I have noted about the people I meet *everywhere* I travel is that *they all want to create a better life for their children.* Even in those societies in which parents are known for working away from their families the longest hours, or driving their kids the hardest in school, they usually do so with the belief that it will make their children's lives better.

In addition to this core value, there are many small threads of life that unite people around the world. Outside of the United States, the rituals of cigarette smoking are still strong forces that bind people. Back when I was a smoker, I came to the conclusion that the most universally valuable currency on earth was a carton of Marlboros. Other universal languages include movies, sex, sports, and music. Beer ranks fairly high on the same list. Increasingly, the English language is also a bond—starting with a simple "Okay" or a "Hello."

But for every similarity we see, there are probably a dozen differences. This reality came home to me when I was traveling the island of Bali in Indonesia. My guide, like thousands of other Balinese, was named Wayan. After he got to know me and felt comfortable speaking his mind, he told me that one of the most perplexing things was "Why you Europeans walk so fast and eat so slow." This statement made me aware that I was a European in his eyes, because of my language, my culture, and the color of my skin. Like other "Europeans," I tended to walk more briskly than the Indonesian people, but then to stop and linger over a meal that a Balinese might gobble down with no conversation. Wayan could not understand what all the hurry was about when we were walking, if we lost all the time saved when we sat down to eat!

In looking at differences, I think it particularly dangerous to assume that moral values are the same everywhere. To be sure, there are a few virtually universal ethical standards. The world is unified in its opposition to murder and slavery. But there are many other moral areas where standards differ dramatically from place to place. Attitudes toward alcohol, drugs, gambling, prostitution, abortion, and pornography differ greatly around the world. They even differ within our own country over time—forty years ago gambling (in casinos or lotteries) was legal in only a few states; now it is allowed in almost all. Whether to tip the waitress or not, whether bribes are evil or part of a civil servants' pay, varies greatly. In Singapore, chewing gum is evil and against the law, while in other countries even ministers do it. No matter what your own beliefs on issues like this, remember that not everyone feels the same way.

A World of Many Cultures

There are books like *Culture Matters,* by Lawrence Harrison and Samuel Huntington, about the importance of culture in determining the degree of material success of different peoples and nations. While such books provide many interesting insights and provocative ideas, they strike me as dangerous—like relying on stereotypes—to assume that cultural differences are the make-or-break factors in determining whether people are wealthy or poor. For example, to imply that Brazil will not succeed in realizing its potential because of its Catholic heritage seems to me to underestimate the potential of its people.

Nevertheless, it is important to look at cultures and to know how they differ in order to understand the role that your enterprise can play in the world. Perhaps the most basic aspects of culture are religion and language. The following table shows 1999 estimates of total global adherents in the major faiths.

Major Religions—Millions of Adherents 1999

Christians	1,974
Roman Catholics	1,044
Protestants	416
Orthodox	214
Muslims	1,155
Hindu	799
Buddhists	356

GATEWAYS

Further Readings on World Cultures and Religions

Two interesting books are *The Clash of Civilizations and the Remaking of World Order,* by Samuel P. Huntington, and a book of readings by different authors, *Culture Matters: How Values Shape Human Progress,* edited by Lawrence E. Harrison and Samuel P. Huntington. Another very interesting book is *When Cultures Collide: Managing Successfully Across Cultures,* by Richard D. Lewis—a very practical but highly opinionated guide to doing business in the cultures of the world. For a better understanding of world religion, try *The World's Religions,* by Huston Smith, the best introduction to the world's major faiths, told story-style, or *The Eliade Guide to World Religions,* by Mircea Eliade and Ioan P. Couliano, an alphabetical guide to the beliefs of the world, including secondary groups.

16

Thinking Regionally

We tend to think of the world in traditional political boundaries—nations, states, provinces, city limits—or in terms of the continents we learned in grade school. But often, the real world that people live in, commute in, and do business in is made up of regions—ranging in size from "Southeast Asia" and "Scandinavia" to "Northern Italy" and "Southern California." Here are eight ways to look at the world and its regions that may stimulate your thinking in new directions.

Eight Thoughts About the World

1. The "Pacific Century" is probably an American myth.

We have gotten into the habit of talking and thinking of the "Pacific Century," an outgrowth of the supposed "Pacific economic miracle" of the past two decades. This is usually phrased in the context that the previous era was the Atlantic era, and now we are switching to the Pacific. But the reality is that the "economic miracle" has primarily taken place in East Asia and Southeast Asia. It could be argued that we are at the beginning of the Chinese or East Asian century, but we are probably not on the threshold of the Pacific Century.

Furthermore, American writers describing "the Pacific Century" may be just trying to cut Europe out of the Asian opportunity. While the west coasts of North and South America have benefited from sharing access to the Pacific Ocean, they are actually no closer to Asia than is Europe, as shown on the next page.

Air Mileages Between Key Cities

	Los Angeles	London
Tokyo	5,470	5,959
Singapore	8,767	6,747
Delhi	7,011	4,181

When I travel around Asia, I see some elevators and escalators manufactured by Otis (an American company) and some by Mitsubishi (Japanese), but just as often I see ones manufactured by Schindler (European). Neon signs on the Shanghai riverfront include advertisements for such European brands as Nestlé and L'Oreal. A visitor to Asia sees as many signs for Unilever as for Procter & Gamble, and the streets contain a lot more Mercedes than Cadillacs or Lincolns. My guide tells me that there are forty-five thousand Santana taxis in Shanghai, manufactured by Volkswagen.

The bottom line is that both Europe and the Western Hemisphere have the opportunity to participate in the Asian miracle, but only through hard work and paying attention to the needs of the marketplace, not by relying on any mythical shift of oceanic power.

2. It's pointless to speak of one Asia.

Asia is best understood if it is broken into four regions—East Asia, Southeast Asia, South Asia, and Russia. While Russia is in many ways more closely related to Europe, most of its landmass is in Asia. It is easy for Americans to think of Asia as one big continent and to think of its people as having a great deal in common—millions of poor people, good at math, and so on.

The "Asian miracle" has taken place in selected countries, from Japan to Thailand. Many others have not participated: Communist Myanmar remains locked off from the rest of the world, much like Cuba in our hemisphere. South Asia, anchored by India and including Bangladesh and Pakistan, vies with Africa for the dubious distinction of being the poorest part of the world.

Singapore, Hong Kong, South Korea, and Taiwan have sometimes been referred to as the "dragons," up-and-coming nations following in the steps of Japan. But it's risky to group these places so glibly, because they are all very different. Singapore and Hong Kong are the world's two remaining city-states—compact, powerful port cities, completely urban, dominated by and reliant on vibrant international trade. But Singapore is in the heart of Southeast Asia, which has dynamics of its own, and Hong Kong is now a "special administrative region" within China. Taiwan, formerly part of China, may remerge with China at some point in the future. The path to that end may be very rocky, but twenty years ago the peaceful reconsolidation of East and West Germany appeared impossible. And South Korea, perhaps the most dynamic of all, remains separated from North Korea—the same traditions yet so different—after fifty years.

The following table compares the economic growth of some of the "dragons" with selected other nations around the globe. You can see why economists get excited by just a few percentage point differences in annual growth rates.

Gross Domestic Product (GDP) per Capita
(inflation adjusted)

Nation	1950	1989	Percent Annual Growth Rate
United States	$8,605	$18,282	1.95
Japan	$1,620	$15,336	5.93
Mexico	$1,594	$3,728	2.20
Brazil	$1,434	$4,402	2.92
Thailand	$874	$4,008	3.98
South Korea	$757	$6,503	5.67
Taiwan	$706	$7,252	6.15
India	$502	$1,093	2.02
China	$454	$2,538	4.51

3. The nation to watch is China.

"There is no people in the world wealthier than the Chinese." So wrote Ibn Battuta, the "Marco Polo" of Islam, in the fourteenth century. His words may well come true again during this century.

Share of the World's Gross National Product (GNP)

	China	India	Japan	Europe	U.S.	Russia
1700	23.1%	22.6%	4.5%	23.3%	0.0%	3.2%
1820	32.4%	15.7%	3.0%	26.6%	1.8%	4.8%
1890	13.2%	11.0%	2.5%	40.3%	13.8%	6.3%
1952	5.2%	3.8%	3.4%	29.7%	28.4%	8.7%
1995	10.9%	4.6%	8.4%	23.8%	20.9%	2.2%

Based on the work of Angus Maddison; see "Gateways."

You've probably heard that China is going to become *one* of the most powerful economies on earth. Don't believe it. China is going to become *the* largest economy on earth. It is just a matter of when. Even the Chinese government cannot decide for or against this; it can only accelerate or slow down the inevitable process. The nation has 1.2 billion people, and its economy is already ranked in the top seven today. And after China's conversion to capitalism, I believe its conversion to Western-style democracy is inevitable.

The President of the People's Republic of China, Jiang Zemin, is possibly the most powerful man on earth, in terms of his ability to influence the way the world will change in the years to come. The rise of China is being fueled by a smart, hard-working, disciplined citizenry. They are eager, reaching, and ambitious. Their children will not grow up in the same country that they grew up in. Change is taking place at breakneck speed. If you go to Shanghai today, you will see more neon than anywhere outside of Las Vegas. Ten years ago, there was none. As of 1999, there were fifty-four KFC fast-food outlets in Shanghai. Across the river, they are building Pudong, an entirely new business city, replete with some of the world's tallest skyscrapers.

When China "recovered" Hong Kong, it got back its commercial center, its New York City. When it got back Macau a few years later, it recovered its Las Vegas—its playground and den of forbidden pleasures. When and if Taiwan reintegrates into the mainland, then China will recover its Silicon Valley, with all the entrepreneurial and technological prowess that implies.

There is no turning back for China. Its leaders have said that they will not tinker with Hong Kong's capitalism for at least fifty years. By the time those fifty years pass, those leaders will be long dead, and the new leaders will be children of MTV and KFC. They will have been raised with freedom of action, freedom of choice, and capitalism. I'd like to celebrate my one hundredth birthday in Shanghai just to see how it changes, how it all turns out.

It is unlikely that China will completely lose its traditional cultures in its transition to modernism. It is more certain that China will have an enormous impact on the lives of the world's people. Our language, our music, our movies, our clothes, our thinking—all will be affected by the depth and intensity of historical Chinese culture.

As we deal with this powerful emerging nation, we only look like colonialists when we behave as if we have all the answers or "know what's best" for these people. The Chinese people were powerful and innovative long before the rise of the Western world—and they know it. Only they can control their own destiny.

4. Malaysia and Singapore are nations of the future.

Two of the clearest examples of strong leadership, in which elected politicians have tightly controlled the evolution of their countries, are the neighboring nations of Singapore, long ruled by Lee Kuan Yew, and Malaysia, led by Mahathir Mohammed. While Lee recently retired and Mahathir may soon do the same, the effects of their leadership will last for generations. For these are two unique leaders—unique in their practical wisdom, their depth of vision, their ability to develop political systems customized to their nations and peoples, and in their readiness to put the welfare of the average citizen ahead of their own self-interest or the interests of powerful friends. In the west, Mahathir is often berated because he is cantankerous and opinionated. But the evidence I saw on my recent first visit to Malaysia suggests that he has been one of the most profound leaders of the twentieth century.

If you want to see people of all races living together in harmony, visit Singapore and Malaysia. Malaysia is roughly 60 percent Malay, 30 percent Chinese, and 10 percent Indian. All three groups are participating in the growth of the national wealth.

When I tell Americans that everyone gets along in Singapore, they sometimes respond, "In a little city, that's easy to accomplish." But Singapore is not so small—its population of 4 million people is greater than that of Ireland. How many U.S. cities of comparable size are noted for racial, ethnic, and social harmony?

If you want to see a city of the future where everything works, visit

Singapore or Kuala Lumpur, the capital of Malaysia. Both cities are remarkably clean and safe. You check in for your airline flight downtown and are whisked to the airport on a high-speed rail system that would be the envy of any U.S. city.

If you want to see neighborhoods of the future, where fiber-optic cable is laid before any homes and offices have been built, visit Cyberjaya outside Kuala Lumpur.

If you want to see intelligently planned urban growth, take a look at the Klang Valley, extending outward from Kuala Lumpur, where they are building three cities of a half million people each rather than one overblown and overcrowded metropolitan center.

If you want to invest in a stable economy built on the strong base of a well-educated population with a large middle class, invest in Malaysia or Singapore. I think of them, despite their different political and cultural heritages, as the Netherlands and Switzerland (successful smaller nations) of the future, although Malaysia already has as many people as those two countries combined. Its potential is enormous.

5. Europe has a sunbelt, too.

Europe, too, is often subject to oversimplification in the minds of Americans. We're aware of Germany's enormous economic and industrial power, and ties of language, culture, politics, and ancestry give us some insight into the peoples of the British Isles. But we often overlook the growing influence and importance of other regions of Europe. In recent years, economic power is accumulating in surprising places—in high-tech manufacturing powerhouses like Nokia (Finland), in world-class retailers like IKEA (Denmark), and in banking powerhouses like Santander (Spain).

One starting point for Americans in understanding Europe is to realize that, like the United States, Europe has a colder, slower-growing north and a warmer, booming south. While we do not normally think of Spain, Portugal, Italy, Greece, Turkey, and Malta as the Arizonas and Floridas of Europe, such a view can be helpful.

In addition, Europe probably has a lock on being the tourism center of the world. Spain, Southern France, and Italy combine sunshine, history, and a tourism infrastructure like few other places on earth. Some call Europe the world's Disneyland—like it or not, there is some truth to it.

In addition, we tend to think of the former Communist nations as a unit, when in fact there are enormous differences among countries like Poland, Romania, Albania, and the Czech Republic, and even among the several states that emerged from the ruins of the former Yugoslavia. It's a mistake to assume that all of these regions are educationally backward, ecologically ruined, and hopelessly impoverished. If you visit Poland, Hungary, or the Czech Republic, you can sense the opportunity in the air. Talk with some of their hopeful, energetic, bright young professionals and you can see that these nations will be far more powerful and prosperous twenty years from now than they are today.

6. The Middle East, North Africa, and the culture of Islam are much more complex than we may think.

One of the fastest-growing religions in the United States (and the world) is Islam, now with an estimated 4 to 7 million practicing Muslims in America. As this is also one of the most misunderstood faiths, it is worth examining in more detail.

Often we think of Islam as being an "Arab" religion. Certainly most Arabs are Islamic, and Islam started with the Arabs. But Christianity started in Palestine, and we don't think of all Christians as Palestinians. Today Islam not only stretches from Morocco to Indonesia half a world away, but is very present in such varying countries as Russia, Britain, France, and the United States. The following table lists the largest countries that are majority Islamic.

Largest Nations That Are Majority Islamic

	Population (in millions in 2000)
Indonesia	224
Pakistan	141
Bangladesh	129
Egypt	68
Turkey	65
Iran	65
Algeria	31
Morocco	30
Iraq	22
Saudi Arabia	22

To put these numbers in perspective, remember that California has 33.9 million people and Texas has 20.9 million.

Indonesia is a particularly interesting country. As the largest Islamic nation on earth (more than 90 percent Islamic), it is the second-largest country after the United States that shares the monotheistic Judeo-Christian-Islamic heritage. In all three of these religions, children learn stories from the Hebrew Bible, such as those of Noah, Abraham, Moses, and Joseph. Muslims believe in Jesus Christ as a prophet before Mohammed and are allowed to marry Jews and Christians. All three religions were born in the same part of the world.

Each of these leading Islamic countries has its own style. Only Saudi Arabia can be considered completely "Arab." In Morocco, for example, Jews have served in cabinet-level government posts, and Morocco was the first Islamic country to recognize the state of Israel. When Nazi Germany took over France, Morocco was a protectorate of France, so Hitler tried to get his hands on the many Moroccan Jews. But the grandfather of the present king of Morocco vowed that no Moroccan Jew would be touched, and his will, not Hitler's, was done.

In Islamic culture, the roles of the judge and the religious leader are

integrated. While this is antithetical to the system we have developed in
the United States, it is not hard to understand its logic. Who should know
right from wrong better than a man of the cloth? Islam, like Judaism,
has a long tradition of studying the Word and learning the ancient laws.
Muslim religious schools include some of the oldest universities on
earth, which have been turning out men of law and men of religion—
often the same men—for centuries.

Islamic scholars preserved the classics of Greece and Rome when the
Christians of medieval Europe were hell-bent on destroying them. In the
year 1000, Cordoba in Muslim Spain was one of the world's greatest
cities, with hundreds of booksellers—four centuries before the invention
of the printing press! Jews, Christians, and Muslims lived peacefully side
by side. Some of the greatest urban civilizations ever known were the
great Islamic cities of Baghdad, Damascus, Cairo, Fes, Constantinople,
and Granada.

In this context, it is easier to understand the idea behind a religious
state like contemporary Iran. But it is also possible to understand
Turkey—the Islamic nation that more than any other has tried to create
a secular society with separation of church and state along the lines of
American and most European practice. In both countries, it is a challenge for faithful Muslims to remain true to the spirit of their religion:
religious Turks ask how church and state can possibly be separated,
while modernist Iranians long for more freedom in their lifestyles.

While Islam may seem foreign to many Americans, it will not stay
that way for long. With more and more people migrating to America
from Islamic nations, and more Americans adopting this religion, you
should not be surprised to see a new mosque being built in your neighborhood in coming years. That will be good for America, because it will
help erode the stereotypes that prevent us from understanding an important and fascinating part of our world.

In large part because of our weak grasp of Islam, it is all too easy to
generalize about the Middle East. We are quick to forget that, for example, under the Shah, Iran had built a large middle-class society, and even
today remains one of the wealthier nations in the region. Jordan and

Morocco have been ruled by brave and progressive kings, both recently succeeded by their sons. Neither has any significant reserves of oil. Nations like Egypt and Turkey remain huge centers of commerce and culture, important to any enterprise doing business in the region. In particular, the Turkish city of Istanbul serves as the crucial link between Europe and the Middle East, a role it has filled for centuries.

Lebanon is currently rebounding from war to rebuild its capital city of Beirut, once the business center of the Middle East. During Beirut's years of decline, the United Arab Emirates (UAE) took on a new role as a progressive economic center of the region. This is a fascinating smaller country where, thirty years ago, seven independent sheikhs joined together into one nation for the benefit of their people. Ever since, they have been building up the nation's infrastructure, its airlines (Gulf and Emirates), its shopping, and its facilities for tourism and recreation.

In this diverse and rapidly growing part of the world (with regards to its high birth rate), it is a mistake to let the affairs of Israel and Palestine dominate our attention. Because our stereotypes about the Middle East are so deeply entrenched, it may take more effort and more study to reach full understanding of this region than of any other part of the world.

7. The three nations with the greatest unrealized potential are Brazil, India, and Indonesia.

These three nations have a lot in common. In addition to their tropical climates and their large and growing populations, they all have incredibly wealthy, deep cultures. They also have huge natural resources, and lots of land with agricultural potential.

At the same time, they have many differences. They are Catholic, Hindu, and Islamic. In the past, they have had corrupt, weak leaders (Brazil), corrupt, powerful leaders (Indonesia), and an often-unfocused form of socialism and central planning (India). Brazil and Indonesia have invested heavily in their infrastructure, from airports and highways to skyscrapers, while India has not. Perhaps most important, Indonesia has invested in its people, achieving very high literacy rates among its children. Brazil has also made good progress in education, but India remains among the worst in the world, especially among its little girls.

In aggregate, especially in India, the average person has not been well served by the leadership of the past. While all of these nations have seen increases in critical measures like life span and healthcare, they have been passed up by many other nations.

I believe that the future of these three nations rests in the hands of the people of these nations, in particular their business leaders and entrepreneurs. At the same time, the government leaders must create an environment that allows those entrepreneurs to flourish and that allows new entrepreneurs to enter the field and prosper, rather than limiting the spoils to those already in the power circles. Distrust of businesspeople and closure to world markets will only continue the poverty of the average person in these countries.

India has been the world's largest functioning democracy for fifty years, and today Indonesia and Brazil are also developing democratic traditions. While the success of some Asian countries can be attributed at least in part to strongmen in power, we also know that open democracies can succeed. But it takes even stronger leaders, ones who both can generate public support for bold programs as well as carry them out and retain their elected offices. It sometimes seems easier when you are the king.

For enterprises from around the world, Brazil, India, and Indonesia present enormous opportunities. But they also present great risks and uncertainties.

Brazilians have a bitter joke: "Brazil has the greatest potential of any nation on earth—it always has, and it always will." Perhaps the twenty-first century will be the time when all three nations finally get beyond potential to achieve full participation on the world stage.

8. The early twenty-first century may be more critical to Latin America than to any other region on earth.

As the United States becomes more Latinized, our neighbors to the south will become more and more important to us. Having suffered under some of the worst and most abusive political leadership in the world, the peoples of this huge region are just now beginning to realize their enormous political and economic power.

I've already discussed the potential of Brazil, the largest of the Latin nations. Here are some very quick observations about Latin America that may be relevant to your enterprise.

In 2000 Mexico elected Vicente Fox as its first alternative-party President in more than seventy years. A long history of institutionalized political corruption and insecurity may be coming to an end. Nothing could be more beneficial to the U.S.

Guatemala, the most populous nation in Central America, signed the peace treaty officially ending its lengthy civil war only five years ago. Guatemala's life as a free, democratic country is just beginning.

Panama, Costa Rica, and El Salvador are all becoming business centers; one or more of these may become the UAE, the Singapore, or the Malaysia of Central America.

After tortured political pasts, Chile and (more recently) Argentina have opened up and joined the world economy. Both are culturally wealthy nations that are now in a hurry to play their proper role on the world stage.

Throughout Latin America, the opportunities for culture, tourism, and commerce are enormous. As in Asia, some nations will be well led, while others will not. But there is no part of the world that is so clearly on the cusp, so clearly at a critical inflection point of history, as Latin America. The same holds true of the Caribbean, which will begin to determine its future course over the next twenty years, starting with the inevitable transition to a post-Castro regime in Cuba.

17

The Rise of the World

Our understanding of the world is best served by connecting change through time and change through space. That is, how is the world changing as we proceed into the next century? Understanding where one stands in time and space is critical to building a successful enterprise, critical to understanding our operating environment. Especially important is understanding the biggest and longest-term factors at work—the evolution of the earth and where it is today. This is where history and geography intersect, where change through time and differences around the globe meet.

The more I study these long-term trends, the more I conclude that the facts are extraordinarily positive. So I call this overview "The Rise of the World."

Wealthier and Wealthier

Over the long term, the world—the whole world—is getting wealthier and wealthier. How do I define *wealth*? I mean *the total accumulation and dispersion of the assets that are most important to humanity*—life span, health, education, food, clothing, shelter, safety, peace, culture, art, music, transportation—every worthwhile asset from hamburgers to Rolexes, college classes to Hollywood movies, clean and well-heated (or well-cooled) apartments to five-star hotel rooms.

In pursuit of these varied goods, we are all climbing the same hill, a shared hill, from caves to the future. Most organizations, enterprises, and societies are either growing or dying at any given point. In aggregate, the world's nations are growing, in multiple dimensions, as we climb the hill of wealth.

As we watch the world progress, we see things move forward in small increments: from black-and-white televisions to color, from propeller airliners to jets, from 16-bit microchips to Pentium processors. But we rarely stand back and look at where we have really come from.

It would be hard to think of a more important measure of wealth than life span. Based on available records, primarily English, European life spans hovered between thirty and forty from the sixteenth century through the eighteenth. Life spans in England and France began to break through forty in the mid-1800s. By the end of the nineteenth century, they were on a steep upward curve toward today's seventies. A similar curve has taken place in China since World War II. These countries are representative of their neighbors.

The rise in life spans has been due to many factors: a decline in accidental deaths, canning and other food-processing procedures that reduce contamination, the general availability of safe water supplies and other improvements in sanitation, advances in health care (especially in dentistry), and innovative pharmaceuticals. The rise has been especially great among women (who do not die in childbirth as often) and children (who live to adulthood more often).

While life expectancy may be the single most important measure of wealth, it is also important to consider the quality of our lives. Worldwide education levels and literacy keep rising. Pollution levels, which are still high, particularly in many poorer countries, are coming down. (Los Angeles today has cleaner air than at any time in the past thirty years;

previously unseen species of fish are spawning in New York's Hudson River.) Total world production of and access to works of film, music, and art are at record levels. The world's great museums are drawing more visitors than at any time in history.

I am focusing on nonfinancial forms of wealth both because they are more important to our ultimate satisfaction and because they are sometimes forgotten when we talk about wealth. But it would be equally regrettable if we forgot the inextricable link between financial wealth and cultural and physical wealth. Nations with high incomes can more readily afford clean air, clean water, great museums, and medical clinics in every neighborhood. Great art collections and great universities are often founded by wealthy individuals with generous spirits. More profitable corporations are more likely to give to organizations that work to help the homeless, the illiterate, and the abused. In short, all the forms of wealth are intertwined and tend to come together. This is especially true when at least some of the wealth is spread among a large middle class.

I do not mean to appear Pollyannaish—there is still widespread poverty and many other forms of evil in the world. As recently as 1994, the government of Rwanda or its affiliates murdered between seven hundred thousand and a million of its own citizens. Those victims who could afford to do so bribed their attackers with money so that they would be shot rather than hacked with a machete. The world has probably not seen the last Hitler, Stalin, or Pol Pot.

Furthermore, even in the most prosperous nations, there continue to be pockets of poverty and deprivation. There will continue to be economic cycles, and in the downturns people living near the edge of poverty are likely to slip backward into true want. And there will always be accidents and acts of nature that cost the lives of millions and bring suffering to even more.

It's the nature of progress that it generally consists of two steps forward, one step back. Sometimes we seem to take two steps back. But we should never lose sight of the long-term trends, the direction in which humankind has been heading for at least the last two centuries. It's the direction that all of us on earth are heading—up. In fact, the largest gains often accrue to those who started out the furthest behind.

The fact that the countries that started further behind often have gained the most is in large part the principle of convergence at work. That is, there is a natural tendency for values to move toward the average. And when the average is rising, those who are furthest behind are often going to rise faster than others.

This same mathematics tends to affect every other group that started behind. For example, the primary beneficiaries of what I call the rise of the world are women. In terms of life span, education and literacy, power and participation in politics, and relative economic status, women have enhanced their position dramatically worldwide. And children are coming right along with them. In many societies, little girls have historically been the lowest on the totem pole, getting less schooling, less access to inherited wealth, and less of everything else. This is one population segment that will benefit the most if we keep moving things ahead. Already, women in college outnumber men in college in about half the world's nations, especially in the middle-income and wealthy nations.

At the same time that most trends are clearly positive, particularly among the poorest countries, it is important to realize that the rate of progress of particular nations is largely under their own control. That is, countries get rich or fail to do so largely as a result of their own actions. Consider, for example, the six countries shown in the next chart, which were economic equals only one hundred years ago.

Gross Domestic Product (GDP) per Capita (inflation adjusted)

	1890	1950	1989
Japan	$842	$1,620	$15,336
Mexico	$762	$1,594	$3,728
Korea	$680	$757	$6,503
Brazil	$641	$1,434	$4,402
Taiwan	$564	$706	$7,252
India	$521	$502	$1,093

Of course, there are many factors that affect how successful each nation is and how fast its people are enriched. These include the broad global factors of success, including democracy and technology. But one other dimension that we cannot forget is the quality of leadership. If you study the nations of the world throughout history, it is a relatively rare and historically recent phenomenon for leaders to make serving their citizens a high priority.

In other words, most kings, emperors, and generals had as their first priority defending their borders or conquering their neighbors. The next priority was making their family and friends and all those who helped put them in power and keep them there comfortable. This applies to the Janissary soldiers of the Ottoman Empire in the seventeenth century or the executives of United Fruit Company in Central America in the early twentieth century. Taking care of your friends has always been high on the priority list of most political and economic leaders. As I write this, the citizens of Indonesia are rioting in the streets as the political leadership tries to sort out the legacy of President Suharto, who did many great things for his people but also made sure his friends and family had well-lined pockets in the process.

Lives of Commonplace Wealth

Compared with all the people who have lived before us, even royalty, most of us in the "developed" world live in unprecedented luxury, with unequalled options and choices. In many respects, the United States was the first nation to reach this amazing level of widespread wealth. Today the average American, not just the wealthy:

- has Internet access in their home

- owns that home

- has access to hundreds of cable channels

- can get a plumber or locksmith to their house in a few hours

- lives within thirty minutes of a shopping mall

- can buy fresh food twenty-four hours a day

- drives at least one automobile

This is a staggering achievement. This twenty-first-century lifestyle is something that has come first to the U.S. and has been developed here. We are the first country that can afford college. I don't mean merely the price of the tuition, I mean the fact that so many of our young people can take four years out of their lives and spend most of that time thinking and learning rather than working. As of 1997, 81 percent of America's college-age residents were in some form of higher education (up from 56 percent in 1980); only in Canada and Australia are the statistics comparable. Germany is at 47 percent, the UK at 52 percent.

In short, the United States is the first giant society on earth that has gotten the basics out of the way—it has fed itself, clothed itself, and housed itself—and is now in some sense sitting back and enjoying the good life. I know it doesn't feel that way when everyone in your family is working long hours or when you are stuck in traffic, but by any rational view through time and space, we are in a unique position. And the inventions of the last twenty years—the CD, the PC, the Internet—take all this to a whole new level.

So now I have drawn this picture of the United States at the head of the pack, leading the world to a new and unimagined place. But what is that place? What happens next?

There is also a dark side to the unprecedented prosperity we enjoy. People in a wealthy America sometimes become bored and do strange things that rarely happen in poorer countries. They spend all their money (and time) on drugs; they meddle in other people's business; they surf the Net for hours a day; they search in vain for a new meaning to life (enriching successive infomercial-makers along the way); they fill tanning salons in cities where the sun shines all day every day; they become addicted to Home Shopping Network; they take their dogs to the psychiatrist. They live alone in big silent apartments and giant houses. A greater share of the American people are in prison than any other developed nation. These are not phenomena you are likely to find in the villages of Nigeria or even in the big cities of China.

As we become wealthier, will we just do more of these same things? Will we lose the drive, the hustle, the dissatisfaction with the status quo that is an American hallmark? And will the other countries who have emulated us in education, in building and buying cars, in promoting home ownership, now imitate us in these ways as well?

I do not have any easy answers to these questions. America and the other wealthy nations will continue to get wealthier and to confront whole new ethical, social, and cultural issues. The rest of the world will be watching us, sometimes admiring what we do and other times aghast.

GATEWAYS

**Further Readings on the World Economy
and Seeing the Big Picture**

Start with *Monitoring the World Economy 1820–1992* and *Dynamic Forces in Captialist Development,* both by Angus Maddison. This fellow is *the* guy when it comes to looking at the long-term economic growth of nations. These two books, and his others, are fascinating. *The State of Humanity,* by the late king of positivism Julian L. Simon, contains a look at every major aspect of the welfare of the world and how it is changing. Finally, *Earth Report 2000: Revisiting the True State of the Planet,* by the Competitive Enterprise Institute (Ronald Bailey, editor), is a look at environmental issues from scientists and others who do not always accept the common wisdom.

The best textbook on world economic geography, with lots of information and great maps, is *The World Economy: Resources, Location, Trade, and Development,* by Anthony R. de Souza and Frederick P. Stutz. *The Geography of the World Economy,* by Paul Knox and John Agnew, and *Regions and the World Economy: The Coming Shape of Global Production, Competition, and Political Order,* by Allen J. Scott, are also very good. For ongoing reading, it is hard to beat the weekly *Economist* magazine. It gives a different slant from the standard U.S. media, and its articles cover the world on a balanced basis.

18

The Seven Big Trends Producing Wealth Around the World

So the world is becoming wealthier and wealthier, led by the U.S. and other nations. Why is this happening? What factors are most important in the world's continuing rise? In the answers to these questions, we find both the factors that got us here and the factors that will carry us forward—the trends we should promote and the trends we should worry about if we see them fading. There are many factors at work, but I will group them into seven master headings.

Note that these are both causes and "co-trends," highly correlated with increasing wealth. They come part and parcel with our wealth, sometimes a little before, sometimes a little after. Consider education as an example—does our rise from illiteracy bring prosperity, or does our newfound wealth finance our increased investment in education? Of course, both are true: education is cause and effect. But that makes it no less important when considering the factors that have fed the growing prosperity around the world.

1. The Rise of Democratic Government and the Democratic Peace

Over the last twenty years, there has been a remarkable global spread of the practice of democracy. From the first real elections in years in Cambodia through the end of military rule in dozens of nations to the victory of the opposition party in Mexico, millions of people around the world are enjoying the right to vote for the first time.

One little-recognized long-term benefit of this trend is likely to be a reduction in international tensions. There has never been a major war between two democracies. When people have a real say in their government, they are not quick to lift arms. Warfare has historically been one of the great destroyers of wealth. Global peace is perhaps the most important prerequisite to global economic growth.

2. The Victory of Capitalism over Communism

In conjunction with the rise of democracy, we have seen the fall of communism in many nations. More such shifts can be expected.

As recently as 1977, many observers still decried capitalism. Typical was this quote from academic author M. P. Todaro: "Capitalism, which postulates that if each individual consumer, producer, and supplier of resources pursues his or her own self-interest, they will, 'as if by an invisible hand,' be promoting the overall interests of society as a whole. Unfortunately, the facts of economic life in both the developed and the less developed world are such as to render much of this theory of negligible importance. . . . Consumers as a whole are rarely sovereign about anything, let alone with regard to what goods and services are to be produced, in what quantities and for whom. . . . Producers have great power . . . in determining market prices and quantities sold."

At the time, giant businesses like IBM, Sears, and AT&T were run by executives who seemed to believe this writer and others like him. They thought they had power. And now those supposedly powerless consumers have transferred the power they actually controlled to companies like Dell, Wal-Mart, and Sprint. I wish that more students in 1977 had been reading *Forbes* and *Fortune* and the *Wall Street Journal* instead of theorists like Todaro.

If you walk the streets of Bangkok and Buenos Aires, as I have—if you walk the streets of Shanghai and Bombay, as I have—you can feel the energy in the air. And that energy is not the energy of generals or central planning committees or think tanks. It is the energy of street vendors, booksellers, Web site designers, free businesspeople of every stripe and color. They're allowed to flourish unshackled by governments that have come to recognize the power, importance, and generosity of the entrepreneurial spirit.

The contrast between North and South Korea is telling. It is like those studies of twins separated at birth, illustrating the powerful effects of environment. The North and South Koreans are the same people, with the same ancient cultural history, the same pride, the same blood. In 1970 every twentieth baby in North Korea died at birth, and in South Korea the rate was the same. By 1998 South Korea had reduced the rate to 1 in 100, while in North Korea the rate had actually risen. In the 1990s, North Korean women died in childbirth at almost six times the rate of South Korea women.

The good news in this is that change is finally coming. Everywhere.

3. The Spread of Universal Education

Once you have a capitalist democracy in place, I believe nothing is more important than education. Research indicates that education is the source of better health practices, of demands for cleaner water, of better organizational practices, of more demanding and aware consumers, of thoughtful population growth, of intelligent voting, and of the desire for more education itself. Education sets in motion a virtuous loop, a host of self-feeding beneficial trends. Education both fuels a people's rise to prosperity and is fed by it. Where people cannot read, life spans are more likely to be short and governments more likely to be evil.

The rise in education is never fast enough for those who don't have it. But it is coming. On a worldwide basis, the percent of the relevant age group enrolled in secondary school rose from 49 percent in 1980 to 64 percent in 1997. Even in troubled sub-Saharan Africa, literacy among young men (ages fifteen to twenty-four) rose from 75 percent in 1990 to 82 percent in 1999, and the rate jumped from 60 percent to 73 percent among their sisters in the same time period.

4. The Rise of Technology and Science

In some ways, American society today seems obsessed with technology. Some investors and career-seekers look nowhere else. We love our gadgets, and their makers love us. Thousands wait in line in the wee hours to be the earliest adopters. Our obsession with technology sometimes causes us to ignore those other things—the aging of the baby boom, the Latinization of the United States, and the rise of Asia—that may be more important in charting our future and the future of our enterprises.

Nonetheless, new technology is indeed a major trend shaping our world. In fact, it's so important and complex a topic that I will treat it in chapter 20.

5. Increasing Urbanization

A significant corollary of the increase in world wealth is the rise of cities. Cities are where more and more of the world lives and where most of our transactions take place. The study of cities is so important to enterprise success that we expand on this subject in chapter 21.

6. The End of the Farm and of the Factory

The single most significant trend in the history of the world's economies is our long, slow progress away from spending most of our time growing things and making things. It is one of the great ironies of the world economy that those nations with the highest percentage of people working in agriculture are also those countries with the worst nutrition and the most people starving. Nations in which everyone is still working to feed themselves are nations in which everyone is not yet well fed. Once a nation can feed itself or produce enough other goods to trade for food, then agriculture becomes less and less important.

Anthropologists will tell you that the family unit must first feed, shelter, and clothe itself. The same is true of a national economy. But once that is accomplished, we go on to the next level, first making more and more diverse goods, then developing creative ways to serve each other.

Of course, agriculture remains a significant industry in countries like the U.S., and technological advances will continue to increase the productivity of American food producers. But the relative fall of agriculture, followed by the fall of manufacturing in conjunction with the rise of services, is an inescapable and powerful trend.

What's more, it is not a new thing, even though the phrase "the service economy" has risen to prominence only in recent decades. According to economic historian Angus Maddison, services were a bigger fraction of the economy than industry (including mining and most utilities) in the United States and the Netherlands by as early as 1890:

Share of Total Employment

	Agriculture	Industry	Services
Netherlands			
1700	40%	33%	27%
1890	33%	31%	36%
1989	5%	26%	69%
United States			
1890	39%	27%	34%
1989	3%	26%	71%

Sometimes you hear skepticism expressed about the notion of a service-based economy. "The world can't just provide services to each other," people say. "We have to make things." While we do have to make things, that activity need not require a very large share of the world's time and energy. In fact, since sometime well before 1980, most of the world's efforts have gone into serving each other. By 1998 it was estimated that 62 percent of the world's gross domestic product was generated by services, as compared to 32 percent by industry and 4 percent by agriculture.

As services continue to rise as a share of world economic activity, especially in the poorer countries, it is important to realize how diverse "services" are. Services include everything from the cop on your block to the ATM on the corner. Services include teaching, legislating, entertaining, thinking, trading, gambling, insuring, speculating, communicating, and curing. Services are at work when we watch professional baseball and when we call UPS, when we visit the supermarket, eat at Chili's, or click onto Amazon.com. Over time, we will think about our economy less in terms of the tradition triad of agriculture/industry/ services and more in terms of the major emerging sectors of our economy. Already, retailing in the U.S. employs more people than the entire manufacturing sector. In the future, travel alone will be bigger than all manufacturing, and health services, education services, and financial services will each be many times bigger than world agriculture.

In conjunction with this understanding, be careful in interpreting statistics on balance of payments or imports and exports. We have a long and tenacious tradition of focusing on manufactured goods. But just as our total economy becomes more and more service-oriented, so do our exports and imports. Between 1980 and 1998, world service exports rose 262 percent, from $363.5 billion to $1.3 trillion, much faster than trade in goods. In particular, the United States' service volume during this period rose from $38.1 to $240 billion, going from 10 percent of the world total to 18 percent, while in this same time U.S. merchandise exports rose far more slowly, from $224 billion to $672 billion. You can see the trend, which will ultimately result in the U.S. exporting more services than goods.

In this context, that American accountant sitting next to you on your next overseas flight, going to work on a project in Russia, and that

European customer buying a ticket on American Airlines both represent service exports. This is where the future—and much of the present—lies for the United States and the world at large. Services have a huge impact on travel and geography. In the old days, when Japan shipped huge numbers of Toyotas to the U.S. (rather than making many of them in the States), the transaction mainly involved moving freight on ships. A few executives crossed the Pacific in each direction, but such interaction was limited. The economic landscape was dominated by huge, immovable factories.

As more and more of our international (and domestic) transactions consist of services, more and more people will move around. Lawyers, doctors, bankers, and management consultants are increasingly moving around—for a day trip, for a week, or for a three-year stint. And every time someone gets a passport to travel abroad for work, they become much more likely to occasionally travel abroad for leisure and to take their families with them.

Finally, the rise of services means that we will have more freelance workers, more people selling their services rather than their skills on the assembly line. This means that more people will have the option of living where they want. Even auto executives formerly bound to Detroit's factories may now become independent business consultants. They'll spend more of their time in airplanes, but they'll spend the remainder of their time wherever they want, whether it's a mountain village or a beach town. People will increasingly congregate near world-class shopping, great universities, natural beauty, and perhaps even great symphonies, rather than near big factories. Over the long run, the rise of services will have significant implications on the role of cities, the value of scenic properties, the importance of feeder airlines and airports, and many other aspects of our geography.

Of course, manufacturing will not disappear. Well-located container ports, deep harbors, air cargo, and efficient factories will be a part of our future. But over time, building, maintaining, and running these facilities will require fewer and fewer people, and they will become a smaller and smaller share of the total global economy.

7. The Boom in World Trade

Few human activities are more powerful than when I give you something and you give me something in return. Transactions move products, of course. But more important, they move people; they move ideas. Historically, trade is largely responsible for the spread of religion, the development and dissemination of math, astronomy, and the other sciences, and our everexpanding awareness of the world around us. The world has been explored and united by travelers like Marco Polo who first saw "the other side of the world" while in search of new trade routes, the Muslim traders who brought Islam to Southeast Asia, and entrepreneur Isaac Singer, who internationalized the ultimate power tool, the sewing machine.

Breakthrough ideas like the number zero (the Romans didn't have it) were invented for trade and spread by trade. The newest concepts in shipping, in paper, in printing, have always spread through trade around the world from the "haves" to the "have nots." In the first half of the nineteenth century, the youthful United States would have never gotten off the ground without imports of English ideas, technologies, and capital. Our first railroads were financed by the British and Europeans. The products we made and the crops we grew were exported to England to support our embryonic economy.

Today we and the other wealthy countries play the same role in the world economy that Britain played for us 150 years ago. It is up to us to continue the long tradition of wealthier nations trading ideas and products with poorer nations to help accelerate their development. China today needs our pollution-control technologies just as much as we needed British steam technologies in 1820. India needs our software techniques just as we needed the craft skills of the French and the Germans. The whole world needs our health knowledge—thousands of lives could be saved and improved through the use of our most basic antibiotics and surgical procedures. The world needs American skills at building and operating universities and hospitals. The world even needs more Rotary clubs—local associations that nurture and encourage industry, trade, and services.

Most of all, the world needs jobs. Today, many of those jobs will be in manufacturing, particularly in the poorer countries. Without the growth engine of "first-world" consumption, the future for the world's poor countries would be bleak indeed. Perhaps the greatest force for world peace is the degree to which our societies are entangled in commercial relationships. The more places we have factories and customers, the fewer places we might be willing to bomb. For all these reasons, the most important single force for enriching the world is trade and communication. We need to trade as many products and services as possible as often as possible; we need *transactions*.

This doesn't mean that all jobs will move from the first world to the third world, or even that all manufacturing jobs will move that way. Germany today has one of the most expensive labor markets in the world, and yet it remains one of the largest exporters of manufactured goods. I recently toured a number of very advanced jewelry manufacturing operations in Malaysia, and I found that most of the jewelers' machines—including their cars—came from Germany. Italy is not a cheap country to do business in, particularly the northern part, and yet that is where most of the world's eyeglasses and many of our finest fashion items are manufactured. Americans once thought we would lose all our car manufacturing jobs to Japan, but instead today the major Japanese companies make cars in the States. When NAFTA opened up free trade between Mexico and the United States, some observers foresaw a huge loss of U.S. jobs, but my Mexican friends report corresponding job losses in Mexico as certain categories of higher-quality U.S. goods have flooded into the market. Japan, another expensive labor market, continues to make products that are shipped around the world.

Each nation combines a unique set of skills and talents, and there will always be some products made in some countries but not others. Most basic, low-skill manufacturing left the U.S. many decades ago and will always seek out the lowest-cost labor. We can only hope that the factories now moving into Indonesia and India will someday move on to Zaire and Nigeria. And right behind them should come more advanced—and higher-paying—manufacturing and service industries.

The Opposing Forces

There are two great enemies to the gradual lifting of the peoples of the world through trade: isolationism and arrogance.

There have always been isolationists. When I was a boy growing up in that GM factory town in Indiana, the leaders at both GM and at the United Auto Workers, the big labor union that represented GM's workers, would have wanted to stop Japanese auto imports if they had understood the changes to come. But if we had tried to keep out Nissan (then called Datsun) and Toyota, today GM and Ford would be dinosaurs, probably bankrupt. Without the spur of foreign competition, they would have kept on making huge cars with big appetites for gasoline. When oil prices spiked in 1973, consumers would have finally demanded more-efficient Japanese cars—or marched on the U.S. car plants.

Because we let in the "enemy," the U.S. car companies were forced to recognize new forces at work and new approaches to the business—from marketing to manufacturing. Ultimately, Chrysler invented the minivan; GM pioneered the Saturn; Ford developed their successful world cars. The U.S. firms began to invest in Japanese car companies. Today GM and Ford retain their historical rankings as the largest and second-largest car companies on earth—thanks to competition from across both oceans.

George W. Bush has said, "The fearful build walls, the confident tear them down." Isolationism is a step toward bigotry, closed-mindedness, technological backwardness, intolerance, and, ultimately, war. *There are few forces more evil or destructive to the ultimate success of the world and its people.*

The other force that is almost equally dangerous is arrogance. And the more successful we are, the greater our capacity for arrogance.

I can make the case against arrogance most vividly by describing our history. To oversimplify just a little, we can say that America rose to greatness from about 1880 to 1920. This is the period when we went from being a secondary world power to the country that "won" World

War I. This is the period when our great cities of New York and Chicago caught and passed the capitals of Europe in terms of size, wealth, and influence. This is the period in which we built our greatest museums and universities and founded our best symphonies. This was the "Gilded Age" in which many of our great family fortunes were formed, some of which still fund philanthropy today. Our railroads reached their peak during these years, and the American West was opened for development.

And during this same period, we largely cut down our forests and polluted our rivers. Our mills were gritty with toxic chemicals and driven by dangerous machinery, our cities were crowded and dirty, and thousands of our children worked long hours in sweatshops.

Today, our kids go to college, our air and water are becoming steadily cleaner, and the overwhelming majority of our population has access to wealth and conveniences that the kings of the past could only dream of. And we turn to China and India and Indonesia and say, "We will not buy your products unless your rivers are clean, your children don't work in factories, and you follow all the rules that we live by today."

In this context, it is not hard to understand why poorer nations might think us a bit arrogant. And the fact that we are more likely to make these demands of the smaller and less powerful nations, but give a pass to the larger and more powerful ones, makes this one-sided dialogue even more irritating to others around the globe.

My point is this: We must have compassion in our dealings with the rest of the world. Each nation must evolve at its own pace. We can work to share our technologies, our management methods, our ethical and social ideals, and any other good ideas we have, but we must offer them in a spirit of sharing and giving, not from the viewpoint of "We know what's best for you." The issues I am raising here are not easy ones. Not long ago, I spent a week in Shanghai, one of the most fascinating and energetic cities on earth—and the most polluted spot I have ever visited. By comparison, contemporary Americans don't even know what pollution is. I want to see Shanghai's air cleaned up more than anyone. But boycotting Chinese trade is not the answer. China has ambitious goals for protecting its environment—and is making progress, slowly but surely.

I am not advocating that we stop our global pressure to end child labor and other such practices worldwide. But I am saying that the best way to end it is probably to trade with as many nations as possible, to urge our companies to do business with the best local suppliers with the highest standards, and to bring our standards to bear on the plants they operate abroad or buy from.

The best example may be Cuba. As long as Cuba is kept out of the loop of global transactions, then attitudes of freedom and change will never have a chance there. Rather than demanding radical change on the part of their government (which hasn't seemed to work in the first forty years that we've been trying it), letting a little Mickey Mouse, Coca-Cola, Nike, and CNN into their society will do much more good for the average Cuban.

GATEWAYS

Further Readings on Capitalism as a Philosophy of Doing Good

Unfortunately, relatively few "serious" writers (such as sociologists and philosophers) understand why capitalism is so successful—its power to serve all that it touches. Here are a few books. *The Spirit of Democratic Capitalism* and *Business as a Calling: Work and the Examined Life,* by Michael Novak. *Capitalist Revolution: Fifty Propositions About Prosperity, Equality, and Liberty,* by Peter L. Berger, and *The Capitalist Spirit: Toward a Religious Ethic of Wealth Creation,* readings edited by Peter L. Berger. All of these are excellent. *The Future and Its Enemies: The Growing Conflict over Creativity, Enterprise, and Progress,* by Virginia Postrel, is a thought-provoking book by a woman not afraid to speak her mind. Conveys the importance of entrepreneurial energy in whole new ways. She calls it "dynamism." *Reputation: Studies in the Voluntary*

Elicitation of Good Conduct, edited by Daniel B. Klein—why doing the right thing is key to survival. A serious look by several authors of how we track trust—even including the role of Dun & Bradstreet! I expect this will become a bigger topic in coming years. A pioneering book. *Capitalism, Democracy, and Ralph's Pretty Good Grocery,* by John Mueller is all about why capitalism gets such a bad rap, and why it shouldn't. Very good.

19

Globalization and Local Culture, and How You Fit In

Go to any big music store, or one with a large selection of CDs. In the bins, you will find a large selection of European classical music. You will find acres of rock. You will find R&B, grunge, movie soundtracks, easy listening, new age, hip-hop, country and western. You will find a jazz section that is now stronger than ever thanks to the skills of documentary filmmaker Ken Burns. You may even find a gospel section and a section of lounge music.

Now wander around and you will surely find "world music." And within that section, you will find maybe two bins of Brazilian music—about the same as half the "M's" in rock and roll. Go further down the row and maybe you will find Indian music, a fraction of the size of Brazilian, and further down maybe Chinese music—perhaps a dozen CDs if you are lucky. That's about it.

This exercise offers an education in cultural wealth and our inability to see it. In cultural terms, China has a history twenty times as long as America, and India perhaps more. The complexity and richness of

Brazilian music is every bit as deep and full of nuances as American and European music. From our distant vantage point, we put the world into bins, and small ones at that, while fully recognizing the depth, breadth, and richness of our own culture. Only by realizing that there is a lot more out there—an awful lot—can we begin to see the world as it really is.

And everything I say about music is just as true about food, clothing, literature, philosophy, architecture, drama, and art. And everything I say about India, Brazil, and China is equally true of sub-Saharan Africa and Indonesia, Egypt and Japan.

As time moves onward, as the world shrinks, as we learn more and trade more, the cultures of the world will combine and sometimes collide, just like the giant tectonic plates on which our continents ride. Absolutely nothing that you or I can do, or that Sony or BMG Music or AOL Time Warner can do, will stop the ultimate rise and confluence of the cultures of the world.

Today when most of us think about models of female beauty, we think about Marilyn Monroe or Pamela Anderson, Gwyneth Paltrow or Michelle Pfeiffer. Our grandchildren will think of beautiful actresses and models from Brazil, India, and China. When we hum a tune, it comes from England or the States. Our grandchildren will hum the tunes of Bali, of South Africa, of Chile, of Tibet.

As you picture this huge and rising force, the cultures of the world, also realize that there is another huge force, and that is the power of the global brands. Everyone can see the spread of McDonald's, the pervasiveness of Coca-Cola, the presence of Western/American culture, from Mickey Mouse to the World Wrestling Federation. Behind these first movers, we know that Wal-Mart and Home Depot will follow, and a thousand others.

Book after book is written about the cultural destructiveness of globalization. The story is often depicted in terms of a struggle by the poor little local cultures to preserve themselves in the face of a global onslaught. But it must be obvious by now that I do not see it this way. I believe that the cultural wealth of the world, the richness of our complexity, is every bit as powerful as the machinery of Sony and McDonald's. In fact, I believe that applying that powerful and flexible distributive machinery to our cultural richness is how such wealth will be preserved and expanded.

Mixing Up the Popular Arts

Step back twenty or thirty years. We had a handful of big record companies with names like Capitol, Columbia, and Decca. There were also a few upstarts like Geffen, Elektra, and Atlantic. The new artists, the most exciting and original young performers, joined the creative, entrepreneurial upstarts. In time, the upstarts got acquired by the giants, which needed new blood. Did the artists die off when they went corporate? No, they just got their records (now CDs) placed in more stores in more places. Come forward another ten years or so and you have Virgin and Island, then Interscope.

The process repeats itself over and over. Sometimes the entrepreneurs and upstarts go off and join together. That's how the movie industry gave birth to United Artists (founded by the rebellious talents of Charlie Chaplin, Douglas Fairbanks, Mary Pickford, and D. W. Griffith) and—seventy years later—SKG DreamWorks. Sometimes yesterday's giants evolve into new forms. Remember RCA Records and CBS Records, now parts of BMG and Sony? Even the geographic focus changes—most of the old record companies were U.S., with one Dutch giant (Polygram) and one British giant (EMI). Today the giants are U.S., German (BMG), Japanese (Sony), and French (Vivendi). Things change in multiple dimensions, but they preserve the vitality and creativity of the artists. All these remarks also apply to the other cultural industries—book publishing, magazines, cable, satellite broadcasting.

Take that model, that understanding of the world, and apply it to the cultures of the world. Apply it to Ronald McDonald and Mickey Mouse, but also to the moviemakers of India (the "Bollywood" of Bombay, now called Mumbai), the young rock bands of Moscow, the innovative choreographers of Korea, the woodworking artisans of Cairo.

To help you along, let me paint some pictures, all speculative, but all possibilities that I believe are more like the world of the future than we might think. Imagine:

- a giant record company based in Shanghai that sells millions of copies of the best North Indian music

- Disney integrating Hindu and Buddhist legends into its repertoire of animated feature films

- McDonald's selling guarana soft drinks from Brazil in the Sudan

- teenagers in Milan partying to the drums of Morocco on an album from a Seattle company

- a large operator of amusement parks that comes from Malaysia and offers a real alternative to Disney and Universal

- books printed on Egyptian papyrus—expensive first editions by Argentine authors

Think of these things, and more like them, and you will be thinking of the world of our children. A world more likely to be the actual one than a world fed only by Starbucks and McDonald's or a world shod by Nike alone. It's an exciting vision.

In order to help this world come along, in order to accelerate this natural evolution, what needs to be done? How do you and I and our enterprises fit in? There are three major concepts to focus on here: branding, cultural wealth and preservation, and specialization.

Global Branding

The rise of global brands is one of the most important developments of the last twenty years. While companies like Coca-Cola have been exporting their products for more than a century, the real global presence of brands is a much more recent development. This trend is good, it is unstoppable, and it will become more complex and more open.

First, it is good because it gives everyone on earth more options, more choices. In Mumbai there is a McDonald's serving Maharaja Macs, along with a full vegetarian menu customized for the Indian market. In Austin, Texas, an Indian can find Indian restaurants to choose from.

In the new world of global branding, access to the world market is easier, not harder. Cable networks and advertising agencies girdle the globe. Consumers everywhere are accustomed to buying the best products no matter where they originate. Now the Internet is facilitating the global spread of ideas, information, and brands.

This trend is unstoppable—the genie is out of the bottle. The people of Russia and Zimbabwe alike want the opportunity to buy a Whopper, Air Jordans, and even a bottle of Head & Shoulders.

This trend is also becoming more complex, in the form of creative alignments and alliances. The most visible example is the airline industry, where major companies around the globe are forming such near-merger alliances as One World and Star Alliance. The groundwork was first successfully laid by the partnership between Northwest and KLM. Integrating their reservations and frequent flyer programs, linking their flights, the airlines increasingly appear seamless to the customer.

Other industries are following suit. One of the most successful companies in India is Hindustan Lever, a locally run joint venture of the Anglo-Dutch Unilever empire. As global retailers like Carrefour and Wal-Mart expand around the world, they are experimenting with new forms of licensing and local partnerships. These newly emerging, more creative forms of the global corporation will become increasingly common. The Internet and other new communications technologies will facilitate and accelerate this process. The net result will be the opening of more opportunities to play the global game for enterprises of all sizes in all nations, including yours.

The spread of global commerce takes place not just in branding and marketing activities. New jobs are created in new places. Dell, Amazon, and Lufthansa are doing more of their service and support work in India, and Microsoft and others are outsourcing programming there. In fact, without Japanese- and German-owned car factories, the U.S.

would today be the second-largest maker of autos, rather than staying in first place.

Cultural Wealth and Preservation

We Americans love our hot dogs and our bagels, our Norman Rockwell and Frank Sinatra; we love our baseball and our blues. As English speakers, we study Chaucer and Byron, Kennedy and Churchill, Dickens and Hemingway. Likewise, each culture, each language, has its own depth and texture. Each has its own arts and sports and heroes. Each is worthy of a lifetime of exploration and contemplation—and preservation.

As we move through the twenty-first century, the continuing development and preservation of humanity's cultural wealth will become one of our most important tasks. I believe we must understand the role of three participants in this process: consumers, enterprises and their leaders, and government. Only through intelligent decisions on the part of each can we preserve our local cultures at the same time that global branding continues to grow.

The Role of the Consumer

Consumers who want to help preserve our world cultures will take the time to look around them, look for independent and locally owned stores and producers, and allocate a portion of our consumption to the locals. We will support our museums and festivals, we will keep traditions alive. Nothing that anyone else does will be more important.

I was recently talking to a friend from Europe and he lamented how the local bistros in the villages of France were closing up as McDonald's spread around the countryside. If this is true, there is only one cause of this problem, only one group to blame: the people who live in those villages. For it is the responsibility of each of us to do our share to preserve our own local heritage, if it is to live on for future generations.

In the U.S., if we want to preserve our remaining roadside diners, if we want to foster traditional regional products like Dr. Pepper (in the South) or Moxie (in New England), then we must give them a share of our business. Maybe not all our business, but a share of it. Drink that Dr. Pepper (ironically now owned by the British), drink that Lucozade, Orangina, Calpis, Antarctica Guarana, and Pocari Sweat. If you want to have strong local merchants around to answer your questions, to inventory what you want, to support the local high school, to provide jobs, then buy your books and cameras and electronics from them, at least some of the time. Give them a chance to earn your business. If they deserve it, give it to them.

The Role of Enterprises and Their Leaders

Again, "Nothing will be more important" than the efforts of consumers to preserve local cultures. But there is one group that is just as important: the leaders of local enterprises. Preservation of our cultural wealth depends on the entrepreneurial spirit of the people entrusted with our traditions.

Local enterprises can compete with the global giants only if they care about their business and treat it with respect and self-confidence.

I'd estimate that only about 20 percent of all the owners of independent mom-and-pop businesses in the U.S. are emotionally, mentally, and professionally prepared to compete with well-organized and disciplined larger organizations. Yet the local enterprise has many natural advantages—knowing the customer, the local market, and local traditions and events. Smaller enterprises can turn on the proverbial dime while their giant competitors go through months of committee meetings. But if the local operator is not willing to study the best business methods, is not prepared to be curious about the customer or to learn from the big competitors, or is more eager to get to the golf course Friday afternoon than to stay late and think harder, he or she will not be able to compete.

I have seen so many people operating a bookshop or a restaurant as a hobby, as something to do in their spare time. When real competition arrives, the results are very sad. Restaurants are not a hobby to the people at McDonald's or Brinker International (Chili's); bookstores are not a hobby to the Riggio brothers of Barnes & Noble. These pursuits are deadly serious occupations to these people, and the small competitor must be just as serious.

As a particular student of the restaurant business, I would mention the example of relating to young customers. As I travel around the world and drop in on McDonald's, I see that their greatest strength may be their Happy Meal, in all its local variations. Often, it is not groups of adults that keep their cash registers ringing, but adults dragged through the door by the tug of little hands. By contrast, in my many visits to mom-and-pop restaurants (which I patronize more often than I go to McDonald's), rarely do I see any effort to attract the little ones. Perhaps the owners would protest, "But McDonald's has Ronald McDonald and expensive tie-ins with the latest hot movie or TV show." True. But the reality is that a real clown, or free kazoos or balloons, or birthday parties or playgrounds, or any slightest sign of caring about the kids and recognizing them, could pay off. Sometimes we spend too much time fighting the competition (or complaining about them) rather than learning from them.

Perhaps the most powerful weapon for local preservation in the face of giant competitors is a successful alliance among independents. Three enterprises come to mind: Ace and True Value in hardware stores, and Best Western in lodging. Each of these organizations is very successful, even in the face of the toughest and largest competitors. They combine national or global branding and advertising with the local touch that can be so powerful. Based in Phoenix, Best Western has grown into one of the largest lodging brands in the world. They have more than twenty locations in Paris alone. Each is operated by a caring local owner, but they all benefit from an international reservations and advertising system.

The best way *not* to preserve your local edge is by taking purely defensive measures. When local merchants get together to lobby local officials to prevent Wal-Mart from coming to town, no matter what claims of civic concern they proffer, they are sending an extremely strong, clear statement to the local consumers: "If you had your choice, you would flock to the big store, so the only way we can compete is by banning it. We know that the big store is better than us and that we cannot compete with them if you have the choice of shopping where you want."

Furthermore, such efforts are almost always futile. If all the restaurants in town get together and keep McDonald's out, the only result will be that McDonald's will build somewhere down the road or come in later, and the customers will drive a little further or wait a little longer. Ultimately, "the big guys" have more money, more lawyers, and more ambition, and they will show up in your marketplace. They also have the consumer as their ally in such battles. It is far better to focus our entrepreneurial energies on competing with the Big Macs, the Wal-Marts, the Home Depots, and the Staples rather than trying to ban them. Let's face it, if we ran one of these giants, we'd probably aim to dominate the market as well. Luckily for all, competition rarely permits such a one-sided outcome.

Another way in which entrepreneurs play a key role in the preservation of our cultural wealth is by promoting and expanding that wealth. A fellow named Dan Storper owned a New York shop called Putumayo, which sold folk clothing from Latin America. As he traveled abroad, he found local music he liked and began selling that in his store. Today the Putumayo recording label sells more than 1 million CDs and cassettes a year, and has just scratched the surface of this opportunity.

When NAFTA came along, many Mexican enterprises were concerned about their future in the face of high-quality American competition. There were no global Mexican companies. But now that Mexican companies have learned that they can indeed compete, we see their huge baker Bimbo expanding into the U.S., their glassmaker Vitro going global, and entrepreneur Carlos Slim Helu taking over the U.S.'s number one retail computer chain, CompUSA. The global stage on which we play is larger than anyone can imagine. When the doors open, they open for all.

Leaders of enterprises of all types, including governments and nonprofits, need to always remember that there is plenty of room for well-run organizations in all categories in all places. If McDonald's reaches all their ambitious goals, maybe someday they will sell 10 percent of all the meals on the planet. That still leaves 90 percent for their competitors, big and small. *There is always room for excellence,* whether from Tom's Diner or Citibank. But there is little room for the weak, the timid, the poor quality, the overpriced, or the badly marketed. You don't have to be an Amazon.com or an e-wizard to succeed in the twenty-first century, you just have to care about your customers and your product and pay attention to the details.

The Role of the Government

There's one more story from the restaurant industry that bears on how we can best preserve our cultural heritage. In the U.S., we used to have big roadside billboards along our highways, available to any advertiser willing to pay the price. Then, in efforts to "beautify" our highways, many states and counties passed laws forbidding the construction of new billboards, and in some cases pulling down the old ones. One of the results was that independent restaurants could no longer appeal to the nation's travelers.

To answer this challenge, the roadside beautifiers developed a signing scheme that placed small, neat roadside signs of uniform size and color near the freeway exits. Each sign indicated, "DINING THIS EXIT," and had room for the logos of the restaurants, but no advertising message. So the traveler would be informed that, at the next exit, they could find McDonald's, KFC, Burger King, and "Tom's Diner." While Tom would do his best to come up with a nice logo to fit in the little space, his message was limited. I saw a defender of this scheme in a TV interview saying, "Now the locals will be on an equal footing with the national chains."

But the fact is that these measures demolished the locals. McDonald's has invested enough in building the awareness and image of their golden arches that those arches say it all. A small sign can be very powerful for them. But without a large sign saying, "TOM'S DINER—BEST BREAKFAST BISCUITS IN HODLEY COUNTY AND FRIENDLIEST WAIT-RESSES ON EARTH," Tom is dead. His name means nothing and his brand has no value to the traveler without some explanation, explanation that is not required by McDonald's.

If you travel around the U.S. and talk to the people who operate the cafés on the town squares, they will often tell you that the federal government built the interstate highways to move traffic away from them, then banned billboards to make sure no one heard about them.

I understand the desire to beautify our highways. But the unintended consequence has been to deplete our cultural wealth. I would argue that, if we allowed 10 percent of the mileage of our freeways to be opened to billboards, our nation would be much stronger for it.

More important than this one example is the overall principle: Cultural wealth requires a certain messiness that may be uncomfortable for regulators and bureaucrats.

As I travel the world, I see the glory in human diversity. But in the more "advanced" and regulated societies I see smaller signs, less color, and more sterile environments. As I walk the streets of any Mexican city, I cannot help but wonder, "As Mexico becomes wealthier, will this society lose its color? Will they ban the street vendors? Will everyone start to dress in black and earth tones? Will vibrant signs be banned, and walls everywhere covered with the statement 'POST NO BILLS?'"

I hope not. I hope that as Mexico gets wealthier, it will continue to look like Mexico, with wild colors everywhere and buildings decorated with hubcaps, not like the antiseptic and manicured sterility of Menlo Park, California, or Plano, Texas. I hope that Japan maintains its giant electronic signs, that India keeps her street vendors, that you will still be able to buy a freshly cut coconut on the streets of Rio. Without these things, we will all be poorer indeed. We are at risk of zoning away the clutter that is human culture, of planning and banning life itself. The cacophony of commerce must be left free to be scrambled, to be diverse, to be colorful and joyful and self-promotional.

Specialization: Niches for Nations and Other Places

Every nation, every region, even every city and village on earth, has a personality. When I drove through Brownwood, Texas, and saw that the feed-and-grain store had a sign offering "FREE CADILLAC WITH MILLION-DOLLAR PURCHASE," I knew that the people from Brownwood had a sense of humor.

Thailand is an outstanding example of a nation with a highly distinctive "personality." Famous as the one people in Southeast Asia who were never colonized, the Thais have a long history of doing business with everyone, letting foreigners trade in their country without ever yielding their sovereignty. I met a GM executive who had just opened a joint venture plant in Thailand. He told me his local partner has informed him at the beginning of the negotiation, "You know, we are also building a joint venture plant with Japanese." The American executive respected the Thais for their upfront honesty, but he also knew that he was not playing with amateurs here. Having a Japanese competitor up the street would keep him honest.

The Netherlands is a small nation with few people, little land, scanty natural resources, and almost no domestic market (by world standards). But by trading with everyone, developing some of the world's greatest ports, and seeking out opportunities around the globe, this little country has given us Shell, Unilever, and Philips.

Poor Switzerland does not even have a port, and sits high up in the mountains. Working from this disadvantageous starting point, the Swiss people have developed one of the wealthiest nations on earth (and enjoy some of the longest life spans). Their hallmarks have been independence, political neutrality, a commitment to international peace, and world-class skills in financial services, pharmaceuticals, and timekeeping. In the future, other "small" nations, like Malaysia and Singapore, will create positions for themselves on the global stage that will give their people wealth just as the Netherlands and Switzerland have done.

Each nation, each state, each city, no matter how small or how large, has a personality—defining attributes that can be turned into competitive advantages.

We have always had room in our global marketplace for Cuban cigars, Italian shoes, Parisian perfume, and Swiss watches. Now it is time to realize that there is a lot more out there—Austrian maps, Caribbean music, Japanese pencils, Indonesian woodcarvings, and Malaysian semiconductors.

Leaders of communities, nations, and enterprises should study their strengths, their distinctive characteristics, and make the most of them. Success is more likely to come from going long with our strengths rather than selling short our weaknesses.

GATEWAYS

Further Readings About Globalization and Diverse Culture

A Future Perfect: The Challenge and Hidden Promise of Globalization, by John Micklethwait and Adrian Wooldridge, two writers from the *Economist* magazine, offers an excellent introduction to globalization. In *The Wealth and Poverty of Nations: Why Some Are So Rich and Some So Poor,* David S. Landes weaves it all together with eloquence. Another book worth getting—actually a three-volume set—is *The Information Age: Economy, Society, and Culture,* by Manuel Castells. You may not always agree with this academic sociologist, but he always makes you think. *Globalization and the Challenges of a New Century: A Reader,* edited by Patrick O'Meara, Howard D. Mehlinger, and Matthew Krain, contains the thoughts of many thinkers, often of opposing points of view. Particularly good.

In Praise of Commercial Culture, by Tyler Cowen, shows how art and music flow from capitalism. Ray Oldenburg talks about an important but often overlooked concept in *The Great Good Place: Cafes, Coffee Shops, Bookstores, Bars, Hair Salons, and Other Hangouts at the Heart of a Community.* Jane and Michael Stern, in the wonderfully titled *Eat Your Way Across the USA,* focus on the very best local eateries across the U.S. In *FoodFinds: America's Best Local Foods and the People Who Produce Them,* by Allison Engel and

Margaret Engel, get a tour of the best regional products. To learn all about the local music of the world, you can't beat *World Music: The Rough Guide,* edited by Mark Ellingham and others—a wonderful two-volume comprehensive set that covers the local music of the whole world, including the U.S.

20

Technology in a Changing World

In truth, the importance of technology is nothing new. It is an old, old story. Entrepreneurial thinkers have always made the best possible use of technology. The railroads jumped on the telegraph. Montgomery Ward made maximum use of Rural Free Delivery. Wal-Mart created its own satellite network linking the stores. BOOKSTOP had a customer-loyalty program with a bar code on the membership card in the mid-1980s. Technology has always been important—important enough to deserve some discussion as a major force in the increasing wealth of the world.

But what is technology? As usual, we should use the broadest possible definition. So let's go with the following: Technology is a better way of doing things. Relax that mental lock that defines technology only in terms of computers and cell phones and maybe software. The odds are that you are right now in physical contact with some of the most revolutionary and important technology in history: the technology of woven cloth. If you don't realize how amazing this is, go see the Historic Mills at Lowell, Massachusetts, or, better yet, the hand looms at the Churchill Weavers in Berea, Kentucky.

Another recent invention with far-reaching implications has been the development of the hub-and-spoke airline system, pioneered by Federal Express in Memphis and Delta Airlines in Atlanta. For centuries, our transportation networks were linear, linking one city to the next. Our canals, our highways, our railroads, and even our early airlines followed common paths. But with the invention of the hub and spoke, everything changed. In the U.S. today, fewer people fly on the same plane from start to finish, but far fewer people change airlines in midcourse. You and I can board planes at adjacent gates in New York in the morning and arrive in the evening at the same time in Salt Lake City, but follow radically different routes on different airlines.

Technology constantly touches us in new ways. CNN political analyst Bill Schneider points out that the Internet is making politics more diverse and making politicians think and communicate differently. We now receive live broadcasts and e-mails from across the battle lines in our wars, from Baghdad to Kosovo. Bioscience is gradually producing new ways to eradicate diseases and to extend life spans. To define technology only in terms of gadgets or "high tech" is short-changing ourselves and the power of the human imagination.

Leapfrogging Technology

An important aspect of technology is technological leapfrogging. That is, those people and places that are behind in technology today will often be ahead tomorrow. Most Chinese people will never own a 35-millimeter camera; their first camera will be digital. India may not take the time and trouble to wire up their nation for old-fashioned copper-wire telephones; they may just skip directly to wireless phones for everyone. As recently as 1985, there were only 3.5 million telephone lines to homes and offices in China. By mid-1998, this was up to 119 million, and new customers were coming onstream at the rate of 83,000 wire lines and 30,000 mobile phones a day.

This leapfrogging can be disorienting if you think that technological progress is linear, allowing one to effortlessly stay ahead of other people and places. Instead, the future may explode somewhere that we in the advanced nations of the West least expect it. If you want to see what an American city of the future may look like, visit Singapore or the capital of neighboring Malaysia, Kuala Lumpur. Here are some of the things you will see:

- Automated subway payment systems in which you whisk your smart card near the turnstile, never taking it out of your wallet.

- Electronic road pricing, through which tolls are automatically deducted from a radio device on your dashboard as you travel about. Usage of a road might cost fifty cents until 7:30 A.M., a dollar till 9:15, then free through midday.

- When you are holiday shopping at the downtown mall, you can hand your packages to a clerk for the post office (which has a location in every store). They will be delivered to your house by six P.M.

- The technologically advanced library is the meeting place for the youth of the city, complete with coffee shop and video rentals.

- Preplanned communities fully cabled with high-speed broadband fiber-optic cable before the first house or office is built.

- Downtown airport check-in where you go through customs and check your luggage, then take a rapid transit train to your flight at the outlying airport.

As nations and cities around the world rise in wealth and can afford better infrastructure and systems, they will not look back to what we did in the U.S. in the 1950s, '60s, or '70s. They will avail themselves of the very latest and most cost-effective methods and ideas available. In some ways, the countries that get their stuff last will also get the best. While my examples above are from Asia, technological leapfrogging will affect every part of the earth, from Boise to Bogotá.

Watching Technology Evolve

Making specific predictions about which technologies will be developed most quickly is almost impossible, but looking at the overall themes in technology is important.

Convergence

Today, we tend to think of television sets and computer monitors as separate gadgets. But the reality is that the underlying technology is exactly the same, and there will be a time when it would be redundant to keep them separated. If you look at real human needs and the way we use our screens, there are really two needs: small screens and large screens. When you want to work on a laptop on an airplane, read a book in bed, or sit at a desk and do close work, you need a screen of only ten to nineteen inches. But when you want to watch a movie or make a slide presentation to a large group, you will want to have a bigger screen. In your home and office, you will have both. The image source might be a computer, a television receiver, a DVD player, or broadband cable. You will have easy-to-use switches on each screen and route content wherever you want it. Just like you pick hot or cold water at any tap. This is convergence in action.

In another example of convergence, it is unlikely that we will continue to carry more and more gadgets in our pockets and briefcases. The idea of a separate cell phone, PDA, and laptop computer is not likely to stand the test of time. While different products and configurations will always be available for specific users, most people will get their phone messages, their e-mail, their radio and TV reception on the same little portable box.

Think creatively about possible convergences. For example, the idea of disposable electronics is not crazy. People buy more than 50 million disposable cameras a year. Yet the technology inside a camera is more complex than that inside a telephone. How soon will cell phones as disposable as diapers come into our lives?

The Three Key Technology Questions

When you study a particular technology, you should ask three questions:

1. What is it capable of doing?

2. What should it be able to do?

3. What might it stumble onto?

Capability is probably the easiest issue to think about, although even here creativity is called for. For example, when people first saw the black-and-white computer printer, most people thought that would be fine forever. While it did not take much imagination (or knowledge of technology) to forecast that printers would go color, most people thought that would be a specialty with limited demand. Few foresaw the $89 high-quality color inkjets that are piled in the aisles of computer stores today.

Harder to envision is, "What should it be able to do?" For example, when considering those first black-and-white dot matrix printers, it was not obvious that you could build in the intelligence to know when they had run out of paper. In the early days of BOOKSTOP, we tried to judge how much paper a report would require so we could let it run overnight. If we misjudged, we'd get to work in the morning to find the second half of the report "printed" on the machine's black roller, with ink slip-sliding everywhere. When printers came out that stopped printing if they were out of paper, we thought we had seen the ultimate genius!

A parallel today would be the potential use of global positioning systems (GPS) in digital cameras. This inexpensive technology (well under $100) is made by some of the same companies that make the cameras, but no one yet embeds it into any cameras. Ultimately, people using digital cameras for real estate or aerial photography will save lots of time and money because the camera will know exactly where it was when it took the picture. (It already knows the time and date.) Add gyroscope technology so the camera knows its angle relative to the earth, and you can automate the process of building models of buildings and cities from a handful of two-dimensional pictures.

Every technology can be used in ways that we cannot yet imagine. But one person or group of people will imagine those uses before others do, and this insight comes more from studying people and their needs than it comes from studying the underlying science.

This is closely related to the third question, "What might this technology stumble onto?" When video camcorders first came out, no one really knew what to use them for. They were first seen as a replacement for the 8-millimeter and 16-millimeter movie cameras (which very few people were using).

Now consider how this technology has changed our lives.

Through most of history, scientists had almost no idea what a tornado really looked like. First, they were able to get a few snapshots, then some early local TV station footage from the 1950s and '60s. But since the rise of the consumer camcorder, there are thousands of hours of tornado footage, depicting every type of tornado conceivable. For the first time, scientists have a visual database of information that enables them to really understand these monsters.

Our criminal justice system has been changed forever by the ready availability of videotape. From the Rodney King beating to footage of highway patrolmen confronting drivers, much more vivid and accurate pictures of police work are available to millions of Americans more than at any time ever before. Consumer news-hounds, from sites of natural disasters to war zones, have reshaped television news worldwide.

None of these trends would have seemed obvious when we first saw that clunky VHS camcorder (and paid $3,000 in 1985 for it). But now we can look at the high-quality, three-megapixel digital cameras on the market and learn something from our past blindness. Now we can predict that these solid-state devices will soon be ten times as good and cost one-tenth as much. They will be capable of being built into a wristwatch or into the lenses of eyeglasses, so we can just blink to take a picture. One day, if someone steals a wallet at the Super Bowl, there will probably be a dozen photographs of the theft.

Most important, by looking at convergence, I can understand that a camera is a camera is a camera, and foresee that the distinction between still cameras and video cameras will probably go away. The barriers that separate still photography and videography today—speed of capture and storage capacity—will disappear. Photographers will simply ask, "Do I want to capture just one image or thirty per second?" and adjust their cameras accordingly.

The most common mistake we make in thinking about technology is that we start with gadgets rather than with people—what they do, how they do it, and their present and future needs and desires. The technology that evolves and becomes prevalent will not be the coolest-looking gadget with the hottest technology. It will be the coolest-looking gadget that somehow makes someone's life easier, more productive, more interesting, or more fun.

GATEWAYS

Further Readings on a Long, Broad View of Technology

The excellent *Technology in America: A History of Individuals and Ideas,* edited by Carroll W. Pursell Jr., contains selected stories by various writers: all the big names, from George Eastman to Alexander Graham Bell and Thomas Edison. A good, overall short history of technology in the U.S. is *Technology and American Society: A History,* by Gary Cross and Rick Szostak. *Technology in World Civilization,* by Arnold Pacey, does the same for the whole world.

For a history of the computer, I highly recommend *A History of Modern Computing,* by Paul E. Ceruzzi; *Herman Hollerith: Forgotten Giant of Information Processing,* by Geoffrey D. Austrian (about the fellow who invented the punch-card machine, which led to IBM); and *Fire in the Valley: The Making of the Personal Computer,* by Paul Freiberger and Michael Swaine—one of the best business (and technology) history books ever written. The ultimate big-picture book on how we got to the information age is *The Control*

Revolution: Technological and Economic Origins of the Information Society, by James R. Beniger. Another great book that will add a long-term perspective to that cell phone in your hand is *Global Communications Since 1844,* by Peter J. Hugill. And, finally, a pure popular book that you can give to your kids when you are through with it: *They All Laughed . . . From Light Bulbs to Lasers: The Fascinating Stories Behind the Great Inventions That Have Changed Our Lives,* by Ira Flatow.

21

Cities: The Greatest Human Enterprise

For modern enterprise, for most of us trying to build a business or in other ways serve humanity, life revolves around the city. The city is where money flows, where goods flow, where ideas flow, and where people live. Most enterprise focuses on cities. Even if you operate a mountain resort, your customers are likely to come from cities. That means that *understanding the city, both conceptually and in specifics, is critical to success* for most of us.

In a thousand years, it is likely that the history books will have forgotten now-familiar names like Bill Clinton and even John F. Kennedy. They will show up in appendices listing long-dead rulers, not unlike Pope Sextus or Pharaoh Mentuhotep II. If they are lucky, maybe they will get a paragraph after the discussions of FDR and Churchill. But in those same history books, it is likely that there will be extensive discussion about New York City at the turn of the millennium. In retrospect, New York today will be viewed as a golden age, not unlike the way we now look back on Republican Athens and Renaissance Florence.

In his small, classic 1948 book, *Here Is New York*, essayist E. B. White described the city as unique, cosmopolitan, mighty, unparalleled.

Today New York may be more vibrant, more unique, more unparalleled than at any time in its history.

We often think of New York as the world's center of art, high culture, Broadway, symphonies, and great museums. It is all these things, and it is stronger in these respects than ever. But New York is, and always has been, above all else a commercial city, a place where people transact with one another. This is not a city where political power rules. It is not even the capital of its own state. But it is, instead, the capital of the world. For no other city on earth has the concentration of power, of media, of finance, of communications and commerce, that are the daily lifeblood of Gotham.

In this regard, human culture today is playing out a pattern familiar from history. Our cities have always been the center of our commerce, of our dealings with one another. We think of the Medicis of Renaissance Florence as art collectors and patrons, but first they were grain financiers and traders—the Cargill Company of their era. Florence was a banking town first; it became an art and music center only with the wealth created from commerce.

Perhaps the city itself is the greatest of human enterprises. The Dutch who first laid out the streets of lower New York could not have imagined how their enterprise would evolve. The Roman founders of Londinium could not have dreamed of Covent Garden or Harrods. No creation of our species more boldly reflects all that is human—the wealth, the poverty, the creativity, the conflicts, the good times, the bad.

It is fascinating how anthills and beehives work. The biological, chemical, and psychological qualities of these social insects are aptly reflected in the remarkable structures they build and inhabit. In much the same way, when we look at New York's Rockefeller Center, London's Victoria Station, or Tokyo's Ginza, we see the natural organic result of the evolution of a species. Are these beehives any less natural than the ones built by bees? Are these anthills any less full of lessons to be learned, interactions to be studied?

The greatness of cities is not limited to their buildings and parks. Great cities are great because of their heart and soul, their spirit, their defining character, their unique sounds, smells, and sights. Like other enterprises, cities grow, die, and compete for position. They even network.

Changing, Dynamic Cities

Urban student Tertius Chandler calls the city "man's largest artifact." It may also be man's most dynamic creation. Change happens at every level within the city—from person to person, block to block, year to year. Perhaps the most dramatic changes are in the competitions among cities themselves—competition for jobs, for trade, for prestige, and, most important of all, competition for people.

As we see a city evolve from one day to the next, or from one visit to the next, we notice a new building here and a new building there . . . a new freeway, a new shopping center, a new skyscraper. But we rarely stand back and see how those changes add up over the years.

In 1850 Chicago was smaller in population than Albany, Providence, Louisville, Charleston, or Buffalo. It was not one of the ten largest cities in America. Just fifty years later, it was not only the second-biggest U.S. city, it was the *fifth-biggest city in the world*.

In 1925 Washington, D.C., despite more than one hundred years as our nation's capital, was only the seventeenth-largest city in the nation, just over half the size of neighboring Baltimore. In 1975, after fifty years of New Deal programs and wartime expansion, the city was eighth—way ahead of Baltimore—and is still rising.

More recently, Phoenix has risen, like its name, albeit from dust instead of from ashes. In 1950 it was the fifty-eighth-largest U.S. city, with a population half that of Scranton, Pennsylvania, and smaller than that of Grand Rapids, Michigan, or Worcester, Massachusetts. Fifty years later, Phoenix ranks fourteenth, ahead of former giants Cleveland and St. Louis.

This dynamic, changing process is at work not only in the U.S. but all over the world, as it has been throughout the centuries. For a little longer perspective on things, study this table.

Most Populous Urban Areas for 200 Years

Rank	1800	1850	1900	1950	2000
1	Beijing	London	London	New York	Tokyo
2	London	Beijing	New York	London	Mexico City
3	Canton	Paris	Paris	Tokyo	São Paulo
4	Yedo	Canton	Berlin	Paris	New York
5	Constantinople	Constantinople	Chicago	Shanghai	Mumbai
6	Paris	Yedo	Vienna	Moscow	Shanghai
7	Naples	New York	Tokyo	Buenos Aires	Los Angeles
8	Hangchow	Bombay	St. Petersburg	Chicago	Beijing
9	Osaka	St. Petersburg	Manchester	Ruhr Valley	Jakarta
10	Kyoto	Berlin	Philadelphia	Calcutta	Lagos

Cities Today

Cities today are more important than ever before in world history.

Cities all over the world are more full of life, full of new restaurants, full of festivals and music and art, than they have ever been in their history. We live in a golden age of the city. However, this late-twentieth-century revival of the city is just one blip on the long-term curve, whose overall direction is up and up and up. Consider, for example, the question of city size. Throughout most of world history, a city of 100,000 would have been considered gigantic. Very few cities ever made it to 500,000. In 1850 there was one city in the world with a population of more than 1 million—London. By 1950 there were 57. In 1990 there were 276, and it is forecast that there will be 380 in 2010.

While most of the people in the wealthy nations live in cities—77 percent in the U.S.—the majority of the world's population still lives outside them. But that is about to change. In 1996 about 46 percent of the world's 5.8 billion people lived in cities. In 2030 the experts say that the earth's population will exceed 8 billion. And that more than 60 percent of these people will live in cities.

Over the next twenty years, doing business in what are today the world's poorer countries will become more and more important. And nowhere will cities play a bigger role. Those countries that trail on the wealth curve are now growing faster than the countries of the first world. And their cities are growing dramatically faster than their rural areas. In that same 1996 to 2030 time frame, the number of people living in first-world cities is projected to increase 15 percent, from 883 million to 1.015 billion. In these nations, few live on the soil—only about 300 million today, and even fewer in thirty years. In that same period, the number of people living in rural areas in poor countries—presently the biggest group on earth—is expected to grow modestly, up only 7 percent (from 2.8 billion to 3 billion). But the number of people living in the cities of those countries is expected to rise 134 percent, from 1.7 billion to more than 4 billion.

If you think Shanghai and Mumbai are important now, just check back in a few years.

Defining the City

We must always make sure we define things accurately before our thinking is formed. And the city is an area where our old definitions get in the way of our understanding. We all know about city limits, those imaginary lines drawn by politicians to define where the turf of one governing body ends and that of another begins. While city limits still have meaning if you are a city council member, or if your house is on fire and you want to know which fire department to call, city limits are of limited value in explaining how people really live and how their economy works.

If you study the areas served by TV stations and newspapers, if you study how people commute to work, if you plan to extend your retail chain into a new city, then all that really matters is the *metropolitan (or urban) area*—the combination of a city and its suburbs. The urban area is one large, living, evolving organism, no matter where the old city limits lie. The city of Boston contains less than ten percent of the population of the Boston metropolitan area.

Unfortunately, the press often does not follow these rules. It is still common to find lists of "the largest cities" that consider only the areas falling within traditional city limits. According to these lists, Houston is the fourth largest city in the US. If you run an enterprise based in Europe or Asia and are planning your US offices, this information might lead you to put an office in Houston before "smaller cities" like Boston and San Francisco. But the urban areas of Boston and San Francisco, and even Dallas, are larger than that of Houston. The same pitfall exists overseas. Most lists show Rome as the largest city in Italy. That's true, if you're talking city limits. But the Roman metropolitan area includes about 2.9 million people, while competitor Milan is up to 4.3 million, making it the third largest urban center in Europe. And Milan is particularly important (and ahead of Rome) in the worlds of business, investment, communications, media, and design.

Our outdated definition of our cities is an enormous hindrance to making those cities better. Older inner cities often contain more poor people and fewer taxpayers, and yet bear higher costs (for law enforcement, fire protection, real estate costs, and taxes). If a city government's power is limited to its historic city limits, it may be impossible to effectively plan the transportation structure (highways or mass transit), school system, or taxes and investment for the *real* city—the urban area.

The Hierarchy of Cities

For at least the last two thousand years, there has usually been a "capital of the world." For centuries, it was Rome. For perhaps more years than any other city, it was Constantinople (now called Istanbul). By the end of the nineteenth century, it was London. Sometime in the first twenty years of the twentieth century, New York took over, and it has remained on top ever since.

Note that the capital of the world may not be a political capital, as

New York shows. The capital of the world need not be the largest city on earth—by the best and most current figures I can find, the New York metropolitan area at 20.7 million people is now fourth largest, behind Tokyo, Mexico City, and São Paulo. (And we don't really know exactly how many people live in any of these places. All we can do is make a scientific guess, and the guesses are less accurate in poorer cities and larger cities.)

But New York is more important than any other single city on earth. And more important in a huge array of dimensions—art, music, drama, poetry, book publishing, magazines, stock trading, insurance, advertising, fashion, corporate headquarters, total dollar amount of transactions, and so on.

The minute we assign "capital of the world" status to New York, we are saying there is a lead city, a main city—center of the universe. But that definition also implies structure; it implies that there is a system of cities. For Los Angeles is more important—in terms of economic and human activity—than San Diego, and Indianapolis more important than my hometown of Anderson. Most people who study these things think of cities as having a hierarchy—a structure from top to bottom. The capital of the world is at the top, and the powerful subsidiary giants—often called "world cities" because of the critical role they play on the world stage, each dominating their own part of the global economy—are right below the capital. Normally people think of this in terms of a city pyramid.

However, I think it is more accurate to think of cities as forming a solar system, with perhaps one city at its center but with the others spread about in all dimensions. I call this image the "city constellation."

This way of visualizing cities gives greater and more appropriate respect to all those other towns. Every city networks with many others. They form a dynamic, ever-changing, growing, and shrinking web of interaction. Austin links to San Jose due to their shared focus on high-tech industry. Orlando in many ways "reports" to Burbank, where Disney's world headquarters are located. Los Angeles is at the center of the film world, but its banking often flows from San Francisco. So the city constellation should really have lots of dotted lines connecting lots of cities. You can draw your part of the universe of cities, and add in the connecting lines that relate to your enterprise.

The Next Capital of the World?

Now that we have built up the pride of all you New Yorkers, here is the other side of the coin: No city gets to be capital forever. The reign of New York has at least fifty years and perhaps much longer to run; the title will pass on sooner or later. Sometimes these things change more quickly than we expect. When the U.S. first built the world's tallest building in the 1890s, and then went on to set new records in the 1930s and '70s, few expected that we would lose that title before the end of the twentieth century—and to Kuala Lumpur, Malaysia, of all places. (The Petronas Towers, built in the late 1990s, are for the time being the tallest buildings in the world.)

What city might be the next capital of the world? This is a question worth considering, because the winner will be on the rise during our lifetimes. In fact, the race has already begun.

First, let's look at some of the contenders that are *not* likely to get the job. Los Angeles is in many ways the prototypical early-twenty-first-century city. We used to talk about how New York had more Jews than any other city outside Israel, more Italians than any city outside Italy, more Irish than anywhere outside Dublin. Today the same kinds of claims can be made about the Cambodians and Guatemalans of Los Angeles. Like the world of our impending future, Los Angeles is large, sprawling, media-obsessed, and largely Latin and Asian. But two things will prevent L.A. from becoming the next capital of the world. First, it divides its power over California with San Francisco. Second, and more important, there are other cities that will be even more thoroughly suffused with Latin and Asian influences, and that will therefore accumulate more people and ultimately more economic clout.

Twenty years ago, one might have thought that the next world capital would be Tokyo. In many ways, this city parallels New York—big, hustling, intense, vertical, all business. Tokyo will have a brilliant future. It is powerful within Asia and will remain the capital of Japan, economically as well as politically. But Tokyo is relatively inward-focused, and it's in a country with limited resources and limited growth. It's one of the few cities where English has not been widely adopted for business purposes. Tokyo lacks large numbers of Italians or Irish or even Cambodians. Look at the past capitals of the world: they have always been very international. Even ancient Constantinople had meaningful enclaves of traders from Venice, Genoa, and more distant cities. By contrast, Tokyo is, above all else, a Japanese city rather than a city hell-bent on being at the center of the world constellation.

I think there are three real contenders for the next capital of the world: Hong Kong, Shanghai, and Singapore. You can make a case for each of the three. All are business and economic hubs, and have been for many years. While Shanghai dropped out of the game during most of Mao's years, it is back with a vengeance. All three have a huge ebb and flow of commerce and people. And two of the cities, Hong Kong and Singapore, are really city-states in the best Greek or Hanseatic tradition.

Most important, all three cities are in East Asia or Southeast Asia, the areas of the world that will see the most explosive growth in the years immediately ahead. We may see this same kind of progress in Latin America, South Asia, and some day even in Africa, but it is not going to happen as soon as it will in East and Southeast Asia. It is happening there now, today. Thus, a head start for these three cities.

The city most likely to win is Hong Kong. Although Hong Kong is now part of China, the Chinese government has pledged to leave its capitalist system in place for at least fifty years. Hong Kong is today probably the most vital major city on earth. The feeling of electricity in the air is rivaled only by New York. With a powerful business infrastructure, leaders with global capabilities, and immediate access to China, the world's largest market, it is easy to visualize Hong Kong's continuing rise.

What could prevent Hong Kong from attaining world-capital status?

First, strong competition from other cities—not just Singapore and Shanghai, but also Los Angeles, Tokyo, and even São Paulo. But the bigger risk for Hong Kong is its limited view of the world. It's a city whose past has changed abruptly and whose future has usually been uncertain. This has resulted in a culture focused on making money, keeping the wolves at bay, and getting rich fast. In Hong Kong shopping centers, you see every prestige brand on earth. But this is not a city with great cultural wealth—you don't see giant bookstores or art students sitting on the streets painting the fabulous views. As in some American Sun Belt cities such as Dallas, the museums are slow in arriving. In order to rise to the top of the world's cities, Hong Kong will have to play a leadership role in more than just money.

The upshot of all this is that there will be a new world capital, and it will almost certainly be in Asia. This same style of analysis can be applied to any set of competitive cities—on your continent, in your country, or in your state. As the service economy allows more people to live where they want, as the airline system and the Internet facilitate more fluid intercourse, and as city power becomes more disperse, the world's capital in the future may never have quite the dominant role of Rome, or even of New York. These three Asian cities will share power more evenly, and other cities like New York, São Paulo, and Milan will retain or achieve enormous power. But your enterprise will be more successful, and your life more interesting, if you watch what is happening among the world's great cities in their competition for dominance and power, and respond to the cultural, political, and economic trends these struggles set in motion.

Signature Cities

Now that we have made a big deal about these giant, energetic, and dominant world cities, you may be feeling pretty bad because your life and your enterprise are centered somewhere else: in Oklahoma City, San Diego, Annapolis, or perhaps in Antwerp or Adelaide. Don't we have anything nice to say about those more modest cities?

Indeed we do. For residents of these cities are living in real hometowns, cities that accurately reflect life for most of us and that are more typical of your nation and its people.

These are *signature cities*. They are more representative, more typical, more true of their countries than the great metropolises—and often more livable.

Can Minneapolis compete with New York? Probably not. Minneapolis is a city where people are apt to say hello to one another on the street, a city with clean streets and (mostly) free-flowing traffic. You don't hear horns honked by out-of-control drivers at other out-of-control drivers. While Minneapolis cannot compare with New York for new experiences, here is a city about which we can say, "What a nice, pleasant, easy, living-room city this is." And the same could be said about Austin, Texas; Antwerp, Belgium; Chiang Mai, Thailand; or Curitiba, Brazil. You can even make a case that the greatest American city is Chicago, a city that genuinely reflects America's strengths and weaknesses in every way, less reflective of Europe and Asia than our coastal giants.

You cannot really understand a country until you have spent at least a couple of days in such a signature city. Each city on earth, no matter where it is on the constellation, is a home to people. It has a history; it has a character; it has strengths and weaknesses. Savor them all.

The World's Two Most Amazing Cities

There are two cities that I love to visit that may surprise some readers: Las Vegas and Orlando (including Disney World). Some of my well-traveled friends, who share my love of Italy and of such further-off-the-beaten-trail places as Indonesia and Morocco, think I am crazy when I promote Vegas and Orlando. Here's why I find these cities so worth visiting.

Stimulation. Vegas and Orlando are the two most successful purpose-built tourism cities on earth. They have based their economies totally on the provision of fantasy for large numbers of people. Therefore, you can see architecture, decorative motifs, light shows, fountains, and live shows like nowhere else on earth.

Operations. As much as I love vision and strategy, the ultimate success of any enterprise depends on the execution of details, of "making it all work." Vegas and Orlando each draw more than 20 million visitors per year. There are probably no two cities in the world that work as well. From your arrival at the airport to the local transportation system (including taxis) to personal safety, these cities are well-oiled machines built to handle huge numbers of people with minimal inconvenience and maximum speed and comfort.

Economics. In the old days, it didn't take much to excite people, to put on a memorable show. Think back to the simple chorus-girl shows of Vegas in the 1950s or the relatively old-fashioned amusement-park ambience of California's Disneyland when it opened in 1955. Today many people have surround-sound and DVD players in their homes. Television, cable, and movies like *Titanic* give us exhilarating, out-of-this-world experiences. So to give us something we can't get at home takes a huge imagination and a budget to match.

Only Vegas and Orlando have figured out how to finance such huge demands. Both do it by assessing a "cover charge." In the case of Orlando, Disney charges visitors about $60 per day per park. With annual revenues in excess of $3 billion, Disney World Orlando is one of the world's biggest "factories"—that is, one of the world's biggest single-enterprise, single-location economic units. In Las Vegas, the cover charge is assessed by the slot machine, and you pay whatever you feel like paying. The totals generated are even greater than they are at Disney World.

Change. The status of both cities is defined by continuous evolution. Disney World gets a major new ride or major new section of the park each year. Las Vegas adds one or more new theme casinos annually. Thus, each repeat visit offers new images, new thoughts, new horizons.

Vision. While Disney World is the vision of a single corporation, a vision first ignited by a single man, Las Vegas has an equally powerful and consistent vision, although it is guided by the invisible hand of a multitude of independent enterprises each realizing the value of a shared vision. In some ways, Orlando and Las Vegas are extremely different from each other. One serves primarily adults in one of America's driest spots and the spirit is "Anything goes." The other serves couples and families in one of the wettest places in America and only very controlled things "go." But they have both continued to build for more than thirty years on a clear and unique vision of their role in the world. It would be hard to find any other cities on earth of which you could say the same.

Global draw and appeal. A diversified economy is usually a requirement for creating a great city, but the concentration of Orlando and Vegas on tourism has served them well. Eventually, almost the whole population of the world will cycle through these cities, drawn by giant conventions in one case and by the tugging hands of small children in the other. They are truly modern-day Mecca's, as indicated by the number of nonstop international flights going to Orlando and the number of international conventions and trade fairs held in Las Vegas.

By now, you may be asking, "How does this relate to my city or my enterprise?" There is much to be learned from these two cities that has parallels in your enterprise. These lessons include:

- The power of vision

- The need to stick to that vision, even when everyone else says you are nuts

- The value of staying current and interesting, of always moving forward

- The importance of operations—of paying attention to details, of making it all work

Finally, the success that these cities have achieved through differentiation of their brand images and appeals can serve as a model for every enterprise, from General Motors to your corner dry-cleaning shop.

GATEWAYS

Further Readings for Understanding Cities

One of the very few books that describes each of the world's major cities in a broader urban-studies context, talking about the factors that matter to builders of enterprise, is *Cities of the World: World Regional Urban Development,* by Stanley D. Brunn and Jack F. Williams. Another excellent book about how the great cities stand today is *Globalization and the World of Large Cities,* edited by Fu-chen Lo and Yue-man Yeung. For a more storylike approach to the great cities of history, there are three great books: *Cities and Civilizations,* by Christopher Hibbert; *Cities and People: A Social and Architectural History,* by Mark Girouard; and *Cities in Civilization,* by Peter Hall. These three wonderful books tell the tale of great cities through the ages. The best books on U.S. cities are *Edge City,* by Joel Garreau, and *Places Rated Almanac,* by David Savageau.

TRYTHIS

Making a City Your Own

There are few things as exciting as getting to know a new city—making the city your own. There are predictable tourist-oriented activities in every great city. Everyone visits the top of the tallest building and eats at the restaurant with the best view or the most celebrities. You should, too. Everyone visits the big museum, and you should, too. But hardly anyone explores the neighborhoods of the city, where people just live. Few tourists sit and eat lunch where the working people eat.

If you do these things, you are likely to discover a city that you did not know existed. A city that is every bit as exciting and interesting as the city of the package tour. Most important, you will develop memories of the city that are your own. You will find favorite places to eat and favorite places to sit where there are no tour bus crowds. You will in fact "possess" the city, making it your own.

In their exploration of new cities, or even old ones, most people follow well-tread routes. We (and our travel books) ask, "What is the best hotel? What are the best restaurants?" But these questions are not the key ones that the entrepreneurial mind will ask. Here is where I start out with any new city:

- Who was it named after?
- When was it founded?
- Where did its people come from, when, and why?
- Where do they work?
- What's the population? How does it rank in the state or the country or region?
- Where do newcomers—immigrants, students, newcomers— tend to settle?

Look at each city's appeal from all viewpoints. Would you want to live there, or just visit there? Should people from other countries visit there? Should students visit there, is it an important part of someone's education?

Finally, after I have gotten to know a city, I try to review where it stands in numerous dimensions. Here is a starter list. I am sure you can add your own city "personality attributes" that interest you.

- Primacy (How far up the pyramid or how near the center of the constellation?)
- Ethnicities
- Languages
- Temperature curve (How hot and how cold does it get?), sunshine, precipitation, and humidity
- Industrialization
- Trendiness
- Energy level
- Nocturnality (Is it a nighttime city, or do they roll up the streets at ten?)
- Masculinity or femininity
- Design-awareness (Some cities don't care much about how

they look; others, like Milan, Houston, and Tokyo care passionately about each surface.)

Before going to a new city (whether on business or pleasure—I make all my visits both), do one or more of the following:

- Listen to music characteristic of that city.
- Study the life of someone important in that city: an artist or writer who worked there, a business leader who helped to build it.
- Study the history of the city.
- Watch a film made in the city.
- Watch a documentary about the city.
- Read a poem from or about the city, or a short story or novel set there.
- Study the city on the Internet.

These same steps will work for a nation or state, as well.

PART TWO

Essence: The Power of Vision

22

The Power of Vision

I began this book by saying that the single most critical ingredient of enterprise success is having a clear vision. Since then, we've covered the foundation that must first be put in place—creative curiosity and an understanding of where you stand in time and space, of how the world is changing around you. With that foundation in place, we can now build our vision. In the following pages, we will answer three questions:

1. What is vision?

2. Why is vision important?

3. What are the characteristics of a successful vision?

What Is Vision?

When I say "vision," I mean *an informed and forward-thinking statement of purpose.*

Above all else, the vision tells us why the enterprise exists, its raison d'être. An enterprise without a clear purpose is a ship without a rudder, a train without a track. The vision answers the question, Just what are we trying to accomplish? In a few pages, we'll discuss how to think about purpose in order to achieve success.

Next, a vision should be informed. The better you understand the world, the better informed your vision will be. An informed vision will reflect the trends at work in your environment. If your vision is to build and sell the world's greatest slide rules, you are probably not going to attract many customers. If your goal is to improve the lives of smallpox victims, you are soon going to be out of business—thankfully. On the other hand, you might today start a magazine focused on people aged eighty and above with the knowledge that the market may "grow into" your business in coming years.

Hand-in-hand with being informed comes "forward thinking." Your vision is not intended to reflect whatever flaws your enterprise may have today. Instead, your vision should reflect what you expect and hope your organization will become. Your vision is by definition a statement of ambition.

A forward-looking statement of purpose informs everyone of the direction the enterprise is moving. Sometimes you move quickly, sometimes slowly, and sometimes even backward a step or two. But the clear vision always lets everyone know what direction you want to be moving in. All priorities flow from a clear vision.

There's no standard "vision formula" that works for everyone. I've read books offering collections of "top company mission statements," and many of them strike me as meaningless words that do not inform the actual conduct of the enterprise but rather reflect generic aspirations to which almost anyone could subscribe.

Instead, a vision should be a highly customized vision that could only come from your enterprise. Uniqueness and differentiation are crucial to a great vision.

Whether it's written or not, whether it's spoken or not, there is a heart and soul within every organization. If you run an enterprise today, ask your employees and their spouses, ask customers, even ask competitors, "What adjectives and phrases would you use to describe us?" Maybe you will hear phrases like "slow to respond," "trapped in the dark ages," "work their people too hard," "always reaching for new business," "a lot of fun," "all business," "great at designing products." Some of the things you will hear may be flattering, others not so pretty. Some things will surprise you, others will not. But every enterprise has such a personality. And inevitably the vision of an enterprise reflects its personality.

I recently met Phil Romano, one of the most creative restaurant entrepreneurs. He dreamed up Fuddrucker's, Romano's Macaroni Grill, and Eatzi's. Phil was speaking to a meeting of young restaurateurs, many of whom had one successful location and were looking to expand. Someone asked Phil, "When it's time to expand, how do you know what is most important in designing and opening your second unit?"

Phil replied, "Look at your restaurant and list those two, three, or four things that, if you changed them, it really wouldn't be the same restaurant or the same experience." Phil went on to describe the many restaurants that had developed enviable reputations, with crowded waiting areas and never enough tables. Often, when those restaurants expanded to meet the demand, they failed. It turned out that their cozy crowdedness was one of the hallmarks that made them great.

Phil noted that, for one restaurant, it might be the décor, for another the menu, for another the attitude of the wait staff, for another the speed of service. But each successful restaurant has something that makes it successful, that sets it apart from its many competitors. That something special is at the heart of its vision.

A great vision reflects your "core values" in the very broadest sense of the term. At Hewlett-Packard, it might be to design the strongest, most durable computer hardware products. At Southwest Airlines, it is to fly reliably, efficiently, and to have fun. At Hoover's, we seek to provide readable, accurate, timely information on companies, industries, and managers. If you study successful enterprises, you always find that they have a "story," an essence. When I first read about the Cross Pen Company many years ago, the article described the company as not competing with Bic and Papermate for the ballpoint writing instrument business, but competing with briefcases and paperweights for the corporate gift business. Whether Cross wrote this down in fancy mission statements or not, their company had a real story, a distinct message that defined the enterprise and set it apart. Every great enterprise has such a message.

Depending on your enterprise and its environment, your vision may or may not include references to customers, suppliers, stockholders, employees, or communities. It may or may not include references to technologies and approaches to the business. It will probably include references to values or business principles. If your company exists in an industry known for dishonesty (used car sales, for example), you may go out of your way to talk about ethical principles. But above all else your vision must reflect what is unique about your enterprise, its personality and attitude. It will reflect what *you* believe is most important, why *you* believe the enterprise exists.

Most important, a vision defines those things that do not change with the vagaries of the marketplace, that do not shift in response to competition, that do not bend with the fads of the hour. When we developed a vision for the first travel superstore, TravelFest, we knew that our stores would carry one of the largest selections of travel books in the U.S. But our vision did not say this. It said we would carry the best selection of *travel information*. We stated it that way because we knew that, in the future, people might be using electronic information sources much more often than books.

Too often, we confuse our tactics with our underlying strategy. What is at the core of General Motors? Is it making cars, or is it making vehicles for transportation? Would GM be comfortable if society went 100 percent trucks? Are our giant retail chains locked into running traditional stores of bricks and mortar, or are they distributors of merchandise that can just as easily move to the Internet and mail order? Don't misunderstand me—I think that some retailers should answer this question, "We are absolutely built around traditional stores, and we will always be," while others should say, "We are ready to sell goods by any channel of distribution that works." Both can be successful if their vision is based on a sound understanding of people's needs, if they believe in what they are doing, and if they execute it well. If I ran a supermarket chain, I might be open to entering the restaurant business but feel no need for e-commerce other than as an advertising and customer loyalty tool. On the other hand, if I ran a bookstore chain, I might view the importance of Internet sales quite differently.

The ultimate purpose of the enterprise transcends the ups and downs of the marketplace, the vagaries of supply and demand, the entry and exit of competitors, the passing of the seasons. Only by looking into the soul of the enterprise can you define the transcendent core of the enterprise and differentiate that unchanging essence from the many tactics used in execution of the vision. Your customers, your competitors, your suppliers change by the year, by the month, by the week. The advertising medium that works one day could be irrelevant tomorrow. Your store location strategy—downtowns versus malls—may need to change. The size, style, shape, and design of your products may change. Whether Hoover's distributes its information in the form of books or CD-ROMs, via the Internet or some post-Internet technology, will change. A vision that is created with foresight transcends those tactics and techniques that not only might change, but often *must* change.

Why Vision Is Important

Some ask, why is vision important? They may say, "I have been leading an enterprise without a vision, and we have done pretty well."

My response is to ask, "But can your enterprise really stand the test of time? If you get hit by a truck today, will the enterprise go on tomorrow?" If the answer is "Yes—everyone around here understands what is important and knows our priorities," then I would say, "Then you do have a vision—you just haven't written it down and made the most of it." But if you have no vision, if you really are running your enterprise with no clear definition or sense of purpose, you are treading on thin ice.

As I have observed thousands of businesspeople, and studied thou-

sands more, one of the characteristics you see over and over is their prag-
matism. They look at the real world in which they live, they adapt, and
they try to achieve. But the flip side of this personality trait is often that
these same businesspeople are not overly introspective. They do not
dwell on why they do what they do or how they got where they got. Just
as the flip side of great philosophy professors is that they sometimes forget where they left their shoes. But those who both do things *and* think
about what they are doing are the ones who achieve the most. Whether
you "do vision" consciously or not, here are the reasons that it is so required, the reasons it is so useful in achieving your organization's
goals:

A vision bonds. The larger your enterprise is, the more likely you will
have workers from diverse backgrounds. The more you grow, the more
you will include different ages, races, religions, backgrounds, and
mindsets. If you grow enough, you will even include many nationalities.
The vision, the purpose of the enterprise, is ultimately the only reason
that all these people come together each day. When bringing together
people of diverse races, religions, ages, and lifestyles, you cannot
overemphasize that "we are different, we all have a reason for being here
at this enterprise, the only thing that brings us together at this work-
place is because we share these values and this purpose."

A vision inspires. As the world becomes wealthier, people have more
career choices. Money becomes less important. While it would be foolish
to think that money did not matter, jobs are increasingly at financial
parity and other elements become the deciding factor—what are the options and other benefits, where is the job, what are the people like, what
do they believe in?

Over time, the values and purpose of the organization have become
increasingly more important, especially to the best people, the ones who
can make the most difference in your enterprise. This trend will only
grow in the future. In short, people are more motivated if they believe
they are doing something that is worthwhile, if they believe that they
can, through participation in the enterprise, accomplish something that
is worthy of their time and energy—something that they could not ac-

complish working on their own. Ideally, the vision of the enterprise is something they believed in before they even joined the organization, whether that be finding cures for cancer or building great cars, operating exciting fashion stores or publishing a fine daily newspaper.

Nothing is a more powerful agent for attracting and keeping talented people than a clear vision, especially if the organization is living that vision and achieving its goals. A clear vision, a sense of purpose, can be a continual motivator and force of inspiration in even the largest of organizations. Perhaps especially in the largest organizations.

A vision is an anchor in hard times and times of change. It is what makes the difference between the flash in the pan and the enterprise that is going to last, to stand the test of time. Those organizations that understand themselves, that have a clear vision and are true to it, have far fewer doubts than an organization without such a rudder. People in a visionary organization can be spellbound by the future and oblivious to the obstacles of the present—or at least have the confidence and the will to overcome them.

A vision is a potent competitive tool. If your competitors have visions themselves, a differentiating vision is required on your part. However, it is often the case that your competitors are without a clear and consistent definition of themselves. If you are so lucky as to be in such a position, you can really make hay out of the weakness of others by being one of the few organizations in your field that knows where it is headed and why.

A vision builds community. Once you have articulated your vision and are confident in it, then it is important that it reach everyone who touches the enterprise. Too often, the vision is either only known at the board level, or only distributed to employees but not to the board. A strong vision is equally motivating to your ad agency, your auditors, your outside lawyers, even your customers. If your story is true, if you really believe in it, then you must use it as the powerful tool that it is, a pervasive tool for inspiration, for longevity, and for unification of everyone involved in the enterprise. A great vision turns your enterprise's acquaintances into advocates.

What Are the Characteristics of a Successful Vision?

I believe that there are four primary attributes in successful enterprise visions. I have studied a lot of companies and nonprofit organizations. I have seen some succeed with only three of these in place, occasionally with just two. But the great enterprises have visions that are all four:

- Clear

- Consistent

- Unique

- Serving

I call these four dimensions the four pillars of vision.

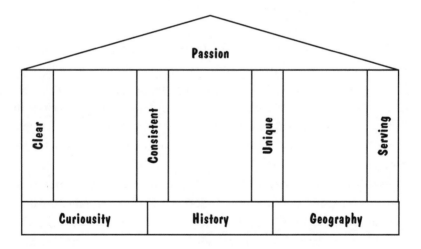

23

The Clear Vision

The English language is a powerful tool. It is used in business meetings worldwide as a common ground of communication. It has an enormous vocabulary of beautiful and appropriate words. Sometimes it seems that the only people who don't want to (or know how to) use the English language are academics, lawyers, politicians—and businesspeople. If you step into a meeting at a Fortune 500 company, you are likely to hear language like, "We are rightsizing and reengineering to adjust to the shifting paradigm of our upscale consumer base emerging from our data warehouse looking for an IT solution." It is no wonder that these companies often have no clue as to what to do, they can't even talk right!

Take a look at the opposite end of the scale. One of the companies with a clear vision is Southwest Airlines. Much has been written on the company and its unique style of doing business. But what impresses me most is the simplicity, the crystal clarity of their message. Since the company's founding thirty years ago, they have held to a handful of key beliefs. These include flying one type of aircraft, the Boeing 737, so that all their crews are trained on the entire fleet and to reduce their investment in spare parts. Southwest has always operated efficiently and without frills—they land, they give the first people to arrive at the airport the first seats (all of which are classless), they throw peanuts at you instead of serving a meal, and they take off—all in less time than any other major airline. In the process, the company also believes in having fun. They have a unique culture and they are proud of it. Beginning from a Texas-only base, they have gone national, consistently delivering reliable and affordable transportation to millions of people.

These are simple ideas. They have not been hidden. If you go to Southwest's Web site, read the company history *Nuts!,* or listen to a speech by any Southwest executive, you will get this same simple message. I call this a "third-grade vision"—any third-grader could understand it. That also means that every flight attendant, every baggage handler, every pilot, every marketing executive—yes, even the CEO—can under-stand it. And put it into practice in every decision the company makes.

One of the hidden values of a clear vision is that it confuses the enemy. People love complex theories and conspiracies. Simple stories seem less interesting, and many people find it hard to accept that the truth can be so straightforward. When the airline America West first started up, they said they were going to be another "no frills" carrier, and I said, "Great, we need another airline like Southwest." But I soon saw that they had several types of planes, they had first class and coach, and they were serving meals. They couldn't even copy the concept accurately! Later, America West got its act more together, but they no longer try to clone Southwest. Some of the giant airlines tried to copy Southwest, but they thought the whole story was price, and missed the simple vision based on reliable, fun service. None succeeded.

So what has this clear vision done for Southwest? Many people still think of the company as a regional carrier. But Southwest has been the most consistently profitable company in the industry, making a profit every year for more than twenty years. None of the other major airlines have done this. It has the lowest costs, too. At the same time—this is re-markable—it also is rated as not only the best airline to work for, but one of the best companies of any type to work for. Quite a trick to be so ef-ficient and a great place to work at the same time! Last, but not least,

Southwest has consistently had the fewest customer complaints, the fewest lost bags, and the fewest late departures. There are few companies that so perfectly embody the ideal enterprise.

What about the stockholders? A key measure of any company is market capitalization—the total value of all the shares of the company. This is how much cash it would take to buy the whole company. As of April 2001, the value of United Airlines' parent company was $1.7 billion; Delta was worth $4.8 billion; and the most valuable of the three industry giants, American, was worth $5.2 billion. That means the three biggest passenger airlines on earth, combined, are valued by the investment world at $11.7 billion. Any guess what Southwest is worth? Would you believe $13.4 billion, more than the big three combined? And of course Southwest's dominance of value was not always the case, as long-time Southwest stockholders will happily inform you.

I believe it is impossible to overvalue the contribution of a clear, simple vision. Anything you can do to streamline your vision, to simplify your story, is a step in the right direction. And critical to that clarity is plain speaking.

Every industry and every profession has its jargon. We throw around acronyms like rice at a wedding. We have to go with TQM and ISO 9000, we put together an RFP for the CIO. Even the simplest of industries has enough jargon to fill several books. The travel agency industry has a simple task—selling you an airplane seat or a hotel room—and yet it can take months, even years, for a new person to learn all the industry acronyms and jargon. Most of us are not in rocket science or brain surgery. We are selling bricks or running car washes. We don't have to invent a new word each week in order to get our jobs done.

At one of my companies, a group of consultants approached me and wanted to teach our company about *kaizen*—the word for the Japanese belief in continuous improvement. No one is a bigger believer in this concept than I am. But why not call it continuous improvement? In rapidly growing companies like those I have built, a major share of your employees are always recent hires. Sometimes more than half the organization are newcomers. If a growing company indoctrinates everyone in an entirely new language, the newcomers either have to go around asking what all these strange words mean or just stay in the dark and feel stupid. A wall is built between the newcomers and the old-timers. That is no way to bond together the organization.

When we are scared or uncertain, when we think we have to impress someone, we often resort to unclarity. A spokeswoman for our local bus system is interviewed on TV and says, "We are a personnel vehicle intensive operation." A NASA rocket blows up and the announcer professionally says, "We have an anomaly." A college student dies when misdiagnosed by student health services and the administration goes on TV and says it was "a scenario we hope never occurs." Newly minted M.B.A.'s speak of "A" financing rounds—I think they mean "first"—and "A" distribution channels.

Try tape recording one of your enterprise's meetings and play it back for any reasonably bright sixth grader. Then ask, "What did we talk about and what should we do?" If he says, "I couldn't understand any of it," then the chances are good that you and your people cannot think clearly about the issues.

The English language is beautiful and powerful. It is worth using well. Having lived a life in business, I know how hard it is to keep from using all the buzzwords. I am sure you can find some in this book. But it is worth a perpetual struggle to keep our words—and our mind—free of doublespeak and alphabet soup. Ask the investors in Southwest Airlines.

24

The Consistent Vision

In this era of rapid, even accelerating, change, it can be difficult to know which way to head. If you want to create a new company from scratch, as I have done three times, you may hear one direction from the venture capitalists today and another tomorrow. If you are running a public company, you will get one signal from Wall Street today and another tomorrow. Your own board of directors or board of trustees may waver from one meeting to the next, from one headline to the next, from one business guru to the next.

And yet, if you study great, lasting enterprises, the evidence overwhelmingly tells us to stay the course. If your course is based on a sound idea, if your direction reflects what you know about people, about trends, and about geography, it should serve you well over time. Your confidence in your vision comes from knowing *what matters*—knowing what you are good at, knowing what is important to you, knowing where your bread is buttered, and sticking to your vision through thick and thin, through bad quarters and good.

As I mentioned earlier, I grew up in a GM factory town. As kids, my friends and I were obsessed with cars (some of us still are). In the 1950s, most of the world's great sports cars were made by the British and the Italians, with a few German cars thrown in for good measure. The two industry giants, General Motors and Ford, decided that this needed to change. GM created the Corvette; Ford, the Thunderbird. Study those two models in the intervening forty-plus years.

The Corvette has always been basically the same: a sports car with a V-8 engine (actually, it was a 6–cylinder engine the first year), two doors, two seats, very fast, sometimes loud, often uncomfortable, usually red. If you have followed GM over those forty years, you know how confused the company has at times been. You know that they must have closets full of consultants' reports urging them to abandon or modify this vision of the Corvette. In the oil crisis of 1973, they probably discussed a 4-cylinder Corvette. It is likely that they are talking about a Corvette sport utility vehicle today. But, at least so far, the car gods have smiled on this car and said, "No, if we are going to make a car called a Corvette, let's stick to what made it famous. The word 'Corvette' means something to people; we cannot afford to lose that. If people no longer want a hot, fast, red, two-seat V-8, then stop making the Corvette, but don't fiddle with that name and what it represents."

On the other hand, the Thunderbird started as a two-door coupe, then became a four-door, a family car, a luxury car, and everything in between. While the Ford Company has outmarketed GM in many of their numerous battles, this is one area where Ford lost its focus. If you study where all this led to, you find that the Corvette continues in production and continues to periodically make the covers of the car magazines. On the other hand, Ford eventually pulled the plug on the Thunderbird and stopped making it. The brand had lost all its meaning. If you take your study one step further, you will find that Ford has now announced a "new Thunderbird," which will be a two-seater modeled on the original. They are trying to recapture what they lost. But it isn't what they lost, it's what they gave away. Because back in the 1950s, the Thunderbird consistently outsold the Corvette by ratios of at least 3 to 1.

It is so easy to get sucked into the fads of the day, to respond to headlines, and to forget your fundamental direction. Two great examples come from two of America's best-known global brands: Disney and Coke.

The Disney Company was built by one of the greatest management teams in U.S. history—two brothers named Walt and Roy. You would have never heard of Walt the animator and dreamer had it not been for his brother Roy, the deal-maker and bean-counter.

As seems to happen, the two men grew old and died. Their in-laws got control of the company, took a look at their big profits, and effectively said, "Wow! Look at these profits! Let's not take any chances, let's not take risks, let's manage what we've got and make as much money as possible today." The company began to slide. It did not go down the tube overnight, because it was a great company. But downhill it went. If you are a movie buff, it is probably sufficient to mention that one of their *most* successful movies in the 1970s was *Tron*. If you aren't a movie buff, never mind—believe me that nothing much happened.

In this environment, some oilmen from Fort Worth, Texas—the Bass brothers—got together with Roy's son (also named Roy) and took control of the company. They put two new guys in charge—Michael Eisner and Frank Wells—who immediately began to refocus the company on the things that had made it great in the first place. In effect, they said, "We are going to be the world's greatest maker of family entertainment—the world's storytellers." When they began an enormous investment in animated feature films, the experts told them they were nuts and would lose their money—the same thing the experts told Walt and Roy in the 1930s when they produced *Snow White* and *Fantasia*. Whether you are a movie buff or not, I think you have heard of *The Lion King, Toy Story,* and *Beauty and the Beast*. Since the Disney Company refocused on its core values, it has risen in value (market capitalization) more than ten-fold.

In Coke's case, CEO Roberto Goizueta apparently decided that he was a little bored with the colored-fizzy-water business. He led his company to buy Columbia Pictures and other entertainment companies. In this case, you have to give Goizueta great credit as he later realized his own misdirection, sold those businesses to Sony, and refocused Coca-

Cola on being the world's greatest maker of nonalcoholic beverages. I believe that competitor Pepsi is one of the world's best-run companies. But the focus of Coke was so fierce that Pepsi spun off its huge restaurant operation (Pizza Hut, KFC, and Taco Bell) in order to focus on being a decent number two in the industry.

Perhaps the most important measure of how well a company uses it resources, the best measure of profitability, is return on assets viewed over five to ten years. By this and other similar measures, Coca-Cola is possibly the most successful major enterprise on earth. Other companies like Intel and Microsoft have generated equally astounding performances, but these companies are mere babes—Coca-Cola is more than one hundred years old and just hitting stride!

Both Disney and Coke are great examples of overcoming adversity and bouncing back from bad decisions, for they had two of the worst business fiascos of the late twentieth century. Disney opened EuroDisney outside Paris. While the company today says that this venture is becoming successful, the project lost more than $1 billion in its first year. It goes without saying that these figures are not what was shown to the board of directors when they gave the green light on this project. And Coke had the infamous "new Coke" fiasco, one of the biggest marketing blunders of all time. But, in each case, the company was strong enough to overcome these disasters. That kind of strength comes from knowing what matters.

As I write this, both Disney and Coke stocks are down. Since the second half of 1998, they have each lost more than half their value. Like any large organization, these companies are not immune to bad decisions and negative factors coming at them from outside. And they are certainly not immune to the vagaries of Wall Street. If I am right about the long-term strength of these two great companies, investors with a longer horizon than two to three years will be rewarded. The same long horizon that the people running these companies have.

When I talk to people about how important a clear and consistent vision is, many say, "But XYZ Company failed because it did *not* change—it didn't adapt to the times." It's true that success in enterprise tends to breed complacency. When something works, you are reluctant to change it, even in the face of clear evidence that the world is changing around you. But a crucial part—perhaps the hardest part—of building a great enterprise is knowing *what to change* and *what not to change*—what is part of the firm foundation versus what is dynamic, ever changing, ever adapting.

The part of an enterprise that does not change is the essence, the vision. Everything else, every aspect of the execution of the idea, every strategy and tactic, every product and every price, is subject to change, sometimes frequent change. Your customers change annually, monthly, weekly, daily, even hourly. To serve them well, your enterprise must also be able to change. At the same time, clear and consistent priorities, the heart of vision, must be in place if leaders (and followers) are to know what to change and what not to change.

25

The Unique Vision

"In real estate, its location, location, location.
In business, it's differentiate, differentiate, differentiate."
—FORMER COCA-COLA CEO ROBERTO GOIZUETA

"Yeah, I'd be back there with everyone else."
—OLYMPIC RUNNER MICHAEL JOHNSON'S REACTION
WHEN EARLY COACHES TOLD HIM THAT HE RAN FUNNY
AND THAT HE SHOULD RUN MORE LIKE EVERYONE ELSE

A successful vision is unique. If you try to accomplish the same exact goal as some other organization, it is not likely that the two if you will be successful. If you try to possess the same position in the market's mind, there will not be enough room.

If you are starting a new company, developing a new division or product, or defining the course for an existing business, uniqueness is of crit-

240

ical importance. The process begins with finding your own space or niche in the world. While size and complexity may satisfy the egos of conglomerate-builders and corporate boards, the reality is that most successful enterprises do one thing, and do it extremely well.

Sometimes it is a small thing, or at least very narrowly defined. Cross Pens and Delta Queen Steamships are famous examples of big fish in little ponds. Club Corporation of America, whose founder Robert Dedman is a billionaire, is the largest operator of country clubs in the world. One of the most successful parts of the Barnes & Noble empire is their college textbook wholesaling operation. The Official Airline Guide is an organization with one database (airline timetables and fares) and a handful of printed publications; at its peak, it sold for $750 million. Big Charts, which provides stock charts to Hoover's and other online services, was valued at more than $100 million. The third-party tech-support or help-desk industry did not exist ten years ago and is today huge. Metro Networks flies traffic helicopters and was valued at hundreds of millions of dollars.

Part of the reason enterprises must have a unique vision is that they will be most successful if they strive to be the best at something, or the best or biggest in some regard. This may take some creativity of definition. In other words, maybe you can't be the biggest (or best) car dealer in the United States, but maybe you can be the best Ford dealer in Central Texas. Once you achieve that more limited goal, you can raise your sights.

One way to differentiate yourself is by finding gaps in a competitor. In all the years I studied Toys "R" Us, they never had a successful toy store competitor. Chain after chain tried to copy them. None of them survived over the longer pull. I told my friends, "You know, someone could build a chain if they just got the business of everyone that Toys 'R' Us has upset." Not that Toys was a bad company or upset more people than normal. But every company has its weaknesses—often, as with people, the flipsides of their strengths. In a U.S. market of more than 200 million consumers, there should always be room for two competitors, even if it requires focusing on the leading company's Achilles' heel or its dissatisfied customers.

One of the most effective differentiators today is the big home-improvement chain Lowe's. Home Depot is one of the most successful and best-run retailers in history, the ultimate example of the superstore. Most of their competitors, such as Builders Square, are long gone. But Lowe's has carefully studied Home Depot and picked all its weak points. Lowe's revised its stores (and *then* its advertising) to emphasize bright lighting, good signing so you can find things, departments that are easy to find, and other attributes in which Home Depot was weak. Today that industry finally has two strong companies. Those that died off were intent on copying Home Depot, the height of folly (and perhaps impossible as well). Lowe's has instead succeeded by juxtaposing itself *against* Home Depot.

After one of my speeches in New England, a fellow came up and described the following situation. I'll call him Rick. Rick was in the local television news business. One of their competitors had changed their format, increasing production values (that is, slicker), focusing on crime and other sensational stories, taking the "easy pickings." Their ratings were way up and they now led the market. Rick had heard my message about the importance of quality and high standards, and wondered if his story proved me wrong.

My answer was that Rick's competitor was profiting because they had broken from the pack and offered something different. Based on my experience in the cities I have lived in, I know that most of their competitors would respond to this move by copying it. If so, they will all end up splitting the market they started with, and none will be differentiated. Of course, there is a real market for sensational crime stories; there are people who want to watch that. Perhaps it is the biggest single slice of the market. But that will leave the other slices—whatever they are—starving for someone to serve them. If I were a competitor in Rick's market, I would do something different. I might have "thoughtful news" (McNeil-Lehrer on a local level), the "sports zone," the "business broadcast," "things that matter to families," "news for the north side of town," or *anything* that set me apart and had a substantial potential audience. Not necessarily the biggest audience, but one that would be big enough to justify the investment to serve them.

For years and years, America watched CBS, NBC, and ABC, usually in that order. They all offered us the same mix of national news, sports, situation comedies, and variety shows. None of them ever stepped outside that box or challenged the definition of a network. But today among the world's most valuable networks are CNN, CNBC, ESPN, HBO, and MTV—networks that are each based on a specialty, networks that do one thing and do it well. If one of the original big three had stepped outside the mold years ago and chosen one of these enormous niches, ahead of the upstarts, they might today be much more valuable.

In thinking about being unique, remember that a Class B idea executed with passion and intensity will usually beat a Class A idea executed half-heartedly. Many times, a fundamentally sound idea is badly executed, often inside a large corporation with multiple and changing priorities. But when a dedicated group of people leave the big organization with the idea and devote their energy to it, it works. The folks at the May Company passed on BOOKSTOP because it was not their thing. Sam Walton tried to convince his employers to open small-town discount stores but they would not do it. Of course, it's hard to beat a Class A idea pursued with total intensity (Microsoft, for example).

But when you are pursuing opportunities, trying to find your spot in the world, and don't lose too much sleep if the single best spot is already taken. Most auto races aren't won from the pole position. Pick a really excellent alternative spot and pursue it with all your heart.

Often differentiation will come from seeing the world in a different way. An excellent example is Volvo. Volvo has never in its history sold a car. Instead, Volvo has sold durability and safety. If they had tried to sell mere cars, they would have been demolished by GM, Ford, and Toyota. But instead, they sold something different. Their current ad slogan, "For life," is one of the best positioning lines in the world, perfectly reflecting their two key values. When Volvo thinks about diversifying its product line, maybe they should make padlocks or child-safety seats instead of minivans and SUVs. Because Volvo set themselves apart from the industry, because they built their own uniquely defined niche, they became worth a great deal of money. Ford bought them. Only time will tell as to whether Ford understands what they bought and how to maximize the Volvo brand.

The bigger your market, the greater your opportunity for specialization. If you build cars, you can find a spot like safety or speed. If you sell groceries, you can be a convenience store or a hypermarket, you can be famous for your produce or your bakery. If you are Coke or Pepsi, even a 35 percent market share means a lot of money. If, on the other hand, you are in the thermometer business or the rubber band business, you have more limited choices of strategy. But you still have choices.

The godfathers of the importance of differentiation are two guys named Al Ries and Jack Trout. Twenty years ago they wrote a book titled *Positioning: The Battle for Your Mind.* Last year they issued a twentieth anniversary edition. They have written many other books that extend and apply their principles. While I have seen a lot of marketing books, I am not convinced you need to read many beyond these. Ries and Trout's bottom line is that you should try to own a word in the customer's mind—"Safety" at Volvo, "Overnight" at Federal Express. I reckon if you are the best dry-cleaner in the Bitterroot Valley, you may have to own a phrase rather than a word, but the principle remains the same.

It is also important to understand that each enterprise has a personality. Once more I turn to Southwest Airlines, about which a great deal has been written. One of the most common themes is that the company has a lot of fun. Some enterprises take this as a key ingredient and try to copy it. Like Southwest, they start sending out birthday cards. Maybe like Southwest, they tell more jokes. I can just see a big insurance company telling all their employees, "You have to tell a joke every morning or you're fired." What people miss is that part of Southwest's personality is it orneriness and its "unprofessionalism." Sending birthday cards and telling jokes in midflight fit perfectly. But they might not fit your enterprise. I, for one, hope that Hewlett-Packard stays closer to a bunch of nerdy engineers than that they start laughing all the time. I hope Anheuser-Busch remains deadly serious about "the Brewers' Art."

On the atrium floor at the headquarters of ad agency GSD&M are the words that define the company's character: "Community, Integrity, Restlessness, Freedom and Responsibility, Curiosity, and Winning." Always remember that human enterprises have human attributes. Is your city feisty? Is your magazine opinionated? Is your college immaculate? Is your endeavor gifted?

Hand in hand with being true to your personality is being true to the facts. I remember when Office Depot, an otherwise fine company, was running TV ads to the effect, "Where America buys computers." The typical viewer, especially those who bought computers, did not need to see a market research report to know that Dell, Gateway, and CompUSA were more likely claimants to this title. While Office Depot's marketing people were exhibiting their goals (perhaps wishful thinking) it was not helpful to their cause to make the statement as if it were already accomplished. On the other hand, there was no gap between advertising and reality when, some years ago, Sears advertised, "Where America shops."

In any communication, your marketing is less important than your substance. When I first began studying business more than thirty years ago, Procter & Gamble was viewed as the world's top marketer. They spent more money on national advertising than any other U.S. company, and their ads were famous for their effectiveness. Their product market shares sometimes seemed invincible, and competitors like Colgate and Unilever could only watch with envy.

But a close look at P&G showed that, at its heart, it was not nearly so much a marketing company as it was a research-and-development company. The reason its ads—which were good ads—worked so well was because they were reminding the public about superior products. P&G invented the commercial detergent Tide in the 1940s; they pioneered flouride in toothpaste with Crest in the 1950s. They continue to this day to refine, refine, refine their products—from diapers to quicker-picker-uppers, from cosmetics to mouthwash.

The P&G lesson is an important one to learn: No amount of great advertising will make up for secondary products, bad service, or other broken fundamentals. But if you *do* have a great product, then you need to support it with great marketing.

Marketing is all about communication. Every enterprise, like every person, is the source of a continual flow of signals and communications, of signs, symbols, messages, gestures, and language. Just hang around any office and look at the desks, the walls, the posters—even when we are silent we are always "talking." Each enterprise is continually communicating, whether planned or not, whether thought through or not. Successful enterprises are aware of their communication flow; they think about it, and they think about what it represents to the recipient. They understand how it has the power to set them apart from others, to differentiate them, to position them.

Differentiation Starts with Your Name

Ultimately, the power of your enterprise's name will be what you make of it. In other words, if you have an awful name, you can still build a great business and people will patronize you. If RadioShack can build a multibillion-dollar business with that name, you can do anything with any name. Even names that seem great are often really the result of the value that has been added to them. When we hear the name of Saks Fifth Avenue, we think of luxury and quality. The name Saks originally meant little or nothing to consumers. While Fifth Avenue already had cachet, Saks has probably done more than anyone to spread the international reputation of the avenue by incorporating that street into its name. In short, names themselves do not have overwhelming value; they become what you make of them.

Having said that, I advise that if you are picking the name of an enterprise or product, or considering renaming something, you should at least try to do it right, and that starts with differentiating yourself.

A few months ago I scanned the usual armada of institutional corporate ads in *Business Week*. These enterprises were putting their best foot forward, spending hundreds of thousands of dollars to get in front of decision-makers via these institutional campaigns. It was their one chance to stand out from the crowd. But what did I see?

First, I saw their names: Aether, Allianz, Acxiom, Agillion, Agilent, Adero, and Aventis. Whoops! Who told all these companies that they had to have names that:

(a) were invented

(b) all started with "A"

(c) were one word

(d) were totally indistinguishable from one another

(e) were sometimes unpronounceable?

More shocking to me is the fact that apparently no one else picked up on this, because since then we have seen even more look-alike names, including Accenture and Agere.

Turning further in that same magazine: Genuity, Flooz, Infinium, Neuvis, Interbiz, and Taligent. Then: Rational, Order Fusion, and Ironside. At least those last three are real words. I got off that plane and walked through the Chicago airport to see more ads—again expensive ads—for Dovebid and Razorfish. Today, the favorite target of my friends' jokes is Cingular—they can't even spell!

This may seem like a 1990s marketing nightmare. But we have been here before. The last time around it was initials—AMR, UAL, NL, SBC, and many others. The former Southwestern Bell was and is a fine company. But when it was called Southwestern Bell, it told people something about the business it was in and something about where it came from. Now, as SBC Communications, it is more firmly linked to global corporate nothingness, cut off from its Alexander Graham Bell heritage.

I earlier said that names were not the end-all and be-all. They are a secondary factor. But in a case this perverse, I would guess that the company's name reduces the market value of the company by 2 to 3 percent. Investors see names; people browsing headlines and stock tables see names. SBC isn't going to trigger any reaction in anyone except those who already know the company—and that's not who we aim most of our marketing budget at. If my 2 to 3 percent number is right, I am saying that renaming Southwestern Bell "SBC" is today costing its owners $3 billion to $5 billion. They have earned the other $150 billion in value by building a great company. But why give away $5 billion in a single decision?

Now that I have upset all my friends who work for these many companies, do I have any positive examples to offer? Yes. I think Great Atlantic and Pacific Tea Company was a great name. I prefer names whose pronunciation is obvious, but Chevrolet has worked out. Once in a while we might try naming a company after a person, like H. J. Heinz, Goldman Sachs, or Ben and Jerry's. If I started a new Internet company today, I'd probably name it like a law firm—Kirshbaum, Spain, and Zacharias (to use the names of three of Hoover's board members) would certainly stand out from the rest of the dotcom world.

My observation is that more than 80 percent of all institutional name changes are for the worse. So when do you change your name? California Packing, a giant food canner, changed their name to match their lead brand: Del Monte. Dayton-Hudson, as it evolved from a department chain focused on those two brands, converted to its leading retail name: Target. These were changes that made it easier, not harder, for people to understand the enterprise. Great names score points in both the "clear" and "unique" pillars of a successful vision.

It is hard to beat putting your primary product or service into your name. In starting three companies I named them BOOKSTOP, The Reference Press, and TravelFest. Only after I left day-to-day management of

The Reference Press, which was founded as a business reference-book publisher, did the board change the name to mirror that of the products: Hoover's, Inc.

In the case of naming BOOKSTOP, I first looked at all the existing companies. They all had very English-sounding names. Dalton and Walden were the industry leaders. Next were Barnes & Noble and Crown. I decided that these were ideal names. If there was only one bookstore in the U.S., it should have the most English name—maybe Shakespeare and Company! (Of course, that's the name of a famous English-language bookstore in Paris.) Because *everyone* else had gone that way, we wanted to go another route. I looked for a name more like Target or 7-Eleven. I took a red octagon and put the word "BOOK" above the well-established word "STOP."

Years later people told us what a great name that was; I could only chuckle. Yes, it was a great name if you were desperate to be different.

Differentiating Visually

Your name is your first act of communication, but close behind that is your "look"—the design of your logo and products, the feel of your ads. If you have delivery trucks, if you have a physical presence such as stores or hotels or branch offices, even if you have nothing more than corporate letterhead and envelopes, you have thousands of opportunities to communicate something unique about yourself.

An example is Bloomingdale's, which in the 1970s not only reflected its obsession with trendy fashions in the design of its stores, but also redesigned its shopping bags and even its type style to match the overall feeling. Historically, excellent companies as diverse as cardboard box makers (Container Corporation in the 1960s) and Fortune 500 giants (IBM and Mobil) have made design a priority. While I believe that Apple's ultimate success will depend on the quality and pricing of their products, they were in large part saved from failure in the 1990s by coloring their computers and expressing their "Think different" attitude through great design.

I believe we have gone into an era in which design has fallen off the map at many companies. Our hotels, which are really in the business of selling living space, often fall somewhere between dull and repulsive. Go to New Orleans and compare two hotels on Canal Street that almost face each other—the monolithic slab of the giant Marriott or the completely restored and New Orleans-style Sheraton. Based on my experience, my opinion is that the Marriott is perhaps better run and a better place to stay, but think of the upside if you combine great looks with great operations.

Roadside inns of today are probably less distinctive than the original Holiday Inns of the 1950s and '60s. In so many ways, we have come a long way since the 1950s—our movies have better special effects, our homes have more advanced televisions. But hotel and motel design, especially at mass price points, has not kept up.

There are some organizations that do understand the importance of design. One of the best examples is Target. When I first studied the department store industry in the 1960s, if you went to a party and asked people what stores they found interesting, you would hear names like Bloomingdale's, Burdines, and Bullock's. But today you are more likely to hear Target. This company has hired some of the world's savviest designers, like architect Michael Graves, to design products from teapots to lamps. Upper-end retailers like Crate & Barrel bring this kind of style to the upscale customers, but Target brings it to the masses.

Retail great Gordon Selfridge always stressed the role of design and showmanship, the importance of (in his words) "capturing the public's imagination." This is lifeblood for top companies like Target and Disney. But is has a role in every enterprise. *Especially* if your competitors are missing it, as Apple found out.

Elements of style—naming and designing—are only the first and most superficial aspects of differentiating yourself. The smart enterprise is always looking for ways to stand out. By honestly reflecting the distinctive personality and ambitions of your enterprise, even by celebrating those differences, you can build a unique place in the mind of everyone your enterprise touches.

26

Built to Serve

The first question I ask the leaders of any enterprise is, "Why does this enterprise exist?" Sometimes the leaders of a business will tell me, "This company exists to make a profit." Some companies fill their mission statements with lines like, "Our goal is to make a 12 percent return on investment every year." These are not the right answers. Saying an enterprise exists to make a profit is like saying automobiles exist to get good gas mileage. Automobiles exist to give us mobility, to allow us to move around. Once the automobile was invented and we want to select the best car, then we look at many measures—gas mileage, maintenance cost, crash resistance, expected years of life. Perhaps one measure, like gas mileage, is more important than any other. But it's not the reason for building a car in the first place. It's not the *purpose*.

I have spent many of my years doing financial projections. I have run every type of spreadsheet since VisiCalc, and I have seen every type of return on investment analysis. If you give me the financial statements of two shoe stores, I can spend hours comparing their gross margins, their sales per square foot, their expense ratios. If you give me the numbers on two airlines, I will stay up all night comparing load factors and block hours. These and other numbers are powerful measures that allow us to compare enterprises, to see which ones use their resources well and which ones waste them. But this fascination with numbers does not change the fact that enterprises do not exist for the purpose of being measured.

The only valid reason to the existence of any enterprise, for profit or non-, is to provide products or services to people—to somehow make the world a better place. Enterprises that forget this will soon perish; those that remember, and put it into practice every day, have a chance at long-term survival, even prosperity.

The Power of the Customer: A Lesson from Wall Street

A vivid example is the rise of Wal-Mart. In 1973, fresh from college, I arrived at Citibank's investment management department as a junior securities analyst covering retailing. I loved retailing, having studied it for ten years, and was eager to learn more. At the time, Citibank was one of the biggest institutional stockholders in the nation. I was blessed to have a chance to learn retailing analysis from a veteran analyst, Pete Wetzel. He is one of the few people I ever met who loved and studied retailing as much as I do.

After I had been around a few months, Pete took me into his office and said, "Gary, the bosses here have given me a budget to bring in a summer intern to study some small industry segment. Do you think we should bring one in to look at the small regional discount store chains?"

At the time, our retail investments were concentrated in the stocks of the three industry giants—Sears, JCPenney, and Kmart. Far behind these industry leaders was a pack of little companies with funny names like ShopKo, Kuhn's Big K, Wal-Mart, Mohr-Value, Caldor, and Alco-Duckwall. None of them did more than $150 million a year in sales, which was a pittance compared with the established giants. Even Montgomery Ward and Woolworth's dwarfed these little regional chains.

Pete and I, "the best and the brightest," decided, No, it would not be worth the time (even of a summer intern) to look at these little outfits. After all, how could any of them survive against the giants? We *knew* that if any of them ever ventured from their small-town, regional bases into the big cities, Sears and Kmart would annihilate them. Our money was safer with the big names, the proven winners.

Of course, over time, Citibank (and every other major investor) changed its tune. In 2000 Wal-Mart made a profit of $6.3 billion on sales of $193 billion. In the same year Sears, Kmart, and JCPenney combined earned $394 million on sales of $111 billion. Kmart and JCPenney lost money, with only Sears making a profit. Wal-Mart today has more than 1.1 million employees, more than three times as many as any other U.S. company. Upwards of 230,000 new jobs were created by the company in the past year alone. They have risen to the uppermost levels of the Fortune 500.

How could we, the best and brightest, have been so wrong?

Try to look back through our intensely analytical 1973 eyes. Do a balance sheet comparing Sears (then the industry leader) and Wal-Mart:

- Who paid their executives the most? Sears.

- Who had the best consultants? Sears.

- Who had the most invested in technology? Sears.

- Who had the best human-resources team? Sears.

- Who had the most experience? Sears.

- Who paid less for their real estate? Sears.

- Who paid less for the merchandise they carried? Sears.

- Who had a better-established brand name? Sears.

- Who had the best and most visible locations? Sears.

- Who had the support of Wall Street and the investment bankers? Sears.

You could go on and on with this list, and you'd be hard-pressed to find a *single* advantage in Wal-Mart's favor in 1973.

But of course, they did indeed have an advantage. To illustrate, let me invent a little fiction:

One sunny spring Monday in the 1970s, the leaders of Sears were at a Wall Street conference. Their private jet awaited them at Teterboro Airport to fly them back to the Sears Tower, a monument to corporate power. They were smart people, hard-working people, nice people. (I know that, because I did meet the Sears people.) Their CEO, an attorney, opened a bottle of champagne and proposed a toast: "To the biggest retailer on earth. We have huge market shares. We employ more people than any other retailer. We are going to take on the residential real estate industry by buying Coldwell Banker. We are going to take on the stock brokerage industry by buying Dean Witter. We are going to build Sears stores around the world!"

Everyone at the meeting seconded the toast. Everyone was happy. Sears was at the height of its power and the future looked bright.

But Sears had forgotten one thing: that the decisions that matter are not made in meetings with accountants and lawyers, on Wall Street or in the board room. The decisions that matter are made on the selling floor, by customers with cash or credit cards at the ready. If there are any meetings that matter most, they are meetings with clerks and assistant managers.

Sears perhaps could have been allowed a slip here and a slip there except for the fact that, on that same sunny day, Sam Walton drove his truck into Poteau, Oklahoma, site of an early Wal-Mart. He walked into the store. He picked up a bag of Dog Chow and said, "Someone could trip over this! We need to put it in a neat pile." He looked at the price and saw $4.99. He said, "I just came from the supermarket, and they have this same bag for $4.49! We can't let them make liars out of our low-price philosophy." Then Sam—also a nice guy, a smart guy, a hard-working guy— headed toward the employee break room to have coffee with the stockboys, to learn what their frustrations were, what their aspirations were.

While I have invented this story, it is an accurate description of how Wal-Mart conquered Sears. Sears, run for more than seventy years by merchants, was now run by lawyers and others far removed from the fray. Wal-Mart was still run by a lowly shopkeeper. Sears began to serve Wall Street; Wal-Mart served Main Street. Everything Sam Walton knew he had learned from the likes of Richard Sears, J. C. Penney, and Harry Cunningham (the inventor of Kmart). Sam was not pioneering a new economy; Sam was focused on the most basic of basics. Sam was focused on the customer. And even the great Sears, Roebuck & Company, with all its assets, with all its brains, with all its accumulated market power, could not stop a force so great as Sam Walton and his organization. Because Sears had taken its eye off the ball.

This same kind of story could be told of General Motors, of IBM, of AT&T, of some of our largest banks. This same story will be told in the future, in industry after industry. In retailing, the story will again be told when Wal-Mart becomes satisfied with its success and deludes itself to believe that power rests in the hands of board members, or Wall Street, or top management. And some younger, more entrepreneurial retailer will come along and unseat Wal-Mart to become the new "largest retailer in the world."

The irony is that as long as Wal-Mart understands their own vulnerability, the company will probably remain on top. The moment they believe they are on top to stay, they will begin the long fall from the top. Study Wal-Mart, Microsoft, and Southwest Airlines and you will find companies that compete with the intensity of struggling startups, despite their enormous success.

It is virtually impossible to overstate the power of the customer. The U.S. Post Office long held a monopoly on deliveries to our home. For some transactions, you had to be home at the right time, or go to the post office on their terms. Their managers felt they had a monopoly that would last forever. But the customer was not being well served, and Federal Express and UPS filled the gap.

Even laws change if enough people want them to change. Thirty years ago, it was illegal to shop on Sunday in many states. It was a violation of the law to discount prescription drugs or eyeglasses in most states. Lotteries and casino gambling were illegal in forty-nine states; today one or both is legal in forty-eight states.

When I was growing up in the 1960s, few people imagined that the Cold War between the Soviet Empire and the capitalist West would ever end. But ultimately, as people behind the Iron Curtain began to get CNN on satellite, as they began to realize that people in Western Europe and the U.S. had access to things like toothpaste and color television, they decided that they, too, wanted a piece of the pie. Leaders like Mikhail Gorbachev jumped on a trend that was well under way, a trend that reflected the power of the consumer, even behind the Iron Curtain.

The only rule is that customers always get what they want. It is just a matter of who gives it to them and when.

Service as Purpose

I've already described the power of a clear and consistent vision to inspire people. Nothing is more motivational than doing something that you think is worth doing. For most people, the key inspirational ingredient in a vision is its stated desire to make the world a better place, to serve others.

Last year, I visited the Department of Transportation in Washington to get more data on the airline industry. I walked into the office on a Friday afternoon and it appeared that half the people had already gone home. I asked around to find what I was looking for, got a few shrugs, and finally was pointed to the man who would know. He said, "Oh yeah, we have that stuff, or most of it. It's back here in this room somewhere. Nobody ever looks at it. We used to print copies and sell them, but our budgets were cut, so you have to copy these. You can make copies on that copier over there. It costs a dime a page."

The books were piled around, not in good order, but I could find most of them with some digging. The copier, which didn't look much used, was out of change, and I didn't have fifty dimes. I went from desk to desk begging for dimes; I finally found one lady with lots of dimes, and I was a happy guy. I stood and copied dusty old reports for three hours, as the rest of the workforce drifted out of the office. By five P.M., only one was left, awaiting my departure.

At first, I felt the classic response of an offended taxpayer: these folks were being paid to sit around and do little, to produce reports mandated by law; they worked as little as they had to, and left as soon as they could. Another government boondoggle, I thought. But then I thought a little more about the people I had met. Ultimately, they were no different from the people at Nordstrom's or at BOOKSTOP. They were normal people trying to make a living. What was missing from the DOT was not well-meaning people; it was a reason for excellence. If no one ever wanted your work, if all your efforts went into dusty piles, would you give your best work, would you stay late? We *need* a purpose, we *need* to be useful to someone.

People need to know that their work matters. Kinko's founder Paul Orfalea continually pointed out to his copy-shop employees that they were helping people announce birthday parties, spread the word on neighborhood festivals, or find lost dogs. Herb Kelleher reminds the people of Southwest that they are helping people get to graduations, to weddings, to be at the side of loved ones who are sick. So often, we go about our business and we forget that we, too, are doing something important. Something that is valued by others. Something that helps others.

At the best of enterprises, this sense of mission becomes almost a religion. Occasionally I have dinner with John Mackey, who founded Whole Foods Market, the nation's largest natural-foods chain. When I first met John, he was pushing grocery carts for the grand opening of his second store (next door to my first). Today Whole Foods does about $2 billion in annual sales, and John is a multimillionaire. But what does he say as soon as we sit down to dinner? He says, "Gary I can't believe you're still drinking that Coca-Cola. That sugar water has zero nutritional value!" Here is a man who went into this business because of his passionate belief in healthy eating. He is still in the business for the same reason, as are most of his eighteen thousand employees.

Southwest Airlines, Nordstrom, and the Container Store are just a few of the other organizations where people behave as if they were on a mission of great importance, a mission based on service.

In all these organizations, you will find workers, from bottom to top, who believe it is *a great privilege to have the opportunity to serve others.* It is the very best possible use of their time and energy. These are not people who think that serving others is beneath themselves. You will not find people who are eager to move up the ladder so they no longer have to wait on people. You *will* find people who always look behind themselves when they go through a door, to make sure the door is not closing in someone else's face. You will find people who always thank other service providers, from waiters to flight attendants. To state it bluntly, these are the people who tell someone at the restaurant when they use the last paper towel in the bathroom.

Service-oriented people, like their leaders, understand that serving is a priority. That other things must come second. Many people today are in heads-down mode, working away on the task at hand, impervious to what is going on around them. The server is always in heads-up mode, always scanning for new ways to serve people. Finishing the report to the boss comes after dealing with the upset customer. Unloading the new arrivals in the back of the bookstore comes after helping at the registers to speed up the lines. Cleaning up the fast-food counter comes after wiping up the spill on which someone might slip. Clocking out comes after announcing on the loudspeaker that someone left their lights on in the parking lot.

Whatever a service person sees, he or she immediately asks, "How will this affect others? How can I take a step that will make life better for other people?" These are people who *care*. They get genuine satisfaction from helping others achieve their goals.

How do you find such people? You must go beyond the résumé and look into their eyes, into their heart. There is a supermarket here in Austin called Central Market by HEB, which is renowned for its outstanding service. If you get in line and realize you have forgotten something, someone on the staff will rush up and say, "No, stay right there, I'll get it for you!"

I met an executive of this store, and asked, "How do you find such great people?" He said it was simple. Every week, they invite applicants to a meeting at their offices, and they put them all in a room with the application forms. They then say, "Our chief of recruiting is a little late, please make yourself at home for a while." Then they watch. The people who fill out their forms and then sit quietly, awaiting the recruiter, are not hired. The people who finish their forms, then turn to the stranger next to them and start talking to them, asking about them, are taken to the next level of interviews.

Central Market first looks for people who care, then looks at résumés. Shared values precede "relevant experience."

I believe that the customer must always come first. They are the reason we are in business, they are the ones we are here to serve. Some of my favorite leaders, including Herb Kelleher at Southwest and Richard Branson at Virgin, espouse a slightly different approach. They claim that *employees* ought to come first. My observation is that every *successful* enterprise that says their employees come first is an enterprise that first selects new hires based on their desire to serve others. Once such employees are on board, these organizations reflect their people-centered nature by putting their employees on a pedestal. They know that one of the best ways to build great service is to have a happy workforce. But it starts with service-oriented people.

"Service First" Means "Other Things Second"

Of course, virtually every company gives lip service to the importance of the customer. Most mission statements talk about serving the customer. But in fact, most companies make their decisions based on what accounting says they can do, what is the easiest procedure to train people in, what their systems allow them to do, what the lawyers tell them to do, or any of a thousand other ways of setting priorities. But the enterprises that survive and prosper the longest always start by asking, "What is best for our customers?"

More than once, the embryonic BOOKSTOP was low on cash. We were working our way toward profitability; we were expanding; we were stretched thin. We might have $100,000 in the bank after payroll but

$300,000 in bills due. Many of our publisher suppliers would have to wait until after Christmas, our big season, to be brought current. But how do you decide which publishers get the $100,000? Was it the publishers who were calling the most often or screaming the loudest? Was it the publisher who had spent the most time kibitzing with the accounting clerk? Was it the publisher who had bought the most lunches for the buyer? Or the publisher who knew the CEO the best?

No, we sat down each Monday morning and figured out which payments would do the most for our customers. Which publishers had bestsellers that our customers were asking for? Which subjects in the store were most depleted, and which publishers should be paid first in order to correct the situation?

One time some computer consultants were visiting us, and I asked how much they could speed up our cash-register process. They said, "For ten thousand dollars you can get only a ten-second improvement per transaction. So of course you won't want to do that."

I said, "Hold on. Have you ever been the tenth person in line at the register on a Saturday afternoon? The one minute and forty seconds that you would save that person is like a lifetime. Of course, let's spend the ten thousand dollars."

When I started in retailing, the giant retailers used their computers to do accounting and a multitude of other "back office functions." At the beginning of BOOKSTOP, with very limited resources ($350,000 total for building and inventorying the first store, advertising, and payroll), we did our payroll and our books manually. We hand-wrote all of our checks. But, even at the beginning, we maintained a computerized inventory system, because that affected the lives of our customers. Go to most great retailers, and see how little they spend on executive offices compared with what they spend on their stores. They know where their bread is buttered.

GATEWAYS

Further Readings on Strategy and Marketing

Of course, there are a million books on business strategy. And nine hundred thousand of them get tangled up in buzzwords and diagrams full of buzzwords. The work of Al Ries and Jack Trout makes real world sense. They may be their own best example of building an enterprise out of one position, as they have cranked out dozens of books extending the same basic theme. And others have jumped on their bandwagon. While most bookstores put these books under "marketing," I believe their ideas are at the core of overall business strategy. In addition to studying the "Ries and Trout school," there are also ideas of merit in the many other approaches to strategy; some basic books in those areas are listed as well. One interesting book that does not fit neatly into any category is *The End of Marketing As We Know It,* by Sergio Zyman, the Coca-Cola wizard who thinks in his own patterns.

Ries and Trout and Related Books

Positioning: The Battle for Your Mind, by Al Ries and Jack Trout is the classic. My favorites among more recent books are *The Power of Simplicity: A Management Guide to Cutting Through the Nonsense and Doing Things Right,* by Jack Trout; *Differentiate or Die: Survival in Our Era of Killer Competition,* by Jack Trout; and *Focus: The Future of Your Company Depends on It,* by Al Ries. Other relevant books include *Identity Is Destiny: Leadership and the Roots of Value Creation,* by Laurence D. Ackerman, which focuses on the concept of being true to yourself; and *The Power of Focus: How to Hit Your Business, Personal, and Financial Targets with Absolute Certainty,* by Jack Canfield, Mark Victor Hansen, and Les Hewitt, in which the *Chicken Soup for the Soul* guys take on clarity—and hit the mark. Jesper Kunde's *Corporate Religion* and Harry Beckwith's *Selling the Invisible: A Field Guide to Modern Marketing* contain more stimulating ideas along the same tracks.

Academic Strategists

The best book that compares all the different strategy theories is *Strategy Safari: A Guided Tour Through the Wilds of Strategic Management,* by Henry Mintzberg, Bruce Ahlstrand, and Joseph Lampel. Other concise overviews include *What Is Strategy—and Does It Matter?,* by Richard Whittington, and *Strategy and the Business Landscape: Core Concepts,* by Pankaj Ghemawat. Kees Van Der Heijden's *Scenarios: The Art of Strategic Conversation* is also worth picking up. Despite the corporate speak of "paradigms" and all that, this book includes a lot of the most important questions to ask and how to ask them. The author once ran Shell Oil's highly regarded "scenario planning" efforts. In an unusual approach for an academic, *All the Right Moves: A Guide to Crafting Breakthrough Strategy,* by Constantinos C. Markides, starts with customers instead of competitive economics. And *Leading the Revolution,* by Gary Hamel—one of the leading proponents of the "rapid change" school of thought—is always provocative.

Business Thinkers Who Realize It Is More Than Just Money

If Aristotle Ran General Motors: The New Soul of Business and *True Success: A New Philosophy of Excellence,* by Tom Morris, are brief and full of straightforward, excellent real-world thinking from a philosopher. Parallel thinking from someone who has built a company can be found in Tom Chappell's *The Soul of a Business: Managing for Profit and the Common Good.* And *King of Clubs: Grow Rich in More Than Money,* by Robert H. Dedman, is a great story by one of the real thinking, curious, liberal-arts billionaires. Finally, *Servant Leadership: A Journey into the Nature of Legitimate Power and Greatness,* by Robert K. Greenleaf, is a kind of quirky book by a very bright fellow.

On service, try *Discovering the Soul of Service,* by Leonard L. Berry, the professor who thinks like a merchant—Bless his soul.

27

Keeping Your Eye on the Customer

As I have worked in and with many companies, I often see them overfocusing on the competition or on outside factors. Being a lifelong learner and observer, I have always kept up with the competition. When I was in the bookstore business, I was in the competitors' stores at least weekly. At minimum, I wanted to know what they were doing wrong, how we could differentiate our company, and maybe spot a potential new employee. But, even with all that scanning, most great enterprises are ultimately introverted.

The idea is simple: If you just take care of the customers you have today, if you focus on the people walking in your door, ringing your phone, or buying on your Web site, you will be on the route to success. If you figure out how to keep these customers happy, how to convert the unhappy customers into happy ones, if you can turn all of them into advocates rather than mere customers, if you can get them to tell their friends, if you can get them to stay longer and buy more, you will have it made. We spend so much time and energy on attracting new customers, but often the most direct route to prosperity is by asking our existing customers, "What else could I do for you? What else do you need?"

Continuous improvement is another key idea. I have consulted for some companies that spend enormous energy looking at the competition and trying to figure how to outsmart them. But if these same companies instead said, "What do we do right and how can we do it even better?" they would be way ahead. How can we reduce the wait time on our phones? How can we reduce the delivery time? How we can we lose fewer pieces of luggage? Looking at your strengths, at your own personality, and making the most of them is critical to building a great enterprise.

One of my favorite stories is that of Continental Airlines. In the 1970s and '80s, they were the talk of Wall Street. Empire builder Frank Lorenzo, a brilliant man, bought Eastern, People Express, and Frontier and consolidated them with his Continental and Texas International (formerly Trans-Texas, or "Tree Tops") Airlines. In this era, Continental expanded aggressively to Europe, and developed big hubs in Cleveland and Newark. The company made the front pages of the *Wall Street Journal* frequently. But the company also made two complete roundtrips through bankruptcy court. Eventually, Lorenzo, embroiled in bitter battles with employees, was driven out of the industry. Maybe he wasn't quite smart enough.

Some investors bought Continental when it was down on its back, its stock cheap. At the time, they appeared the greatest of fools. But they hired a fellow named Gordon Bethune to run the company. Bethune now tells how he did not realize what a mess things were until he arrived at Houston headquarters, and how he gave serious thought to immediately packing up his bags and heading home. But instead he gave it a shot.

He found that flight delays were costing the line millions of dollars a year (to pay for hotels and alternate flights). So he told his people, "I will pay each of you a bonus every time that we are one of the top airlines in on-time departures." These bonuses were small—between fifty and one hundred dollars. But soon his airline was consistently among the top three, sometimes first.

Bethune saw that employee absences were costing the line dearly. So he took every employee who did not miss a day of work for six straight months and put their name in a hat. Every six months, he drew some names out and gave them Jeeps. Gordon Bethune ignored Wall Street. He put all his energy into making the planes fly on time, into not losing baggage, and into treating customers right. Today Continental consistently wins awards for being the best long-haul airline (Southwest usually wins the honors for shorter flights). So far in 2001, Continental and Southwest are the only major U.S. airlines to make a profit. Bethune has written the company's remarkable story in his book *From Worst to First.*

If most companies merely took their present customer base and focused on them, looked at how to serve them better, how to get them to tell their friends and attract more customers, most companies would not have to look elsewhere for business. As Amazon and other New Economy companies have found, the great expense is attracting new customers. Customer acquisition cost has become one of the most closely watched statistics at any company. These new customers are the expensive ones. Once you have a customer, it is worth your while to do everything you can to keep them, to make them even happier. And yet many enterprises, certainly most of the retailers I am familiar with, do not know how many times you have been in their store, how much you have spent over months or years of shopping with them, or how much you might spend during the rest of your life if they keep you happy.

Flying High Versus Staying Close to the Ground

"Whenever you get confused, go to the store.
The customer has all the answers."
—SAM WALTON, AS QUOTED ON A CORRIDOR WALL AT
GSD&M (WAL-MART'S AD AGENCY)

Knowing and serving your customers starts with being close to them—at the lowest level.

It is so easy to get caught up in the clouds. It can be exhilarating to sponsor the Olympics, to get a good seat at a NASCAR race, to throw a party for customers where Bill Cosby gives a speech, or to ride in a private jet. And it can be hard work to sit down and talk to real customers, to visit them on their turf, to listen to their agonies, to help them solve their problems. And yet virtually every great leader spends disproportionate amounts of their time with customers—small customers, big customers, any customers.

When I was first learning the retail business as a buyer at the old Sanger-Harris (Dallas) division of Federated Department Stores, all buyers were required to be on the selling floor helping customers during the noon hour. This was not a put-it-in-a-memo-and-hope-someone-does-it kind of thing. The chief merchant (a title second only to God in a retail company) came storming through the buyers' offices—all of them—every day at 11:50 barking like a drill sergeant: "Almost noon! Time to hit the floor! Double time! Double time! All hands on deck!"

In those days, Federated was the envy of its peers (the Bloomingdale's division even made the cover of *Time* magazine). The company was run as a group of independent store divisions, each led by a chairman who was all-powerful in that division. If they made their goals, they kept their jobs. If they didn't make their goals, they were replaced. In the interim, corporate stayed out of their way. Corporate CEO Ralph Lazarus only visited each division once a year, in a formal, preannounced visit. He kept out of your store, and out of your hair, the other 364 days.

I had just arrived at Sanger-Harris (now called Foley's) when our "Lazarus day" came around. Keep in mind that not only was Lazarus CEO, he was the leader of the founding family, a retail industry icon. As the parade of execs came through the store to my department (books, of course) I stood like a rank private at attention. Our local chairman, Don Stone, introduced me to Mr. Lazarus and I said hello, trying not to show my sweating. I hung on every word that Lazarus uttered, and expected Stone to do the same. But, halfway through one of Lazarus's profound sentences, Stone started moving away, saying to Lazarus and me, "Excuse me a second." He moved through the stacks of books toward a lady customer no one had noticed. No one except Don Stone. After helping her find the book she was looking for, he came back and turned to Lazarus and politely said, "As you were saying . . . ?"

I was now really sweating bullets. I was thinking, Stone has insulted the most powerful man in the department store industry. I was sure to have a new boss by Monday. Maybe I had witnessed the beginning of Armageddon. But did Lazarus fire Stone? No, he promoted Stone, who went on to bigger and bigger things with Federated, peaking at Corporate Vice-Chairman.

What I learned that day, which I have never forgotten, was what is most important. It was something that both Ralph Lazarus and Don Stone instinctively knew—and wanted to teach the new guy—that the person with all the power is that lady looking for that book. Without her, we are all for naught.

It is a continual struggle to stay in touch with real customers, to make sure we operate in the real environment rather than from some ivory tower or lofty peak. The airlines devote great energy to "airside" (seating in the airplane, inflight services) but tend to ignore "landside" (baggage handling, airport parking, check-in process). Banks run elaborate national ad campaigns, but their ATM's don't work. Coca-Cola, on the other hand, keeps running great TV ads, but they also know that their trucks and their vending machines are communications opportunities closer to where the buying decision is made.

One Detail at a Time

"God is in the details."

—TRADITIONAL SAYING, MADE FAMOUS BY ARCHITECT
LUDWIG MIES VAN DER ROHE

A couple of years ago, there was a lot or malarkey going around that you could build a brand overnight. People pointed to Amazon.com (which *was* built quickly, though not overnight) and figured they could run a few ads on the Super Bowl and become a household word. However, unless they wanted to be known in every household as a laughingstock, this did not work.

The reality is that brands and reputations are built very slowly, one customer at a time, one transaction at a time, one experience at a time. All the ads in the world will not tell as many people about your enterprise as their friends and relatives will. And their friends and relatives will spread your reputation, good or bad.

Building your business, serving people, depends first and foremost on paying attention to details. When I was in the book business, I would often visit the two chains that then dominated the industry—B. Dalton and Waldenbooks. In any given year I might find the stores of one chain terribly messy, with books all over the floor. While a first reaction might be to say they had bad store managers, it was more likely they had bad *management*. Management that was too busy in retreats or meeting with lawyers or accountants or each other to hang out in the stores. When I go into a Target store, I can tell from the incredible attention to detail that the CEO of Target lives in his stores. When I tour Disney World, I can tell that management at the very highest level *cares* about every detail of the parks.

An acquaintance told me of being interviewed by Microsoft. They had flown to Seattle the night before the interview. In the morning, the Microsoft person asked, "How was your flight? Is the hotel okay? What did you think of the alarm clock?" What did you think of the alarm clock! Microsoft asks questions like this one because they want to know, "Do you pay attention to details? Do these things matter to you?"

At the other extreme, when I last shopped for a new car, in 1993, I took a look at the new Cadillacs. Here was a car with a great transmission and a great engine, but no lower back support (standard even on cheaper Japanese cars) and no good place to store coins (don't they have parking meters in Detroit?). Until some of those engineers get out and live in one of their cars, I don't think I'll buy one.

Amazon is seen as a great company for building its brand and revolutionizing the way books are sold. But anyone who has spent lots of money at Amazon (as I have) knows that this company is built on nothing fancier than inventory availability coupled with outstanding, detail-obsessed customer service.

I went into a beautiful new retail complex in San Francisco called Metreon. It's a brainchild of Sony and is anchored by one of their product showcase stores. I admired the beautiful fixtures and the plentiful, helpful staff. I saw all the latest that Sony had to offer. I selected one of their little digital pocket recorders so I could record ideas when I travel. I picked the most powerful one they made. The plentiful clerks told me they didn't have any in stock. I asked, "Where can I find one?" They suggested the Circuit City store two blocks away. I went there. No one knew about the Sony units, and I bought an Olympus recorder instead.

All that beauty, all that investment, but no one was into inventory control.

I had heard from my friends that Singapore Airlines was the best airline for business trips to Asia. They always flew business class, so I did the same on my first trip. But a few years later I was flying coach and found out what really separated this airline—they treated you as well in coach as other airlines did in first class. Even the food and video system were outstanding. Unlike some U.S. carriers, you didn't overhear flight attendants joking about having to work "the back of the plane where the Clampetts are." ("Clampetts" is an unflattering airline term for the non-frequent-flyer masses, taken from the old *Beverly Hillbillies* TV show.)

How easy is it to open your package? How strong is your shopping bag? How far is it from the parking lot to the door? How wide are your aisles, how high are your shelves, how slick is your floor? Can people understand your instructions? Can they read the labels on the buttons on the electronic gadget you make? How will our aging population like your latest innovation? How simple is your credit application? How complex is your voice-mail system? Do your Web pages download fast? Do they print out on a single page of paper?

Are you willing to make sacrifices for the benefit of the customer? Most convenience stores and fast-food restaurants profit greatly from "selling their soul" to either Coke or Pepsi. So why did 7-Eleven opt to offer both products in its fountain, running an ad campaign saying "It's your choice" and boldly going where no one else would go? After years of drug stores telling themselves, "Let's keep people waiting twenty minutes for prescriptions, and put prescriptions at the back of the store, so people will buy more," why did Walgreen's break rank and start putting drive-through prescription windows in every store they could? Does your organization have this kind of courage?

Details are everything. There is nothing in the way you deliver your product or service to your customers that does not matter. The CEO's desk doesn't matter, the corporate jet doesn't matter, the latest Power-Point presentation doesn't matter, unless it somehow makes life better or more interesting for your customer.

A Hearty Story

Perhaps my favorite illustration comes from an unusual company called Build-A-Bear Workshop. An old friend of mine, Maxine Clark, of St. Louis, started this company. A few years ago she called me up and said, "I am thinking about leaving the world of big retail corporations and starting my own store. I wanted to see what you thought of my idea. I want to have a shop where people can come in and build their own teddy bear." I think I told Maxine that it sounded like a small market to me, I didn't know if it would work, but wished her luck.

Next thing I know, she has twenty-plus stores (fifty-plus by the time you read this) and is the talk of the industry. So I figure I better get into one of her workshops and see what I had missed in my initial take on her business idea.

I went into the store and found a fascinating process that totally involved kids or their parents. You choose the body, the clothes, and even a pair of eyeglasses for your bear. You stuff it. You choose its name. You go to a computer and print its birth certificate (which is always on file, so if your bear is ever lost and returned to one of the stores, they can find you). I was getting pretty excited, realizing how much more involved the concept was, how much more *involving* it was, than I had ever imagined.

But then I came to the heart department. Here, you chose one of a variety of hearts. The heart goes inside the stuffing, never to be seen again. Why on earth would any rational person want to put something in there, pay good money for it, that no one would ever see? Because this was not about rationality, this was about the total experience of creating your own Teddy Bear. And my friend Maxine (now Chief Executive Bear) and her colleagues had felt that no detail was too small to pay attention to. Certainly not the heart of your bear.

The Value Formula

Let me close this section with a quick review of what really does matter in any product or service. Unlike what some believe, it is not the price, it is not the quality, it is not service. It is the total package. I call it the value formula, which looks like this:

$$VALUE = \frac{Quality + Other\ Factors*}{Price}$$

$$* = Convenience,\ Selection,\ Service,\\ Experience,\ Information \ldots$$

Again I go back to the airline industry. I was at a conference where Continental's Bethune sat on the dais with Southwest's Kelleher. One of the most interesting questions posed was, "Why has Southwest been so successful, while all attempts to copy it have failed?" Kelleher gave many of the reasons I have already described, such as no frills and happy employees. But Bethune, looking in from the outside (and running one of the airlines that had tried and failed to copy Southwest before his arrival) had a different take. He said, "Everyone looks at Southwest and thinks the secret is low fares. They ignore the on-time record, the lack of lost bags. People first and foremost want safe, reliable air travel."

As you have probably gathered, I admire Wal-Mart as much as anyone. But one sad side effect on the rest of the retail industry has been an obsession with price. Low prices, which is indeed the Wal-Mart mantra, is only part of a successful formula. The role it plays depends on your store and your customer. Wal-Mart's cost cutting carries the corollary that the stores have to be pretty bare bones. At one point there was a huge wave of sporting goods superstores that spread across America, including Austin. These companies took something as exciting and evocative as athletics and stripped it of all its appeal, adopting Wal-Mart-style flooring, lighting, and overall plainness. Within a couple of years, most of them were closed.

By contrast, Target realized that the best way to compete with Wal-Mart was not to copy them but to differentiate—in their case largely through store and product design.

When Austin-based Dell Computer first started up, I was sure they would fail. What industry could be tougher than computer hardware? Surely the industry giants (led by IBM) would put them out of business. As the years went by, I kept hearing people say, "Dell computers are really inexpensive." Having bought my first personal computer from RadioShack in 1980, I've seen plenty of ads for computers saying "Ours are the cheapest." It struck me that a low-price strategy would be the easiest to copy. I became even more convinced that Dell would not survive.

But then I started reading new comments in the computer magazines, things like "Dell is fastest of those tested" and "Dell has the best service and support of those we examined." And my friends stopped saying, "Dell is the cheapest" and started saying, "Dell is the best value." And they have not stopped saying it.

My last five computers have been Dells. Arch-competitor (and former industry leader) Compaq just announced they are not going to focus on hardware in the future, moving instead toward software and services. It appears they think that fighting E.D.S. and Oracle will be easier than competing with Dell.

What goes into the value formula differs with each industry, with each company, even with different customer types. There is a different set of details if you are selling jets to British Air compared to the formula for selling Dairy Queen to Middletown. But there is always a value formula, and there is always a mix of things that go into it.

One of the most common mistakes is to forget that what the customer receives is not just a single item, but a combination of factors, a soup. It is not the salt or the vegetables alone that makes great stew, it is the combination. Too often I have seen a retail store drop a product line because it was unprofitable. But the most profitable retail chains usually have at least some loss leaders. Does *Time* magazine really know the exact value of having an obituary section? Do people pick up the *Chicago Tribune* only for the sports scores?

In the same manner, it is a mistake to believe that each transaction must stand on its own. The person who comes into your bookstore today and stands and reads a book for twenty minutes, then puts it back on the shelf, may tomorrow bring in a friend who buys five hundred dollars' worth of books. The man who has been kicking Ferrari tires for six months may complete that real estate sale next week and walk in with a half million dollars in cash. In reality, we often do not make much money on any given transaction. But over the lifetime of a good relationship with a customer, we can earn a lot of money. Ask McDonald's if you can get rich five dollars at a time.

Each day brings new headlines and new books that claim that business is being revolutionized by this or that innovation. But a careful look at the success of the greats, and the failure of the not so greats, lets us know that *nothing that really matters changes* in business. The technologies come and go, new advertising media come and go, but what matters today is what mattered to the leaders of enterprises fifty years ago and five hundred years ago—knowing your customers, caring about their needs and desires, and working around the clock to anticipate and meet those needs and desires.

This remains true today whether you run Wal-Mart, Harvard, or the local luncheonette.

28

Vision for Enterprises Old and New

Let's take a few pages and look at some real-world issues: how you choose a vision for a new enterprise and how you create a new vision for an old enterprise, especially if that established enterprise lacks a clear vision.

New Ideas and the Customer: The Creation of New Products, Services, and Companies

While I have studied more companies (thousands) than I have created (three), I have dreamed up hundreds of ideas in order to get to those three. Of those three, two worked and one did not. I have spent more hours working on the creation of new businesses than I have studying other businesses. I have a long list of new business ideas at all times. This is a very tricky pursuit, one that is in vogue right now (that's good) but one about which there are a lot of myths (that's bad).

Look for example at all the people in recent years who have wanted to start "Internet companies." These include many of my friends and neighbors. People who want to start Internet companies or operations usually have one of three mindsets:

1. My neighbor or someone in an article got rich on the Internet, and I want to get rich, too.

2. My competitor has a website, so I should, too.

3. I have a burning desire to improve industry X, and the Internet is a great tool for doing so.

People motivated in the first two ways will likely be disappointed. If they have enough money and patience, they may survive the intense process that is a startup business. However, the people who are most likely to succeed are those who see the Net as a tool to serve customers, to meet real needs. If you have always wanted a better way to buy and sell used cars, or a better way to offer insurance, then the Internet might be the right tool for you. Hoover's is a company with an intense desire to offer people information about companies—accurate, interesting, affordable. The books in which we first offered our company profiles could not be timely; the Internet can, so that's where most of our energy goes today.

I am always looking at business plans, helping people evaluate their new concepts. Too often I hear things like:

- The venture capitalists told me this kind of idea is what they'd like to back.

- The stock market really loves companies like this.

- I think I can create this company and Intel or Cisco will want to buy it in a couple of years.

- I will create this company so it's a thorn in Home Depot's side and they will have to buy us out.

- I will create this company that will not generate revenue but it will get a lot of buzz so someone will want to buy it out.

- I have assembled a great team of people, so the idea does not matter that much.

- We have the cleverest name you have ever heard, and wait till you see our great logo!

All of these paths, and more like them, are dead ends. Because there is only one valid reason to start a business. No surprise here: the only valid reason is to provide goods or services to people. The most compelling explanation I have ever heard of how to dream up businesses is also the first one I heard: *Find a need and fill it.*

So where do you look for opportunities for new ideas, whether that be a new product or division, or a whole new company? Here are some of the most basic approaches, which can often be used in combination.

- Copy an existing idea into a new geographical territory. Every day, someone somewhere on earth seems to start a local version of eBay. I met the prosperous fellow who introduced "tilt-wall" construction methods in Australia, having seen them in the U.S.

- Copy an existing idea from one industry to another. When I first saw Toys "R" Us and read their annual reports, I knew their idea could be adapted to almost any category of merchandise. I picked books.

- Chain it up. Many industries remain highly fragmented, dominated by independent companies. B. Dalton's and Walden Books were the first chain bookstores. Walgreen's, Whelan's, and Rexall did it in the drugstore business. Quality Courts began to pull together independent motels; Best Western and Holiday Inn took the concept to the next level. Service Corporation of America went around buying up local funeral homes, and Coach USA consolidated local charter bus companies. Today this approach is often called the "rollup."

- Brand an unbranded field. Disposable pens were made into a branded item by Bic. Power tools were not seriously branded outside Sears before Black & Decker rose to prominence. Today even miniblinds are branded, and some of our most powerful brands grace the once-lowly sneaker.

- Split things into finer specialization. We have had sporting goods stores for a long time, but only in recent years have bicycle stores, outdoor stores, fishing stores, and running-shoe stores come to the fore. We had general TV networks for many years before we had news, sports, and old-movie networks.

- Make a dramatic breakthrough in a business or improve the way things are done. Hoover's changed the way business information is distributed. Kmart took the discount store approach to retailing first pioneered by New York's E. J. Korvette and others, and "perfected" it. Wal-Mart took the Kmart approach and further "perfected" it. There is always room for improvement, in any business, if you watch it closely enough. Especially if the business is dominated by old, profitable companies. I have been waiting thirty years for a department store to organize the men's dress shirts by size (the way people shop for them) rather than by supplier (which is what the suppliers want).

- Invent a whole new business. Federal Express came from Fred Smith's mind. WD-40 came out of nowhere. eBay came from even less. Metro Networks figured out how to build a company by offering pooled traffic helicopter reports to local radio stations. Kelly Girls met a need no one was focusing on.

The beginnings of success are not usually too complicated, as this excerpt from a Hoover's company profile shows:

In 1918, twenty-two-year-old John Jacobs opened a Chicago car rental business with twelve Model-T Fords that he had repaired. By 1923, when Yellow Cab entrepreneur John Hertz bought Jacobs's business, it had revenues of about $1 million. Jacobs continued as top executive of the company, renamed Hertz Drive-Ur-Self System. Three years later General Motors (GM) acquired the company when it bought Yellow Truck from John

Hertz. Hertz introduced the first car-rental charge card in 1926, opened its first airport location at Chicago's Midway Airport in 1932, and initiated the first one-way (rent-it-here/leave-it-there) plan in 1933.

Gaps and Intersections

Many times, the best ideas come from two sources:

1. Looking for gaps in the present structure.

2. Looking for intersections.

Take looking for gaps. When I studied the bookstore business, I found that people had numerous and excellent choices when they shopped for toys, but not when they shopped for books. When I look at the consumer-banking industry, I see an industry that is years behind where most U.S. businesses stand (in terms of paying attention to the customer). There are literally thousands of gaps like these, you just have to find them. (Try the curiosity tools in the early chapters of this book.)

Looking for intersections means finding ways to combine two existing ideas. Perhaps more than two ideas, but usually two is enough. For years, I kept noticing that iced tea was one of America's most popular beverages. But, twenty years ago, you could not find iced tea in bottles or cans. I kept asking, where are the cans of iced tea? Only in the 1990s did the tea companies (Lipton and Nestea) get together with the canned drink folks (Pepsi and Coke) to create products that people want—and buy. Toys "R" Us was really taking the economic structure of Kmart and applying it to a new business—toys. Innovators are combining Laundromats and cafés. Put together coffee and cool lifestyles—and you get Starbucks!

One way to look for intersections is to draw a grid, with one type of thing running vertically and another classification horizontally. In the grid below, I have put technologies (broadly defined, of course) on the vertical lines and product types on the horizontals. Note that I have been loose in my definitions, letting books fall on both axes. Then look at every possible crossing point and give it some thought—is there a business opportunity there?

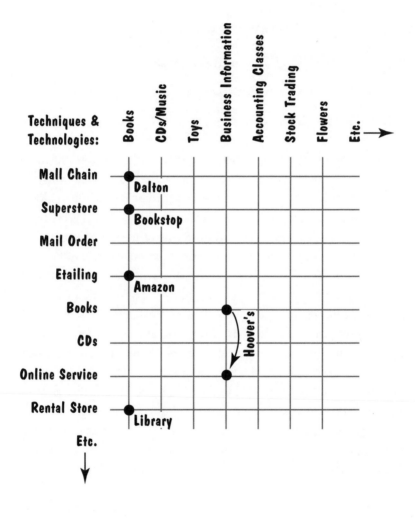

Knowing What People Need

Throughout this process, the key thing we are looking for is real needs or real desires felt by real people. Without that, our concept will never get off the ground. Does that mean that if everyone says your idea won't work, you are wrong? No. Most great ideas start with most people not believing. You will hear everything from, "If it was such a good idea, the big companies would have already done it," to "It was tried years ago and it didn't work." In fact, if everyone's first reaction is, "That's a great idea! I wish I'd thought of that!" then you probably have an idea that is *not* a real breakthrough, and possibly an idea that would be easy to copy. No, people not believing in your idea should not bother you.

Next, you may ask, "Should I go ask people if they would buy this service if I offered it?" Yes, I usually do ask people that, but I don't always listen to their answers. There are two reasons.

First, when you come up with a whole new idea, there is no way someone else can visualize it like you can. Not even your mom.

Second, customers do not always consciously know what they want. In each of the three companies I started, I started them because I wanted them for myself and thought that my fellow baby boomers would also like them if they saw what I had in mind. When we surveyed people and asked, "Would you shop at a giant discount bookstore?" many of them shrugged. Only when we opened the store did they say, "Oh, I had no idea you meant a store with this many books!"

People did not go around before Federal Express complaining about how they couldn't live with first-class packages taking three to seven days to deliver. People did not walk around in the 1950s bemoaning the lack of personal computers. No one spent the 1850s griping that they couldn't find a phone to call home on.

However, you *can* extrapolate what customers want based on their behavior. The crowds in the Toys "R" Us stores told me what my surveys did not—that people would beat a path to BOOKSTOP. In dreaming up Hoover's, I knew from the success of *Leonard Maltin's Movie Guide,* the *Rand McNally Road Atlas,* and the *World Almanac* that people would eagerly consume affordable reference information if done right.

I am not saying that any of this is easy. Of my three ideas, two worked and one did not. No matter how good any enterprise's batting average, almost nobody hits 100 percent. Ask Coke and Disney. But your chances of success will be multiplied dramatically if you continually ask, "Is this something that people will really like? Is it something they really need, whether they fully realize it or not?"

New Visions for Established Enterprises

While I often speak with startup or early stage entrepreneurs, I even more often consult for and speak to more established businesses and nonprofit organizations. Many times they do not have a clear vision, or their old one is inadequate. In addition to the basics of clarity, consistency, service, and the ever-evasive uniqueness, here are two ideas that may be helpful: (1) Streamlining and (2) Redefining and Subdividing.

Streamlining

Perhaps the most common challenge in today's enterprises is their effort to do too much. Clarity of vision is tantamount to simplicity of vision. Great enterprises usually do one thing, and do it very, very well. Over and over again. But as companies are driven to grow by managers and stockholders, they sometimes grow into strange dimensions, losing focus. Ask yourself and your organization these questions:

- How many key priorities are on your to-do list?

- What structural changes could we make in the organization to reduce this list? (Should we be selling operations rather than looking for acquisitions?)

- What do we do well?

- What are we known for?

- What does that mean we don't do as well, or what we aren't known for?

- Is our heart fully into every task on our organizational to-do list?

- How much time do we spend in meetings?

- In working on deals?

- How could we reorganize to reduce these activities and increase time spent with customers or serving customers?

- Have we really milked our basic business in every possible way before heading off into new directions?

- What share of our energy goes into our basic business?

- How sad would we all be if we lost our market position in that basic business?

I was speaking to entrepreneurs in Asia, where almost every company is in at least a dozen industries. While this might not be the crowd to respond to my message of "focus pays off," I told them, "if you have ten businesses, try to get it down to eight; if you have eight, aim for five. Any step toward simplicity is worth taking." Always seek opportunities to streamline your enterprise.

Redefining and Subdividing

Step with me back to the mid-1960s. Look at two industries. Start with retailing in midtown Manhattan, then (as now) the highest volume retail district on earth. The industry was led by a number of middle-market department stores: Gimbel's, Altman's, Ohrbach's, Saks Thirty-fourth Street, Macy's, and Stern's. Or look at the computer business, in which the list of largest competitors included RCA, GE, Honeywell, Burroughs, NCR, Control Data, Sperry Rand, and IBM. Like the department stores, all of these companies competed for the same market—they targeted dead center in a huge and growing market.

Now step forward to today. In both cases, retailing in Manhattan and computer sales, the business has grown dramatically. But, in each case, only one or two of the old "everything for everybody" companies is still in the business. And those are usually the companies (Macy's and IBM) that started out being the largest. This pattern could be found in many other industries. Number one and sometimes number two have survived. But fate has not been kind to numbers three, four, five, and six. The question is, "If this industry grew so much, why did most of the companies fail?"

From a strategic viewpoint, we find that the surviving companies, including new companies that came along and took market share (Barnes & Noble, Gap Stores, Sephora, Amazon, Dell, Hewlett-Packard), followed "redefining and subdividing" strategies. They either picked niches or they developed different technologies, including distribution technologies (such as Dell's direct sales and Amazon's Internet usage). In fact we can make the case that the growth of the industry in itself allowed for this finer fragmentation and specialization in the industry, reducing the relative appeal of mainstream, dead-center products and services. If I now have the option of buying one hundred small computers instead of just one big computer, if I can now shop for books at B&N, Borders, and Amazon, then the mainframe makers and the department stores lose share. Market growth gives rise to opportunity to boutiques, boutiques provide alternatives to mainstream producers, and mainstream producers do not get the lion's share of the growth as customers move outward from the center.

Some of the ways in which competitors move away from center include:

- Changing the cost structure, in conjunction with the pricing structure (Wal-Mart and Dell lowered their prices but also their rent and distribution costs).

- Changing the service and price structure (Saks Fifth Avenue and Lexus spent more and charged more).

- Pioneering or adopting new technologies (the superstore, Amazon).

- New attitudes (Apple, Nike).

- Specialization (Home Depot, Best Buy, Jeep). Finding "niches," some of which are enormous, is perhaps the main form of subdividing.

Many times the redefining involves revisiting the entire economic process, from producer to consumer. Let's use a forward-looking example. Perhaps today's bookstores should consider themselves not as booksellers, but as merchants of entertainment (novels and stories) and information (nonfiction). Customers may move away from paper-and-ink books toward new technologies like downloadable books (which they are likely to do in some categories while not in others). If so, the bookstores may better weather the changes if they redefine their industry and themselves. If you came in wanting a story, the bookseller-turned-storyseller might say, "We have old rare first editions, we have a library, we have new books for sale, we have books on floppy disk, we have fiction on audio cassette, and we have videos for rent." Some bookstores could choose the entertainment business while others chose the information business, rather than trying to be all things to all people (department stores of books). I believe the demand for entertainment and information will grow dramatically in coming years. But companies like booksellers and book publishers may have to become "format agnostic" in order to maximize the opportunity. At the same time, their focus may be most laserlike if they limit their scope to a narrower piece of the pie than "everything for everyone."

If your business is struggling to see a clear future, take a look at the way you define your industry and the way you define your role within it. Look at what customers really want, and what they are likely to want in the future. Along such paths great opportunities often lie. Now let's turn to the industries and companies around us and think about what to look for when we observe those companies. Maybe we will find some opportunities there as well.

PART THREE

Execution: Enterprises at Work

29

Looking at Industries and Enterprises

This book started by laying the foundations of enterprise building: understanding the world around us, its people, its places, and the trends that affect them all. But the enterprise-builder must also examine and understand the economy, industries, and individual companies. The better we understand other enterprises, successful and unsuccessful alike, the better we can answer such questions as:

- Would I want to work in this industry?

- Could I start a new company in this industry? Would I want to?

- Would this industry make a good customer for my products or services?

- Would this industry be a good supplier, partner, or affiliate for my enterprise?

- Would I want to invest in this industry by buying stock in it or (if it is nonprofit) by contributing to it? Or invest my time and energy?

- Do I want to compete in this industry and, if so, how can I compete most effectively?

In these questions, "industry" could be replaced with "enterprise." Most important, even if none of the above questions apply, the entrepreneurial mind is *always* asking, "What can I learn from studying this industry or this enterprise?" For all these reasons, looking at all kinds of enterprises around you is one of the most important exercises for the enterprise-builder.

We will first take a quick look at some of the factors to consider when looking at enterprises. Please remember three things:

1. There are exceptions to every generalization. One of the secrets of all great enterprises is differentiation. Sometimes that means breaking the rules, even my own.

2. Things change. Think about how quickly the so-called New Economy was born, blossomed, and receded, all within five years. Some of the specific things I say may be dated by the time you read them. But the underlying principles remain valid.

3. Few things are harder than running an organization. It's hard to understand the pressures, obligations, and intensity of the CEO's job until one has been there. Having been a CEO three times, I know it is far easier to second-guess decisions than it is to make them. While I may be critical of some companies or their CEO's, I also have sympathy for them. I also know that we have all made plenty of mistakes—it is not how few you make so much as how fast you correct them that matters. Please read my comments and critiques in this light.

My tool kit for looking at industries and companies includes several key elements:

- a clear definition of the industry

- an understanding of its economic fundamentals

- an understanding of its structure and of the structural trends in the industry

- a look at how customer-centered the industry and its leading companies are; and, within that focus, a look at the strength of innovation and branding in the industry

Industry Definition

The first step in understanding any industry is to define it. If we were to ask the people at Carnival Cruise Lines what industry they are in, we might expect them to say "Cruises." But, in fact, the answer the company gives is "Escape vacations." What's the difference? While their competitors, who define themselves strictly in terms of cruises, are chasing Carnival, Carnival is looking at Disney World and Las Vegas as competition.

Does Harvard compete only with Yale (and other universities), or does it also compete with other options for well-heeled and intelligent young people: for example, four years spent traveling around the world, or a stint as an intern in Washington or at the United Nations?

Economic Fundamentals

You might assume that a focus on the economic fundamentals of any industry would be obvious, but I'm amazed at how often these are ignored. To analyze the economics of any industry, try asking the following questions:

- Is this industry part of the resource extraction, manufacturing, or service sector? ("Resource extraction" includes agriculture, timber, mining, and the oil and gas industries.)

- Is its share of the overall economy rising, stable, or falling?

- Is this industry growing faster or slower than the overall economy?

- Is this industry in its early stages, or is it mature? (Remember, it might be mature in the "first world" but still relatively young elsewhere.)

- Does this industry produce a commodity that rises and falls in price, with little differentiation from one supplier or distributor to another, or does it produce a product or service that can be differentiated and effectively branded? (Examples of commodities are oil, paper, and grain.)

- Is the demand for the industry's product stable or cyclical? (Purchases of cars and houses, for example, rise and fall with interest rates; demand for semiconductors varies in tune with the overall business cycle. Such swings are rare or nonexistent for products like toothpaste and beer.)

When you begin to study any industry, first research these questions, then think about the answer to each of these questions. What does it mean for the challenges of the enterprise? For its attractiveness to investors and ability to raise capital? For the nature of competition and the psychology of the industry?

The Evolution of Industries

It's also important to understand where an industry stands on what I call the *evolution curve*. In the last forty years, most industries in the U.S. have gone through substantial restructuring. Those that have not experienced these changes are likely to do so in the future, and these same changes will likely affect enterprises around the globe.

One of the first major industries in America to go through these changes was the steel industry. Dragged down by old methods, old facilities, old technologies, old managements, and old attitudes, our once world-class steel industry by the 1960s was in no position to compete with rising Japanese and Korean competitors. In order to survive, the old leading companies like U.S. Steel and Bethlehem Steel had to slim down, reduce layers of management, cut out waste, adopt new attitudes, drop the costly perks enjoyed by their executives, and begin taking the new competition seriously.

This was a tough transition that rattled the steel industry to its core. In fact, the old industry leaders were not even capable of doing it all themselves, and new innovative companies like Nucor Steel took leadership positions alongside the old players or displaced them. This painful process lasted many years, and even today it may not be completely over.

At first, most observers assumed the problems of steel were unique to the industry. Even those who saw a broader trend emerging believed that it reflected mainly the flaws of the old heavy-industry segments of our economy. Few thought that the trend would ever touch America's best companies, such as AT&T, Sears, and IBM.

But as time went on, this sweeping trend reached more industries. General Motors and the other car makers were among the first to follow steel down the path. Banking and, more generally, the financial services industry were close behind. By the 1990s, even such historically powerful consumer products makers as Procter & Gamble and the pharmaceutical makers were facing layoffs, management restructurings, early retirements, and a reduction of management layers. One by one, most of America's giant industries had to look in the mirror and ask, "Are we as competitive as we need to be?" Even AT&T, Sears, and IBM, all once seen as providing jobs for life, had to lay off thousands of workers in an effort to become streamlined and efficient.

Despite the pain involved, U.S. industry has survived this series of revolutions, often emerging more competitive than ever before. In some cases, new companies lead the pack (Wal-Mart, Dell, Microsoft, Intel), while in other cases reinvigorated old leaders are in the forefront (Alcoa, International Paper, GE).

I believe that this trend is far from over. In fact, I would argue that America's most important industries are just beginning to feel the heat.

In the 1990s, the health care industry began to be buffeted by waves of change. Employers in Minneapolis and other cities said, "We aren't going to send our employees to your hospital anymore unless aspirin is less than ten dollars a pill," and things began to change. Since the health care industry is so huge, so entrenched, so important, so good at much of what it does, and so important in our daily lives, the management revolution that is happening in health care is perhaps the most painful and challenging to digest yet. And yet, based on the history of other industries that have passed through similar changes, we can predict that U.S. health care and all of us who rely on it will emerge "healthier" than before.

We have still more giant, entrenched industries that have not yet felt the sweeping waves of change. The first of these is education. While our higher education system of colleges and universities is the envy of the world and one of our nation's strongest industries, it is also one of the few that continues to allow costs (and prices) to outpace inflation. This situation can't continue much longer. There are other signs that the higher education industry is headed for change. The rise of privately owned education empires like Knowledge Universe (backed by investor Mike Milken) and Apollo Group (including the eighty-thousand-student University of Phoenix) is producing competitive pressure that will only accelerate creative change in the higher education industry.

Similar turbulence is in the cards for other nonprofit industries, from museums and symphony orchestras to libraries and philanthropic foundations. Another big entrenched industry that is behind the times is government.

The historical patterns are clear. Therefore, in studying any industry, I believe it is important to ask, "Has this industry been streamlined yet? Is it lean enough to compete? If not, when will it happen?"

Entrepreneurship Versus Institutionalization

When looking at the nature of an industry, another factor to take into account is the degree of entrepreneurship versus the degree of institutionalization. An entrepreneurial organization is resourceful, flexible, ever adapting. The final chapter of this book is devoted to examining this mindset. If you show up five minutes after closing time, you're likely to be let in the entrepreneurial business. By contrast, an institutional organization is built around rules and procedures. You won't get in after closing time. Most enterprises lie somewhere on the scale between these extremes.

If a manager with an institutional mindset sees a mosquito in his office, he will fill out a form (in triplicate) to start the process of hiring a pest-control company. A request for bids will be sent out to the leading exterminators, and—with luck—someone will be on the job with mosquito spray six months down the road. If a manager with an entrepreneurial mindset sees a mosquito in his office, he runs to the corner store and gets a can of Raid.

Most of the economic fundamentals of a business can be analyzed from a distance. The Internet makes it easy to track down the key numbers about most enterprises. But sensing whether an organization is entrepreneurial or institutional requires more work. You will probably have to visit the company or at least talk to some people who work there. And you may have to read between the lines to interpret the corporate-speak you're likely to hear. Most companies like to claim they are entrepreneurial in spirit; very few truly are.

I have been active in education all my life—as a student, as a proponent of adult literacy, as a bookseller, and as a supporter of the University of Chicago. When I sit with educators, particularly those in the public schools, and I question some of the rigid and inflexible policies and procedures they follow, I often hear an answer like, "Well, we have to do it that way because we want to make sure that every student is treated the same." This is the institutional mindset in a nutshell. The entrepreneurial leader wants to make sure that *no one* is treated the same. *The entrepreneurial ideal is to customize every relationship.*

Today some of the airlines are trying to get the airports to enforce size limits for carry-on bags at the security checkpoints. This would save the airlines the hassle and take them out of the role of disappointing customers. But Gordon Bethune at Continental thinks differently. He'd rather empower his people to make the right decision in each case. If the flight is half full, you can bring a larger bag on board. Bethune says that the airlines who want strict rules placed on all flights are trying to lower their competitors to their own low standard of service and flexibility—a level at which those weaker airlines can compete, where their people are not required to think for themselves.

Where you find institutions, you find rules and regulations printed up and widely distributed. You find systems designed to be airtight enough so that robots can do the work. You find buzzwords and consultants. You find complacency and smugness.

By contrast, at the entrepreneurial end of the scale, you find power and initiative distributed well down into the organization. You find straight talk. You find leaders who are dissatisfied and hungry for improvement.

Between these two extremes you find almost every major corporation in the world. One of the most important things you can know about any enterprise is where it falls on the entrepreneurship scale. Entrepreneurs see opportunity when they see industries or companies that are rule-bound institutions. Always ask, what's most important in this enterprise or this industry:

- Paying people based on years of service or quality of service?

- Being efficient and conserving resources or developing and following procedures?

- Trying new things, being proud of failure, or avoiding embarrassments and mistakes?

- Serving the customer or following the rules?

- Doing your best or meeting minimum standards?

GATEWAYS

Further Readings About Economics

Hidden Order: The Economics of Everyday Life, by David Friedman, is exactly what the title says, by one of the clearest economic thinkers around. Also by David Friedman is *Price Theory: An Intermediate Text,* the real stuff of microeconomics if you want to take the time to really think and understand. *Basic Economics: A Citizen's Guide to the Economy,* by Thomas Sowell—a top economic thinker makes it accessible to the rest of us (I just wish he had illustrated the book with some graphs). *The Making of Modern Economics,* by Mark Skousen, tells the fascinating story of the evolution of economic theory.

30

Merger Mania

Industry structure is the study of questions like the following:

- Are there a multitude of enterprises at work in the industry, or is it an oligopoly—only a few giants—or even a single-company monopoly?

- Is it easy for new companies to enter the industry or has it been the same players for years?

- What is the rate of mergers—high, low, or nonexistent?

- What is the rate of spinoffs and breakups?

I first studied this field—sometimes called "industrial organization"—more than thirty years ago. At the time, it was a pretty esoteric field limited to a few economists (including the great George Stigler) and antitrust lawyers and scholars. But I believe this is a field that everyone should look at.

Some of my observations run against the "common wisdom." For example, I believe that one of the most common signs of corporate (and industry) illness is the merger between two giant companies. While Wall Street and the financial press rarely pick up the signals, many mergers reflect a sad state of affairs, particularly at the acquiring corporation. Most companies react to merger news (or rumors) as though the opposite were true. When their competitors announce big mergers, they respond by desperately trying to arrange mergers of their own. However, most mergers should be seen not as threats but as opportunities for the competition. Why do I say these things, which may seem counterintuitive? For seven reasons:

1. Mergers are rarely done for the right reasons.

2. Size is not all it is cracked up to be.

3. Vertical integration is even less what it is cracked up to be.

4. Big merger deals tend to take management's eye off the ball.

5. Mergers are always more difficult to carry off than expected.

6. Great companies are usually focused on a single business.

7. Great companies usually prefer to grow from within rather than through acquisitions.

First, let's consider the reasons for mergers—most of which, as I've suggested, are misguided. Major reasons that are publicly cited for merger deals include:

- "Our competitors are merging, and so we must merge to stay competitive."

- "The large size of our newly combined companies will allow tremendous cost-savings as we eliminate duplication."

- "We will pull off tremendous synergies—one plus one equals three."

- "We will get better control over our sources of supply and our distribution channels through vertical integration."

Of course, many business leaders *want* to believe these things. CEOs and board members fall prey to the lure of the big deal, the "transforming transaction," and the desire to make their company the focus of industry-wide attention. The strategic consultants and investment bankers present at the high-level meetings (who may profit from merger activity) are unlikely to say, "Forget about doing this deal—send us home." Everyone gets caught up in the sex appeal of the merger.

The Myth of Size

Probably the number one wrong reason given for a merger is sheer size. The assumption seems to be that bigger is better, so merging will make us better, stronger, more competitive. But consider these facts:

Size is the enemy of the customer. Larger firms tend to become more bureaucratic, more institutional and procedural, and more rule-bound. They often have less room for unique and entrepreneurial individuals. By contrast, smaller firms are usually more able to "turn on a dime," to be responsive to the customer, and to involve the owners or leaders of the business in customer interaction.

Size is the enemy of vision and culture. A clear, consistent, unique vision is easier to maintain in a smaller organization than it is in a big one. If you study the greats like Southwest Airlines or Home Depot, you will see companies that are always growing because they want to bring their greatness to more people, they want to create more jobs, and they want to enrich their shareholders. But the bigger they get, the harder these companies have to work to maintain their culture, their vision, and their unique spirit. Every new city they enter, every new store, every new division makes life harder, so they must be certain that each increment to their size is a valid expansion that continues along their visionary track. The great companies understand that growth must more than compensate for the inevitable loss that comes with increased size. And they regard the benefits of possible acquisitions with skepticism.

Size brings complexity. Especially when an organization acquires a company that is in a different business, even a slightly different one, the complexity of the leadership challenge increases enormously. Complexity is the enemy of simplicity, the enemy of clear vision.

Size alone does not win. Twenty years ago, IBM was the largest software company and the largest computer hardware company. Sears was the largest retailer. Zenith was the largest TV company. None of these is number one in its field today. Clearly there are other things that are more important than size.

Size brings "dis-economies" of scale. People talk of economies of scale but they haven't reread their old economics textbooks. Because right after economies of scale come "dis-economies" of scale. That is, up to a point you get more efficient as you get bigger. A car factory that makes one hundred cars a year cannot buy supplies and schedule workers as effectively as a plant that makes twenty thousand cars a year. But manufacturer after manufacturer comes to realize that there is an ideal size for factories in their industry. Hewlett-Packard learned years ago that the ideal plant size is not that huge. It is big enough to be efficient but small enough to maintain a sense of community and to be manageable by humans, by people who can stay in touch with the plant. Our education system is more likely to improve when educators realize that *class* size may be less important to success than *school* size.

So the goal should not be to build the largest plant on earth—or the largest farm or bank or retail chain. Those often fail to achieve their aims. The goal should be to build the best. If you become biggest because you *are* the best rather than through helter-skelter acquisitions, as Wal-Mart has done in discount stores or John Deere in tractors, that is a different story. These companies still have to fight the demon of size, but at least they can fight it with a unified culture and vision.

The benefits of vertical integration are usually a fantasy. Most mergers fall into one of two traditional categories: horizontal mergers and vertical mergers.

Horizontal mergers are mergers of peers. When the Burlington Northern Railroad took over the Santa Fe, they created an end-to-end system that was in the same exact business in different parts of the country. When a Houston dry-cleaner merges with a dry-cleaning chain from Dallas, that's a horizontal merger. But when companies acquire other companies that are "up the chain" or "down the chain," that's a vertical merger. For example, from time to time in their history, the moviemaking companies have decided they should own the theaters so that they can control their distribution of their products. At one time, retailers owned textile factories, and most of the big newspapers bought paper companies and forests. These are vertical mergers. And one thing that history teaches us is that vertical deals often do not work.

A good example from the 1990s is the acquisition of ABC by Disney. Both were great companies. The surviving parent, Disney, is still a great company. But I believe that Disney would be greater still had it not bought ABC. Go back to the 1950s, when Leonard Goldenson's ABC and the Walt Disney Company were both struggling. The two firms cut a deal under which ABC aired a Disney show every Sunday night. ABC got a real boost to its lineup on the most important night in prime-time TV, and Disney got an invaluable promotional vehicle for its new theme park, Disneyland. Two creative, driven entrepreneurs put together an arm's-length deal that benefited both companies—perhaps rescuing both from failure.

Fast forward to today. If Disney has a great idea for a new TV show, can they play off ABC against NBC in search of the most advantageous deal? No. And if CBS has the perfect spot in its fall lineup for a new family-oriented show, do they call Disney? Probably not. Instead, they start talking with one of Disney's competitors.

Apple has recently announced that they are opening twenty-five retail stores in an effort to halt the decline in their share of the personal computer market. I fear that this excellent company may soon learn, as Viacom, Gateway, and Warner Bros. already have, that running profitable retail stores is not a sideline. It is a tough business. Apple has hired key managers from some of the best large retailers, but running stores for a big, established retail company is not the same as starting a chain from scratch. Believe me, I know from experience. If Apple sees their stores purely as an advertising vehicle, maybe they can justify them—and the money they are likely to lose. But the odds are against a company with no retail experience achieving their published projection of "a profitable chain by the second year." The company made this projection even before a test store was up and running, really tempting fate.

I think Apple would have greater odds of success in spreading the gospel of Apple computing if they used existing retailers more aggressively rather than striking out on their own. Who knows? Maybe Apple will be the exception and beat the odds. But I doubt it.

A vertically integrated system in which suppliers are inextricably linked to specific customers is inflexible. Henry Ford's famous River Rouge Plant was one of the most amazing industrial facilities ever built, enabling Ford to put together a complete car from raw materials in one location, even making its own steel and glass. Today the auto producers are spinning off their parts plants, and none of them want to be in the steel or glass business.

In the same vein, Wal-Mart is perfectly happy letting Sony make the television sets; Sony is happy letting Wal-Mart sell them. They both retain the flexibility to serve customers and to carry out their mission—with or without each other.

Mergers are always harder to pull off than people think. When Boeing bought down-on-its-luck competitor McDonnell-Douglas, it seemed like a straightforward move by a strong company taking over a weak sister. But years later, Boeing was still wrestling with how to merge the cultures of the two companies and make sense of the resulting hybrid. Boeing has never been the same since the merger.

Integrating companies is even harder when different industries are involved. Over the years, many enterprises have tried to diversify, believing that this would reduce their vulnerability to slowdowns or market reversals in specific business. Some have even sought to become conglomerates, holding companies that brought together dozens of diverse, unrelated firms under a single corporate banner. In the great conglomerate era of the 1970s, Beatrice Foods, ITT, Litton Industries, Gulf & Western, and other conglomerates were formed by strong leaders like Bill Karnes, Harold Geneen, Tex Thornton, and Charlie Bluhdorn, respectively. But in each case, the conglomerate was dismantled soon after the end of the founder's reign. One of the few diversified enterprises to stand the test of time is General Electric—and even there, I can make the case that the parts might be more valuable than the whole.

The future will bring more big mergers, but it will also bring spinoffs of unrelated businesses and dismantlings of diverse corporations, like those underway today at AT&T, GM, RJR Nabisco, and Philip Morris. There will also be a continuing rise in creative alternatives to mergers— strategic alliances, partnerships, and joint ventures. The global airline alliances like Star Alliance and One World are perhaps the most prominent examples today.

Not Everyone Is Merging

Having heard this litany of the disadvantages of mergers, you may ask: If mergers are so unproductive, then why do all the big companies do them? In the first place, many of our greatest companies do not "do mergers," or do them only very rarely and with the greatest of care. They understand that most great companies are created from within, based on products and services that naturally evolve inside the company rather than on outside acquisitions. Study the history of the greatest enterprises and you will see that the vast bulk of their growth has usually come from internal sources. I would mention Microsoft, McDonald's, Home Depot, Wal-Mart, and Hewlett-Packard for starters. Wall Street calls such a company a *pure play*, because they do one thing and if you want to invest in that thing, you can do so on an undiluted basis.

When the business headlines declared that the pharmaceutical companies must merge in order to stay competitive, how many mergers took place at Johnson and Johnson or Merck? Very few.

While United Airlines was investing a great deal of time and money in trying to buy USAir before killing the deal, Southwest was zooming past them in market value and profitability, with almost none of its success (or growth) attributable to mergers.

A few years ago, computer giant Compaq became the talk of the industry when they acquired established industry player Digital Equipment. Some asked, "Whom will Dell buy to keep up?" Michael Dell took a different tack. He told the press, "This is a great day for Dell. Now we can pick up all those customers who aren't happy with our competitors' merger." Most people thought he was just whistling in the dark. But in the first quarter of 2001, Dell sold 12.5 percent of all the PCs in the world, while Compaq sold 12.1 percent, the first time Compaq has lost the lead. Now Compaq has announced that it is "de-emphasizing" hardware, perhaps a precursor of completely pulling out.

When Do Mergers Make Sense?

Are there any mergers that make sense? You may have good reason to consider a merger if the merger will help your enterprise:

- make better products or provide superior services

- improve life for your customers

- save jobs that otherwise would be lost

- balance strengths with weaknesses, downtimes with good times, East with West

- acquire valuable assets cheap

Mergers can be a powerful way to extend the geography of an enterprise—not cheaply or easily, but perhaps quickly. Or to extend the reach of the enterprise to different customer classes.

I am in the minority today in believing that the DaimlerChrysler merger may turn out to be a smart one. Today those companies are embroiled in all the agonies of integrating two companies, paying the prices described above. But if they are smart (and lucky), when the dust settles they will have combined a global luxury brand with an innovative North and South American brand, a company strong in trucks and sedans with one that is strong in minivans and sport utility vehicles, an innovative styling and design team with one of the world's greatest engineering organizations. Given how risky any merger is, I can't be certain that things will unfold this happily for DaimlerChrysler. But I would give them pretty good odds of long-term success.

Mergers that allow one company to pick up the pieces of another can also pay off. The May Department Stores Company has posted more than twenty consecutive years of record earnings per share in a mature industry. Their acquisitions are rare; they spend more energy spinning off things that don't fit than looking for new things to take on. But in the spring of 2001, May acquired a number of vacant Montgomery Ward stores after that company's closure. This is a pure real estate (asset) play, and one that probably makes good sense from a business standpoint.

In other cases, companies are acquired to get their talent, their management, their customer list, their technology, their faded brand name, or other assets (an archive of great old movies or a pipeline full of promising new drugs). While acquisitions like these can be just as tough to carry off as any others, at least they sometimes make more economic sense than mergers consummated for size or ego alone.

GATEWAYS

Further Readings About the
Structure of Industry

The Structure of American Industry, by Walter Adams and James W. Brock, is the classic textbook about how industries are structured, using real industries for examples—from beer and computers to college sports. Great book.

31

Customer Focus: Innovation and Branding

Companies and industries sometimes forget about the customer, giving precedence instead to the whims of Wall Street, the demands of operations, the limitations of systems, or the perks of management. This is when alert, service-oriented enterprises find opportunities. Two of the areas to review closely in looking at an industry or company are innovation and the establishment of brands.

Many industries are not innovative from the customer's point of view. Even as manufacturing, the back office, and the technology of operations take giant leaps forward, the customer is left behind. Despite e-commerce, cell phones, computer capabilities, and the Internet, some parts of our lives have not changed in years. The experience of cashing a check at a bank is fundamentally the same today as it was twenty years ago.

Innovative industries have high rates of experimentation and offer the consumer many options. Does this description fit your industry?

Branding

Companies touch customers most effectively through the establishment of a unique, differentiated identity—a brand. Yet there remain many "brand wastelands"—industries in which no great brand exists.

Perhaps you can recall when many of today's branded industries had no major brands, or only weak ones. For example, when I was growing up, the leading brand of rubber-soled footwear was US Keds, a secondary division of tire company US Rubber. Among serious basketball fans, the Converse brand carried high recognition. But strong branding in this business did not really take off until the great Nike-Reebok wars of the 1980s.

Some companies have been around for a long time but have only recently become household words. A good example is United Parcel Service, founded in 1907 and bearing the UPS name since before World War II. We always knew they were around, but only with the coming of the Internet and the rise of e-commerce have they really penetrated the awareness of consumers as a great American brand.

Companies rising to the top of their fields have especially strong impact when their field is also growing in prominence. Even if Nike had existed in the 1950s, being number one in sneakers would probably not have meant much in terms of total dollars and social and psychological awareness. Few remember the name of the largest cruise line in 1950, since relatively few people took cruises then. Today, Carnival has carved out a dominant position in an industry that is becoming significant. If they manage their brand well enough to maintain or enhance their position, the company's long-term upside could be staggering. Being the largest maker of software for personal computers in 1981 implied a garage-sized business at best. Today we call it Microsoft. As a category grows in size, its leading names also grow in impact.

Note that a brand name is not really meaningful if it has no strong connotation in the mind of the consumer. If Random House were to try to market a book as being "From the publisher who brought you James Michener," it probably wouldn't work; readers have no clear image in their minds as to what a "Random House book" is. Similarly, Twentieth Century Fox probably can't market its movies with the line, "From the folks who brought you *Titanic*," since most moviegoers associate that movie's success more with the "brand names" of director James Cameron or stars Leonardo DiCaprio and Kate Winslett. On the other hand, Disney has established a meaning (quality animation) in the minds of moviegoers.

Extending this logic, I would make the case that CBS, NBC, and ABC, while very powerful and interesting companies, have not succeeded in creating brand names. When you think of NBC-TV, what do you think of? Probably nothing that is dramatically different or special compared with the other two, at least nothing that lasts more than a season or two.

Thirty years ago, the CBS of Walter Cronkite *was* a brand in the news business, but that unique prestige is long gone. Rather than strengthen it, build on it, and extend it to other CBS News products, they let it dissipate and vanish. (Similarly, Sears was once a differentiated retailer in auto parts, tools, and appliances. Today, like CBS, Sears is still a player, but it is no longer *the* player.) By contrast, MTV, ESPN, HBO, and CNN are clearly defined leadership brands. Even when under siege (as CNN is today, given FOX News's strong challenge), they are still perceived as the ones to beat.

In the future, business categories will continue to rise and fall in relative importance, and with them the dominant brands. Media (information and entertainment) will become more and more important. But the components will shift—video games and video rentals are already as large as movie ticket sales. Health, financial services, education, and travel will grow dramatically. At some point in the future, categories like these will generate more revenue and employ more people than many industries that were once much larger. Not only will travel become bigger than manufacturing, but even segments like "adventure travel" or "bed and breakfasts" will grow into major industries in their own right. Mutual funds, investment management, adult education, and many other niches will become larger than even some of today's biggest industries.

As a result, new industry leaders and great new brand names will be created. Ten years ago, no one had heard of Amazon.com. Today, Jeff Bezos adorns the cover of *Time* magazine. Today's largest private for-profit higher-education enterprise is the Apollo Group, which operates the University of Phoenix. On a global scale, few have heard of the University of Phoenix and even fewer have heard of Apollo. But in fifty years, whoever is on top of this industry, or any of its key segments, will be as well known as Amazon is today.

At the same time, many prominent brands of today will fade and vanish. As I write, we are about to lose Oldsmobile and TWA, two of the greatest names in transportation history. We have already lost brands as varied as Woolworth's, Ward's, McDonnell-Douglas, and Columbia Records.

In looking at branding, keep in mind that brands can be especially durable if they really connect with the customer, if they have some emotional content. In other words, "The pause that refreshes," "Think different," or "Just do it" are more likely to stand the test of time than "Since 1876" or "Low low prices everyday." Simple technical or economic devices are easier to copy than cachet, prestige, or beauty. Would you rather own the Mercedes name or the Hyundai name?

It's especially hard for complex or diversified enterprises to manage brands. Keeping many varied brand names strong at the same time is a real challenge. Look at General Motors, which started the postwar period with some of the strongest brands in the world. Today, many of those brands are floundering. Chevrolet has little meaning outside of trucks and Corvettes. The people entrusted with the former automotive gold standard, Cadillac, don't know whether to introduce trucks or sports cars—so they're doing both. And as we've noted, Oldsmobile is already heading for the scrap heap. Only Pontiac and Buick have maintained their brand power.

As a result, the company as a whole has a vague and uncompelling image. If you work for General Motors, who do you work for? A sporty company, an aggressive company, a luxury company? The people who work at such well-branded companies as Wal-Mart, Dell, Nike, Coca-Cola, and Southwest Airlines have no such questions in their minds. And neither do their marketing planners and strategists.

Most successful diversified companies let each brand stand as an independent entity insofar as possible. Procter & Gamble, a master at maximizing the value of competing brands, is famous for this. The Head & Shoulders brand manager and the Pert Plus brand manager may carpool together on the way to P&G headquarters in Cincinnati, but they don't plan their marketing together. They see each other as different as they see Unilever or Revlon. They just know that the P&G competitor will be especially tough. They're careful to keep their own brand images clear, crisp, and distinct.

Perhaps you are in charge of a brand, whether it's Joe's Service Station or Pontiac, Sheraton or Fidelity. Will your brand be one that rises to prominence among its competitors, or one that's left in the dust?

On the preceding pages, we've discussed the importance of industry definition and structure, of innovation, and of branding. If you'd like to see my application of these ideas to specific industries, including banking, retailing, hotels, airlines, media, the Internet, education, religion, the arts, and government, please visit www.hooversvision.com.

32

The Right Stuff:
What It Takes to Succeed

"Work is love made visible."
—KAHLIL GIBRAN

We're nearing the end of our journey together. We began with ideas about how to see things in new ways—even to see things that others do not see at all. We looked at how to seek those new visions in the past, in the future, in your own neighborhood and around the globe. We've considered the importance of defining a purpose, of crafting a vision that is clear, consistent, unique, and—above all else—focused on serving others. All of these are ideas are vital in the building of successful enterprises—no matter the field, no matter how big or how small the enterprise.

But what is your role in all this? How do the participants in the building of a successful enterprise feel about themselves and the world around them? When we study those who have done it, do we notice any patterns? What attitudes and values are shared by the entrepreneurs who build great enterprises?

Let me begin to answer these questions with another story.

Passion and Profit

It was the late 1980s. I stared at the newspaper story and shook my head. Yet another giant toy superstore chain had bitten the dust.

First, a little background. From the time I first decided that retailing was the business arena that most interested me until I targeted book-selling in particular, I studied the retail industry with much of my time and energy. I was getting paid to do this research, first as a stock analyst on Wall Street, then as a department store buyer and planner. But the real reason for my studies was my own desire to understand what separated successful retailers from the many failures.

During this period—the late 1970s—perhaps the most successful U.S. retailer was Toys "R" Us. Founded by Charles Lazarus, Toys "R" Us was the first superstore. In city after city, Toys held an unprecedented market share, selling as much as 50 percent of all the toys. It was the kind of market share that Sears or Wal-Mart could only lust after. The reason for this success was simple. Toys "R" Us offered a never-before-seen selection of toys at the lowest prices ever. As a result, customers were enriched. In fact, everyone who got near Toys was enriched. As Toys converted the business from a two-month Christmas market into a year-round business, toy manufacturers were enriched. Every employee of Toys received stock options, so workers were enriched. And of course, thousands of Toys "R" Us stockholders, from the investor next door to the largest institution, were enriched.

Obviously, I borrowed many lessons from Toys "R" Us when creating BOOKSTOP. However, as I followed Toys "R" Us in the 1980s, another chapter in the story unfolded. In that era, several clones were created—companies whose backers had looked at Toys and decided they could create a similar business. Their names ranged from Child World to Lionel Play World. However, the success these clones hoped for proved elusive. In fact, every single one of these firms is gone today, most of them bankrupt.

This was a puzzlement to me. How could one company be so outrageously successful, while all these clones were failing?

In some industries, you might assume that Toys had some trade secret, some patented recipe for success. But there are few secrets in retailing. Every store is an open book (a fact I greatly appreciated when doing
my research into the industry). If you want to know what a store pays its
employees, just ask for a job application. If you want to know where they
buy their merchandise, just look at the labels. If you want to know their
pricing strategy, just look in the newspaper or on the store shelves.

In truth, the Toys clones had done a great job of following the leader.
They had the same aisle widths, the same Barbie doll section, the same
Nintendo section, the same cash-register set-up. They were excellent
clones! So what was the difference between the one company that succeeded and all the others that failed? Was it magic?

As I studied Toys and its unsuccessful copycats, I discovered an intriguing difference. Charles Lazarus and the people who worked for him
had two things at the forefront of their minds: (1) We love toys; and
(2) we love customers. I was struck by the unabated passion for toys and
for toy customers that everyone connected with the company seemed to
share. When a retail chain honors its "Store Manager of the Year," the
prize is usually a resort vacation or a cruise. However, at the peak of
Toys' success, their best people were rewarded with a trip to the giant
New York Toy Fair, where they had the opportunity to walk the aisles of
a huge trade show, spending night and day learning more about toys.
The toy business wasn't work for these people—it was pure joy.

By contrast, the people who ran the failed clones also had two key
things in mind: (1) Copy Toys "R" Us, and (2) Get rich. As good at copying as the clone companies were, none of them succeeded because none
of them had the burning passion for the business and for the customers
that was the cornerstone of Toys "R" Us.

There's an important underlying truth here. While people may give
effort toward the goal of easy riches, ultimately most will not work the
long hours, put in the strenuous work, or think the innovative
thoughts that are required to succeed in today's competitive world if
wealth is the only objective. It is easy to believe that clever management
techniques, technological innovations, or cutting the right deals will

make your enterprise great. All those are secondary. *Passion is at the heart of every great enterprise.*

Each year, I speak to a group of high school juniors who are interested in entrepreneurship. One time, a young man came up to me after my talk and said, "I love poetry. But my parents and guidance counselor say I have to make a living, so I am going to study accounting instead. Am I doing the right thing?"

I told him—I wonder whether his parents ever forgave me—that we had plenty of accountants who do not love accounting. If he loved accounting, go for it. But if not, then he should go with his heart. You don't know what might happen to you as a poet—poet Maya Angelou has made millions of dollars.

One of the greatest tragedies in our world is all the people who hate their work, or merely tolerate it. If you don't love what you do, you'll never go the extra mile, work the extra hour, dream up the new idea. *If you are doing something you love, if you have your heart in it, at least you have a chance to excel.*

Passion intersects our lives at many points. Sometimes it touches us at a fundamental decision point, like the one faced by the young poet-accountant. Sometimes it affects the most detailed level of carrying out our vision. I have mentioned the rise of nostalgia in our lives—our sense of history coupled with our individual interests. This is the force behind much of eBay's success. People have made a veritable industry out of Coca-Cola collectibles. Coca-Cola itself has gotten behind this development by operating a museum, now one of Atlanta's most-visited tourist sights. Nike, Warner Bros., Disney, and others try to make the most of their logo, their history, and their fundamental association with our culture. Even software companies that have trouble selling their software can't restrain themselves from offering sweatshirts and coffee mugs.

So it was with great interest that I walked into the McDonald's in New York's Times Square a couple of years ago and spotted a display case offering "McDonald's merchandise." There are few companies in America with a greater attachment to us and our culture. All those

Happy Meals, all those promotions, those golden arches—this is the most natural of opportunities. Especially here in Times Square, which has become "the Valley of the Brands," with big signs and big stores for some of the most prominent brands in the world. But, in the right business at the right time in the right place, how did McDonald's approach the opportunity? They had this small unattended glass case of logo merchandise. No one was there and it was not even clear how you go about buying the stuff. It was a long way from the cash register. It was gathering dust. The odds are that this effort went down in the corporate memory as "we tried it and it didn't work." But the real issue here was that their heart was not in it. This was an afterthought, not a vision. Not even a small vision. No one *cared*.

At BOOKSTOP, our lives were centered on making more books available to more people. We tried to venture into software and video when those categories first appeared. We failed in both of those experiments. Why? Our hearts were just not in it.

Whether planning the course of your life or the merchandise displays in your corner store, whether thinking about how to sell magazine subscriptions or how to manufacture computers, there is always a place—a winning place—for passion. Without passion, without heart, all the analysis and study in the world is for naught.

I mentioned earlier my penchant for visiting bus stations, including the one in Brisbane, Australia. When I got all the way up to the third floor of that station, where the long (long, long) distance busses came and went, I stopped in my tracks. There, patiently awaiting his bus was a lone man, his pile of luggage, and his seeing-eye dog. Every time I hear someone say they can't travel because they don't have the time, money, or ability, I think about that man. If you want to do it badly enough, nothing can stop you. With passion, all things are possible.

Persistence for the Long Journey

"Knowing trees, I understand the meaning of patience.
Knowing grass, I can appreciate persistence."
—HAL BORLAND

From passion flows many other qualities, all of which can give extra oomph to our enterprise and increase its chance of success. The first of these is persistence, the endurance to continue the journey. For building any enterprise is indeed a journey, often a long one.

Imagine being a college student in Boston. One summer, you and three friends decide to drive to L.A. Everyone is gung ho and excited. You stock up on road maps and pack the car with clothes and CDs and sodas and snacks. Heather has her travel pillow, Joe has his favorite trail mix, Jack has his headache pills. The four of you set off with high hopes and excitement.

But when you get to Buffalo, Jack says, "This has been fun, I'm tired, let's go back now." He grabs the next plane back to Boston. You keep going. When you get to Cleveland, Heather says, "I really just wanted to go to L.A. to see the art at the Getty. There's a show at the Cleveland Museum that will do, let's stop here." She stays in Cleveland, you keep going. Joe throws up outside Toledo; you blow out a tire just west of Chicago; you lock the keys in the car at the Denny's in Denver. You run out of money; you run out of time; you and Joe are constantly squabbling.

There are a million reasons to turn back. They are obvious, clear, and indisputable. There is only one reason to go on—*because you want to get to L.A.* And only with that kind of single-minded dedication will you ever make it.

Most enterprises begin with one person starting out alone. You are the only believer. Eventually you find someone who will listen to you and who comes to see the same vision. That person becomes your partner, your investor, or your first employee. Now there are two of you. In time, there are three, then ten, then one hundred. Eventually, if you are persistent enough and dedicated enough, the whole world sees the vision.

It's a long march. You start out uncertain of your ability to generate any sales. In time, you make some sales, but you're not sure you can make any profits. Then you make some profits, but you're unsure of your ability to sustain them. You start out with nothing but unanswered questions. Then you proceed to answer them, one by one.

The hurdles are enormous. The experts will tell you it can't be done:

- "You can't be open long hours in a travel agency."

- "You can't carry a huge selection and discount prices in a bookstore."

- "You can't run a hotel on twenty-four-hour pricing."

- "You can't give away free newspapers on an airplane."

- "You can't appeal to in-town residents in a hotel."

- "You can't have a drive-through prescription window."

- "You can't create an online bookselling operation from scratch."

Accomplishing anything worth accomplishing takes enormous endurance. As of the end of 1998, Wayne Newton had given 26,000 live performances in Las Vegas. He'd also made 142 albums. Let's not even talk about the TV appearances and concert tours. No matter what you think of his music, you have to admire his energy.

When Steve Case took AOL public in the early 1990s, he had been working at it for seven years, and his own stock was worth less than 1 million dollars. Most people would have given up long before that. Lots of folks thought AOL would perish, that its business model wasn't working.

Years later, Steve Case might have been the *only guy on earth* who wasn't shocked when his company acquired Time Warner.

Overcoming obstacles is one of the most common patterns you see in the building of great enterprises. When Carnival Cruise Lines first started, the company couldn't afford a new ship—so they bought an old, slow, beat-up one. Their cruises took longer than the competition to get to the same places, so they added discos and such to keep the passengers entertained. From that make-lemonades-out-of-lemons start, Carnival reinvented and reinvigorated the cruise industry, and today it holds a market share in excess of 50 percent.

Energy

Another quality that entrepreneurs have in common—and one of the first things you notice if you spend much time with them—is their high-energy level. This is an intense group of people. Yet their styles vary greatly. I remember sitting at dinner with a group of members of the Young Entrepreneurs Organization. One of them talked on and on about his gorgeous house, his sporty car, and his many business accomplishments. Everyone nodded politely; if you know a lot of entrepreneurs, you know people who wear their egos on their sleeves. But at the same dinner there was another fellow who never said a peep. My curiosity got the better of me, so when we stood up to leave the restaurant, I introduced myself and inquired as to his involvement in YEO. The shy fellow quietly told me that he had sold his first company for $6 million and was now building a second enterprise, a nonprofit dedicated to helping the less fortunate.

I can assure you that anyone who accomplishes things like this may appear shy, but he has a fire burning inside—a fire just as hot as the fire inside a person whose heat can be felt from fifty yards away. Some people just have their engines set on high, and entrepreneurs are among them.

Self-confidence

I run into plenty of people who are timid, lacking self-confidence—but not successful entrepreneurs. Many parents tell their kids, "You can do anything you put your mind to." The entrepreneurs are the kids who believed them.

Entrepreneurial self-confidence isn't a simple quality. It refers to a combination of courage, optimism, self-esteem, and self-reliance. One reason most entrepreneurs rarely use consultants is that they trust themselves. As a result, they sometimes err, but the smartest among them are usually quick to know when they are wrong and correct their mistakes.

I said that entrepreneurial self-confidence includes optimism. While entrepreneurs hold a wide variety of views about the future of society in general, they *must* be hopeful about themselves, their own organizations, and their industry. Pessimists usually don't build anything. Why invest in a bleak future? Entrepreneurial optimists are not blind to the problems around them, but they see them as opportunities for innovation.

You might think that most business leaders would have high self-confidence. They often appear self-confident on the surface. But look at these common traps of thinking that people fall into every day:

"We don't have enough money to achieve our dream—we need a partner with deep pockets."

Influenced by the thinking of investors and investment bankers, many would-be entrepreneurs get caught in the trap of equating money with the power to effect change. There are plenty of cases where deep pockets accomplished nothing. Giants IBM and Sears joined to form the ill-fated Internet portal Prodigy, while the undercapitalized outsider with passion and vision on its side—AOL—struggled and won. In 1970 Sears had a lot deeper pockets than Wal-Mart. No more.

Yes, there are times when you need money to do the right thing and to accomplish your goals. And when necessary, the entrepreneur finds the money. But for every such example, there are a dozen cases where people were needlessly frightened away from pursuing their goals by the deep-pockets myth.

"The big competitors will steal our ideas and demolish us."

This argument is just as familiar as the deep-pockets myth—and just as frequently wrong. Did Hilton demolish Holiday Inn? Did Howard Johnson destroy McDonald's? Did Waldenbooks crush BOOKSTOP? The fear of entrenched competitors is often overblown.

So is the fear that some other businessperson will steal your idea. Many would-be entrepreneurs have their lawyers create NDAs—Non-Disclosure Agreements—they insist on having signed before they'll talk about their ideas. In reality, no real entrepreneur wants to steal someone else's idea—they have way too many ideas of their own.

I'm far from being the world's most prolific entrepreneur, but I've kept a list of promising business ideas ever since I was a teenager. At the moment it contains about seventy active ideas. The last thing I need is another new idea for my list. A real entrepreneur would no more want to borrow your idea that he would your underwear.

"Everyone says my idea is silly—maybe they're right."

This is just pouring gasoline on the entrepreneur's fire. Proving the doubters wrong is one of the most powerful motivators of the entrepreneurial spirit. Nevertheless, I have many times heard people say, "I want to create a business idea so that when people hear it, they all say, 'Of course that will work, what a great idea, I wish I had thought of that.'" If your idea is that straightforward, maybe it is too simple, maybe it is too easy to copy. When you study most of the true breakthrough ideas, you usually find that people's response was not like that. It was, "What a stupid idea, it will never work." This is how the movie studios felt about sound in the movies, this is how the railroads felt about airlines.

Robert Galvin of Motorola said that every great idea at his company started out as a minority position, originated by a person on the edge, often laughed at. The originator had to be thick-skinned and persistent to be heard. That's the way entrepreneurship works.

And centuries ago Italian Renaissance thinker Machiavelli said:

> And it ought to be remembered that there is nothing more difficult to bring to hand, more perilous to conduct, or more uncertain in its success, than to take the lead in the introduction of a new order of things. Because the innovator has for enemies all those who have done well under the old conditions and lukewarm defenders in those who may do well under the new.

"We've got to move fast—the window of opportunity will soon be closing."

Once in a while, this is true. Back in the 1920s, when AT&T tried to sell the movie studios on the use of sound, Warner Bros. woke up a year before everyone else. Starting with *The Jazz Singer* (1927), they made hay with the new technology and were transformed from a secondary studio into one of the biggest, a position they retain to this day. But for every instance in which there really is a rapidly closing window of opportunity, there are hundreds of imagined windows. Three years ago, friends were telling me, "If you want to start an Internet company, do it this year before all the spaces are taken." The truth is that many of the leading Internet companies of 2010 have yet to be founded.

We hear much about the so-called first-mover advantage. But history shows that being best is more important than being first. If you can be first *and* best, like Federal Express or Home Depot, great. But Microsoft, Wal-Mart, and IBM often have been followers—really excellent, and very profitable, followers.

"We need the right team—a group that has done it before."

Recently I was sitting amongst a group of bright young M.B.A.'s who had gathered to talk about current trends in venture capital. One of the brightest remarked, "You can usually tell which venture ideas are going to work and which ones won't. It's the management team. If a company is run by a group of talented executives who have created a successful business before, you know they can do it."

In contrast, just a few months later, I heard that one of the biggest VC firms had decided never to back second-time entrepreneurs—because so many had failed them. They had come to believe that someone who has done it once before often assumes—incorrectly—that he (or she) can do it again without much effort. (By the way, this firm *does* back third-timers. They figure that, when an entrepreneur goes back to the well for the third time, he's beyond any such delusions).

The bottom line is that what matters isn't how many times you've done it, it's how badly you want to do it. Alfred Sloan had never built an auto company before he created GM. Bill Gates never had a real job before he founded Microsoft. Starting Dell Computer was Michael Dell's first real job, too. Fred Smith's experience in the airline business (before launching FedEx) was as tiny as Ted Turner's in broadcasting. And many of these entrepreneurs got very little big-time venture capital backing in the early stages.

There's another problem with the we-need-a-great-team myth. Most great teams follow the idea, not the other way around. I met one fellow who was certain he was going to start a great company. "What's your business idea?" I asked.

"I don't know yet," he said, "But I've gathered the smartest group of people, and we work together like clockwork, so I know we can do anything."

Unfortunately, the truth is that they won't do *anything* without a shared vision that they really believe in. This dream team may find out the hard way that nothing can break up friendships faster than trying to build an enterprise together—except, they tell me, remodeling an old house together.

Another form of this myth is the widespread tendency to hire people based on their résumés alone rather than their hearts. Smart companies know better. A Nordstrom executive was asked, "How do you train your people to give such great service?" He answered, "We don't. Their parents do."

Of course, a résumé can tell you a lot about a person, but no more than the look in his eye, the sincerity of her smile. Great companies are not built by hiring a bunch of warm bodies with the right skill sets. They are built by hiring people with the right skills *and* a passion for what they are doing.

"We've got to know the right people if we want to get ahead."

Of course, this is the myth most favored among "the right people." It's true that, once in a while, some useless person makes it to the top because of their daddy's friends, where they went to school, or the money they inherited. But these are not often the people who build lasting enterprises. How many powerful people did Michael Dell know when he began? How many of the right people did Sam Walton know?

True entrepreneurs understand that working with the best people is critically important, but they do what it takes to find them. Some are deep inside their own organizations, some are new hires right out of school, and some even are "the right people"—working for big established companies or Wall Street firms. It's the connections you create—not the ones you are given—that are the most powerful.

"Let's build a business that the venture capitalists and institutional investors will love."

If you can find me a venture capitalist who is looking for the same thing today that they were six months ago, I'd like to meet them. If you manage your business based on what Wall Street tells you, you are probably going down a dead-end street. Note that this is different from *you* telling Wall Street what to expect: those promises you must deliver on, unless you want to be spanked by the market and sent out behind the woodshed.

But using the theories of venture capitalists, Wall Street investors, or any other group of experts to guide your enterprise rarely works. It does not have a good track record. The experts are usually enamored of the last big thing, not the next big thing. They will ask, "If this is such a good idea, why hasn't someone else done it?" They will say, "What other business can I look at to understand what you are doing? Who has proven this concept?" They might even say, "You don't have enough money, you don't have the right team, and the window is about to close."

Don't listen to them. Listen to yourself and listen to your customers.

Entrepreneurs and leaders who think like entrepreneurs believe the following:

- We can do anything.

- We can learn anything.

- We can make this world a better place.

- We can make a difference.

- We can figure it out.

- We can lick the toughest problem.

- Few things if any are outside of our control.

- No competitor scares us.

- We will focus on what matters.

In my travels, I meet with many people who dream of starting their own enterprise. Once in a while, I meet someone who is timid, who says, I would love to do it but I don't think I can. Well, they are right. For whatever silly reason they don't think they can do it, they have made it true by thinking it. Most any excuse is adequate to stop the creation of a new business: not enough time, not enough money, not the right skills. Just as often as I meet people like this, I meet folks who say, "I want to start a business and I know I can do it." They are equally right. I don't have to ask about their time, money, or skills. All of these will of course be needed, but they are tools that will never be picked up unless you, in your heart, know that you can do it.

If you have this entrepreneurial self-confidence, you will be more decisive, more prepared to act.

Action Orientation

Any observer of both large corporations and entrepreneurial enterprises quickly notices one difference. In the time it takes a large company to research, debate, propose, approve, and launch a single new idea, an entrepreneurial organization has already dashed through the stages of, "Let's give it a try. Whoops! That was a disaster! Let's try this instead. Hey, that seemed to work. How can we do it better? Yes, it's a hit! Okay, what do we try next?"

I met a fellow who had been a senior officer at Tandy Corporation (parent of RadioShack) when it was still run by founder Charles Tandy, one of the greats of American retailing. Tandy died in his fifties, shocking the company. But this fellow told me that the first five years after Tandy's death were the most productive in the company's history. While he was alive, he wanted to try too many things, too fast—no one could keep up with him. But after he died, they finally had a chance to carry out his ideas. Unfortunately, five years later, the company began to falter—because no one had come up with any new ideas since "the old man" had died!

Passionate, visionary, driven people never want to sit around. They want to do things, to learn, to experiment. Failure is an expected part of the process. Rather than sitting around waiting for or planning the giant effort, they are willing to move ahead step by small step, making constant progress. The only thing they can't stand is inaction.

Resourcefulness, Creativity, and Risk Taking

The entrepreneurial spirit is capable of creating great things out of nothing. Stories about entrepreneurs who created companies starting with nothing but $2,500 and a credit card are part of the common lore. But you may not realize that being well funded, fat, and happy is not only *not* required by the entrepreneur, but can in many cases be *harmful*.

I met a would-be entrepreneur who told me, "I've been a very successful residential realtor all my life, but now I think that the future lies with lower-cost distribution systems. So here's my idea: I want to open a 'home store' where buyers and sellers can get together more easily and cheaply than through traditional realty."

"Not a bad idea," I commented. "So when are you quitting your old business so you can pioneer the new?"

"Oh, no," he replied, "I'm going to keep the old business going in case the new one doesn't work." As soon as he said that, I knew that the new venture would probably fail.

If you hope to scale Mount Everest, you don't practice on a fake rock wall with a safety net. Like any other muscle, entrepreneurial self-confidence must be exercised in order to grow strong. Only taking on real challenges, with all their inherent risks—including failure—is sufficient.

Being backed by investors with deep pockets can be as much of a problem as a benefit. Here in Austin, a group of experienced retail executives raised several million dollars to build an exciting new store. They leased the store and began to spend on construction. But something was wrong in their projections, and they ran out of money before they got their doors open. The result: more than 5 million dollars down the drain! Ironically, if they had started out with a million dollars—and spent it as frugally as if they had *half* that amount—they might be thriving today.

Australian movie director Scott Hicks tells about the benefits of learning to make movies on small budgets. During his days running a shoestring film operation, he learned to conserve resources, to plan shots with care so as to get the best take quickly, to build drama through character development rather than relying on costly special effects. Later, when he got big budgets, he knew how to make pictures that looked as if they had even bigger budgets.

A corollary of resourcefulness is creativity. I sometimes meet successful entrepreneurs who say, "I am not very creative." Their ad agents laugh at their efforts when they try to come up with a clever or artistic campaign. But then these same people tell me, "I found out that if I walked through the floor of the plant and gave the best employee of the day the next day off, it really paid off. And over here, we figured out how to save a few thousand bucks by sharing the floor-polishing machine with the company next door. And we built this special rack so we could knock twenty minutes off our order processing time." That's the kind of creativity I'm talking about.

In making every decision, from deciding what to pay someone, to how to handle customer service, to what kind of telephone system to install, the true entrepreneur is always thinking, "There must be a better way to do this." This kind of hard-working, everyday creativity pervades the successful entrepreneurial enterprise.

People talk about how entrepreneurs are great risk-takers. Maybe so. But most of the risks that entrepreneurs take are small risks—trying a new way to lay out the cash-register area or creating a Web site that shows competitors' prices as well as your own. When entrepreneurs take big risks—the risks of startup or bet-the-company risks—most entrepreneurs are as risk-averse as anyone else. The only difference is that they assess risk differently.

For example, when I decided to leave the May Company to found BOOKSTOP, my parents' first reaction was, "But, Gary, you're doing so well, why take the risk?" I responded by saying, "Have you read the headlines lately? Do you know many corporate staff execs are getting fired or laid off these days? There's risk in either path."

Sometimes the greatest risk lies in not taking one. The true entrepreneur remembers this truth and is prepared to act on it.

Individuality

"Distrust any enterprise that requires new clothes."
—HENRY DAVID THOREAU

Maybe Thoreau was talking about real clothes, but I doubt it. I think he was talking about the need to remain true to yourself rather than donning a false front.

Entrepreneurs are, above all else, true to themselves. And they are as individually unique as any group of people you could meet.

I opened this book by talking about enterprise as an art form. Like artists, entrepreneurs are highly individualistic. If you held a big party and invited the greatest artists of all time, you would have all sorts of strange characters—bohemians, rebels, loners, romantics, dreamers, even one fellow with a missing ear. When you get a big group of entrepreneurs together, it is the same—the only thing they'll have in common is the label "entrepreneur."

What are some of the ways in which entrepreneurs differ?

Personal goals. First, they differ in their underlying goals.

- Some are out to build a great business to pass along to their children.

- Some are out to prove the naysayers wrong.

- Some are out for the pure joy of building something.

- Some just enjoy the excitement of nonstop action and challenge.

- Some want to build a nice little business that fits a local niche.

- Some dream of creating a global empire.

- Some want to work at one goal for the rest of their lives.

- Some want to build a business for a few years, then move on to the next thing.

Vision. Every entrepreneur is unique in his or her breadth of vision. Of course, every successful entrepreneur has some special vision of the future. But that vision can be broad or narrow. If your vision is a golf ball that flies farther, that might make you a million dollars. But if your vision leads to revolutionizing the whole game of golf, that might make you a hundred million dollars.

Some envision the Weather Channel; some envision the whole evolution of cable and wireless entertainment. Some envision a better produce stand; some envision ways to feed the world. The breadth of your vision depends especially on how good you are at exploration and how well developed and broad your curiosity is.

I do not really believe that some people are visionaries and others are not. We all have the potential to see the future, whether it be a small part or a great part. And I believe that, by using the techniques described in the first part of this book, anyone can enhance their ability to see things that others do not.

Paradoxically, vision is in itself blinding. Berkeley Rice said, "Visionary people are visionary partly because of the great many things they *don't* see." That is, most true visionaries are so obsessed with their own vision that often they can see little else. This is a mixed blessing. The visionary can ignore obstacles that would daunt a lesser man, but he can also discount or disregard the visions of others that are in fact as valid as his own. Henry Ford, clearly a visionary in his own field, thought jazz was silly. It's very common for entrepreneurs to think their fellow entrepreneurs are just as crazy as everyone else does.

Entrepreneurial Leadership

Passion and vision combine to give the entrepreneur strength and self-confidence. But how does this entrepreneurial passion translate to the rest of the organization? How does it reach every nook and cranny?

The answer, of course, is leadership.

I recently spoke to a group of the top executives of a major company.

The fellow in charge talked about what it was like when he was first appointed president. He said that nothing in his experience as a vice president or even a senior vice president had really prepared him for the job. He had made his mark in marketing, so at first he put his energies there. Then he realized he'd better pay more attention to finance. Then it seemed that human resources was where he needed to focus. It took him a while before he realized that, as CEO, he was really in charge of two crucial things: strategy and culture.

Look back over this book and think about the huge range of things we have talked about. In a sense, they can all be boiled down to strategy and culture.

Having studied hundreds of entrepreneurs, I have to say that some are great managers, some are lousy. The lousy ones who succeed either learn to be better managers or surround themselves with great ones. A common mistake made by those who fail is trying to do it all themselves. They think they can do it best or fastest—and this is often true—but as a result, no one else in their enterprise learns how to do it.

In a way, they're like overly protective parents. At every step, the kids hear, "Don't touch the stove, watch where you walk, how can I help you?" When they finally leave the nest, they may be helpless. But if kids are raised with some leeway to learn for themselves—and to make a few mistakes—they are more likely to be able to adapt and survive in the real world.

Some entrepreneurs I know complain that they can't trust anyone; they moan about how hard it is to find good help. What will happen to the businesses they are trying to build if they get hit by a truck tomorrow? In building my businesses, I could sleep well at night only if I honestly believed that the business could continue successfully without me. This may be impossible at most startups, but the sooner you develop organizational depth, the better.

Leadership versus management. Developing strong people through coaching and teaching is critical to success, yet many entrepreneurs fail in these areas. Superior managers are outstanding in these regards. This is one reason why both leadership and management are needed by any lasting enterprise.

One of the myths prevalent among venture capitalists is that it takes one kind of person to start a company and another to build it or run it. The implication is that the visionary and the manager are never united in the same package. The problem with this theory is that most of the really great innovative companies have been run by the founder until he died or retired. It's true of Home Depot, Wal-Mart, Toys "R" Us, Microsoft, Dell, HP, Intel, Oracle, AOL, McDonald's, Hilton, and many others. Admittedly, the person who combines entrepreneurial vision with management skills—the Bill Gates or the Michael Dell—is a rare bird. But not nearly so rare as venture capitalists seem to believe.

Management is a world of budgets, of hiring and firing, of deal making, lawyers, and accountants. By contrast, leadership is a world of passion and of vision. Leadership is about seeing what needs to be done and having the courage to do it. Management is about knowing how to fit together the details to make the vision real.

An apt illustration of the difference between management and leadership comes from railroading. When you stand at a country railroad crossing and watch a freight train pass, it is hard not to be impressed by the miracle of railroading. A train longer than a mile, weighing millions of tons, glides by at 65 mile per hour, with almost no friction. But if you study how trains really work, you find that this is not when the locomotives do their greatest work. For the very hardest part of any railroad journey is the first inch. Getting that multimillion-ton train to move off the dime is the most difficult task ever asked of a locomotive. And so it is with enterprise. The hardest task is to get people to change, to try new things, to have the courage to break out of the mold and move ahead.

The leader is the one who shows the way, who holds up the torch to the future so it is clear for all to see. From the leader's passion the whole organization draws strength.

I will leave you with one parting message. Perhaps it will help you maintain your fire, your burning passion. I have carried this thought with me for many years; it is the only quote that has always hung on my wall.

If you have ever stood and admired Washington's Union Station, New

York's Flatiron Building, or Chicago's manicured lakefront park system, you owe what you see to visionary architect and planner Daniel H. Burnham. Here I (in parentheses) update his century-old comment for our changed world:

> *Make no little plans. They have no magic to stir men's blood and probably themselves will not be realized. Make big plans; aim high in hope and work, remembering that a noble, logical diagram once recorded will never die, but long after we are gone will be a living thing, asserting itself with ever-growing insistency. Remember that our sons and grandsons* (and daughters and granddaughters) *are going to do things that would stagger us. Let your watchword be order and your beacon beauty.*
> —DANIEL HUDSON BURNHAM

GATEWAYS

Further Readings About Entrepreneurship and Leadership

Innovation and Entrepreneurship, by Peter F. Drucker—still the best mind in the business. Try *How to Think Like an Entrepreneur*, by Michael B. Shane—the other extreme; a practitioner rather than an academic viewpoint. Great little book with lots of nuggets of wisdom. Two excellent textbooks are *New Venture Creation: Entrepreneurship for the Twenty-first Century*, by Jeffry A. Timmons; and *Entrepreneurship: A Contemporary Approach*, by Donald F. Kuratko and Richard M. Hodgetts. Amar V. Bhide's *The Origin and Evolution of New Businesses* is the best serious academic study of entrepreneurs and the causes of success and failure.

Further Readings about Leadership

After Alfred P. Sloan's book *My Years with General Motors*, my favorites are *Control Your Destiny or Someone Else Will: How Jack Welch Has Made General Electric the World's Most Competitive Company,* by Noel M. Tichy and Stratford Sherman; and *Built to Last: Successful Habits of Visionary Companies,* by James C. Collins and Jerry I. Porras. Also recommended: *John P. Kotter on What Leaders Really Do* and *Leading Change,* by John P. Kotter; and *On Becoming a Leader,* by Warren Bennis. Finally, the psychologist Abraham Maslow is no longer with us, but his ideas about motivation live on in *The Maslow Business Reader: Abraham H. Maslow,* edited by Deborah C. Stephens.

Using Reference Sources for Further Exploration

Spend a few hours with a basic data reference book, flipping from one section to the next. The two best are *The Statistical Abstract of the United States* and *The World Almanac*. Stop on a random table and think about what it means. Close your eyes and picture the activity or event (from shipping grain to winning the World Series) represented by the data. Or try *Understanding*, by Richard Saul Wurman and the TED Conferences, a wonderful book of data by one of the top fellows in information design.

Key Reference Works That Everyone Should Have

The World Almanac.

The Almanac of American Politics, by Michael Barone and Grant Ujifusa. Published every two years (most recently for 2000), this is the definitive reference book about our governors, senators, and congressmen, including how they voted on key issues. To me, it is even more useful for its descriptions of each congressional district and its people. No other book paints such a vivid portrait of the people in every part of the U.S. I could not live without it.

Places Rated Almanac, by David Savageau.

Statistical Abstract of the United States: The National Data Book. U.S. Bureau of the Census. Annual. An essential source of data about every aspect of the U.S. Also available on CD-ROM. For historical trends, see the companion two-volume set, *Historical Statistics of the United States.*

And, for every business researcher, *Economic Census 1997.* Available online or on CD-ROM from the U.S. Bureau of the Census. Updated every five years, then fully released after three or four years. This is where I start every analysis of an industry; see www.census.gov.

For additional U.S. data, try the Bureau of Labor Statistics. Especially useful is the Consumer Expenditure Survey, which looks at how people spend their money, available at stats.bls.gov/csxhome.htm. A good source of government statistics and publications is the Bernan Press, www.bernan.com. Hoover's sells numerous business reference books; see www.hoovers.com.

Key Works on World Statistics

World Development Indicators, by the World Bank. Annual. Data. Indispensable guide to all the latest numbers for all the nations of the world.

The Statesman's Yearbook: The Politics, Cultures, and Economies of the World, edited by Barry Turner. Annual. Alphabetical by country, covering every nation on earth. Lists of leaders, lists of states and provinces, lots of words and stats. I always keep the current issue near at hand, as do many of the world's diplomats. The 2000 edition was the 136th annual number.

World Development Report, by the World Bank. Annual. Data and text.

Human Development Report, by United Nations Development Program. Annual. Data and text.

The World Bank Atlas, by the World Bank. Annual. Maps and data.

The Global Competitiveness Report, by Harvard University and the World Economic Forum—Michael Porter, Jeffery D. Sachs, Klaus Schwab, et al. Annual. Consolidates several measures of the "vibrancy" of each nation. Very good.

Index

About
TEXERE

TEXERE seeks to become the most progressive and authoritative voice in business publishing by cultivating and enhancing ideas that will illuminate the global business landscape. Our name defines the spirit of our vision: TEXERE is the ancient Latin verb "to weave". In an increasingly global business community, we seek to create an intersection where authors and readers can share the best thinking and the latest ideas. We want to leverage the expertise and insights of leading thinkers by weaving them with TEXERE's capability to deliver them to the marketplace.

To learn more and become a part of our
community, visit us at:
www.etexere.com
and
www.etexere.co.uk

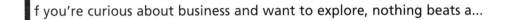